The Complete Low Sodium Low Cholesterol Cookbook

Edith Tibbetts & Karin Cadwill

Foreword by Philip Chiotellis, M.D.

 Sterling Publishing Co., Inc.   New York

Edited by Timothy Nolan

Library of Congress Cataloging-in-Publication Data
Tibbetts, Edith.
    Complete low-cholesterol low-sodium cookbook / Edith Tibbetts and
Karin Cadwell.—Rev. ed.
        p. cm.
    Rev. ed. of: Complete low-sodium/low-salt cookbook. 1984.
    ISBN 0-8069-5852-9
    1. Low-cholesterol diet—Recipes. 2. Salt-free diet—Recipes.
I. Cadwell, Karin. II. Tibbetts, Edith. Complete low-sodium/low
salt cookbook. III. Title.
RM237.75.T53 1989
641'.5'632—dc20   89-21670
                                                                            CIP

1 3 5 7 9 10 8 6 4 2

Copyright © 1990 by Edith Tibbetts and Karin Cadwell
Published by Sterling Publishing Co., Inc.
387 Park Avenue South, New York, N.Y. 10016
Original edition published under the title
"The Complete Low-Sodium/Low-Salt Cookbook"
© 1984 by Sterling Publishing Co., Inc.
Distributed in Canada by Sterling Publishing
% Canadian Manda Group, P.O. Box 920, Station U
Toronto, Ontario, Canada M8Z 5P9
Distributed in Great Britain and Europe by Cassell PLC
Artillery House, Artillery Row, London SW1P 1RT, England
Distributed in Australia by Capricorn Ltd.
P.O. Box 665, Lane Cove, NSW 2066
Manufactured in the United States of America
All rights reserved
Sterling ISBN 0-8069-5852-9 Paper

Contents

Conversion Guides

CUSTOMARY TERMS

t.	teaspoon
T.	tablespoon
c.	cup
pkg.	package
pt.	pint
qt.	quart
oz.	ounce
lb.	pound
°F	degrees Fahrenheit
in.	inch

METRIC SYMBOLS

mL	millilitre
L	litre
mg	milligram
g	gram
kg	kilogram
mm	millimetre
cm	centimetre
°C	Celsius

GUIDE TO APPROXIMATE EQUIVALENTS

Customary:				Metric:	
ounces; pounds	cups	tablespoons	teaspoons	millilitres	grams; kilograms
			¼ t.	1 mL	
			½ t.	2 mL	
			1 t.	5 mL	
			2 t.	10 mL	
½ oz.		1 T.	3 t.	15 mL	15 g
1 oz.		2 T.	6 t.	30 mL	30 g
2 oz.	¼ c.	4 T.	12 t.	60 mL	
4 oz.	½ c.	8 T.	24 t.	125 mL	
8 oz.	1 c.	16 T.	48 t.	250 mL	
2.2 lb.					1 kg

Keep in mind that this is not an exact conversion, but generally may be used for food measurement.

Foreword

I am convinced after reading this book that the authors accomplished their goal of providing all the needed information for a heart-healthy diet. Today, cardiologists have no doubt that a sedentary lifestyle and dietary habits, i.e. eating food high in salt, fat and cholesterol, smoking, obesity and diabetes are risk factors for elevated blood pressure, angina, heart attack and stroke.

Some individuals are genetically predisposed to high blood cholesterol and need to be more cautious in their food intake of cholesterol. If you have a family history of heart disease, learn about your risk factors and do something about them.

It is more likely today than in past years that your physician will check your cholesterol. You will hear more about bad cholesterol or LDL and good cholesterol or HDL. The latter exerts a "protective" effect and should be kept high by diet and exercise. The higher the cholesterol and LDL cholesterol, the more the risk of hardening of the arteries and a more strict, lower cholesterol diet will be advised by your physician. Occasionally a cholesterol-lowering medication may be prescribed. Individuals with high blood pressure need to restrict their salt intake. Consult your physician about your blood cholesterol level. The book in front of you provides easy reading and should be of great help to you in gradually changing to healthier eating habits.

Philip N. Chiotellis, M.D., F.A.C.C.
Cardiologist
Hyannis, Massachusetts

Acknowledgments

The authors want to thank the people who helped with the manuscript:

Louann Walther, who has cheerfully and patiently typed endless revisions, whom we couldn't get along without;

Betty Dennis, the world's fastest typist, who typed the entire manuscript for American cooks and then retyped the entire manuscript with metric measurements;

Donna Byerly, who checked and double-checked the recipes in addition to typing;

Jean Meers, who led the taste testing;

Joanne McIlhenny, who computed the sodium and calorie content of the recipes;

Theresa Gutsch, R.D. and Sylvia Mortenson, R.D., who reviewed the manuscript from the dietitian's point of view;

All the people who participated in our low-sodium classes and tested the recipes in their own kitchens.

Preface

We wrote this book for people like you—people who love good regular cooking but who want to cut down on salt and cholesterol. This book is different from all other low-salt low-cholesterol cookbooks. How is it different?

The Complete Low Cholesterol Low Sodium Cookbook provides an understanding of sodium and cholesterol restriction and gives practical help in the types of situations you encounter daily—restaurant eating, travelling, visiting, shopping, cooking, planning meals, selecting low-sodium low-fat ingredients, natural and commercially prepared kinds.

This book tells you how to cook the foods you and your family really like. Recipes include pizza, pancakes, tacos, egg rolls, hamburgers, onion dip, lasagne, curried tuna canapés, barbecued chicken and spareribs—tested for you and written with clear directions. Most recipes also include the amount of sodium and calories in each serving.

Our work in conducting classes for people on special diets produced the ideas to begin and complete this book. In talking to hundreds of men and women with high blood pressure and high cholesterol, or their spouses, we found that they needed a lot more than the traditional advice, "Just cut down on your salt and fat."

Above all, they needed to know how to make low-sodium low cholesterol food taste good. Working with many people and two dietitians who checked the nutritional content, we chose the most delicious recipes—using ingredients available in your grocery store.

WHY CAN'T I JUST STOP EATING EGGS AND SALTING MY FOOD?

THIS COOKBOOK DOES have recipes and you can flip ahead to them if you want to, but we would like to ask you to read over the early chapters. Why? Because you will be in a much stronger position to help yourself if you learn more about healthy eating.

Cutting down on table salt and dietary cholesterol is something you can do to help yourself. But giving up the salt shaker and limiting the number of eggs you eat are only a small part of a better diet. Recent studies show that salt added at the table is only 10 percent of a person's total sodium intake. The other 90 percent of the sodium is hidden in other foods. Although egg yolks contain cholesterol, we know now that it is the amount of fat you eat and the kind of fat you eat, as well, that determine the amount of cholesterol contained in those egg yolks that ends up in your bloodstream.

The first step must be to learn what sodium and cholesterol are all about.

What Is Sodium?

Sodium is a chemical element. Table salt is sodium chloride—part sodium and part chloride.

What Is a Milligram?

A milligram or "mg" is a unit of measure: 1000 mgs equals 1 gram. A milligram, a very small amount, is the way elements, such as sodium, are often measured. In order to know how much salt is in a person's diet, you count the number of milligrams of sodium.

Doctors tell people to cut down on salt, but it's really the *sodium* that you need to cut down on. Sodium is found in many foods in addition to

table salt. It is just as important to avoid all ingredients that have the word *sodium* in them. You can do this by reading the labels. Don't buy foods that say on the label that they contain salt or sodium in any form, such as *sodium* nitrate, or mono*sodium* glutamate (also called MSG or Accent), or bicarbonate of *soda* (baking *soda*). Even a "little bit" can hurt!

Did you know that the ingredients on a label must—by law—be listed in an order that represents the relative quantities present in the entire product? The ingredient that is listed first is present in the largest quantity. If you read the label on dried chicken soups while you are still in the store, you can see that there is more salt and MSG than chicken. They might be more appropriately called salt soups.

Read the labels carefully. Ask yourself this question: "How much sodium does this food contain?" People who are placed on a strict level of sodium restriction are limited to 500 mgs of sodium per day!

Talk to your doctor about how many, or approximately how many, mgs of sodium you should take in each day. You will be better able to plan your diet once you know how many mgs you should be aiming for. Use the charts in the back of this book to help you learn more about which foods are high and low in sodium. Because it is important for some people to monitor the amount of sodium they take in each day, we have calculated the amount of sodium per serving in each recipe.

Your diet may be called "cutting down in salt," "low salt," "low sodium," or "sodium restricted." The name is not important. What matters is that you have an idea of the amount of sodium that you should allow for in your daily meals.

If you have questions about your diet, ask your doctor or dietitian for help. Your doctor also may have told you to take medication or make other changes.

If your diet has been severely restricted (to around 500 mgs of sodium per day), you will need to choose your foods very carefully and keep track of how many mgs of sodium are in each serving of food you eat. A moderate restriction might allow you to take in 1,000 or more mgs of sodium per day. In some cases, the doctor does not tell you how many mgs of sodium to take in, just that it would be wise for you to cut down on your salt intake. If you are "cutting down on salt," you will have to learn which foods are high in sodium so that you can avoid eating them.

Of course, some people decide on their own to cut down on sodium (and cholesterol). Even the healthiest person would be wise not to take in more than 3000 mgs of sodium per day.

Is Cutting Down on Sodium Worth the Trouble?

Excessive sodium intake has been identified as a contributing factor in various health problems, such as high blood pressure, congestive heart failure, kidney ailments, migraine headaches, and premenstrual tension.

Cutting down on sodium has helped people suffering from all of the above. For kidney problems and congestive heart failure, sodium restriction is an accepted part of the treatment. With other problems, discussion continues on the question of whether or not restricting sodium should be universally recommended. The quantity of research connecting sodium intake to high blood pressure is enormous, but there is some lesser interest in using sodium restriction for other problems.

There is also anthropological evidence linking high sodium intake and high blood pressure. In the United States, Canada, England, and Australia, where the average sodium intake is high, blood pressure is expected normally to rise as people get older. But among other groups of people who take in very little sodium, essential hypertension, or high blood pressure, is virtually unknown and blood pressure does not rise with age. In countries such as Japan, where people take in very large amounts of sodium, high blood pressure is fairly common. A chart has been made to show the relationship between salt intake and the percentage of people with high blood pressure in various populations.

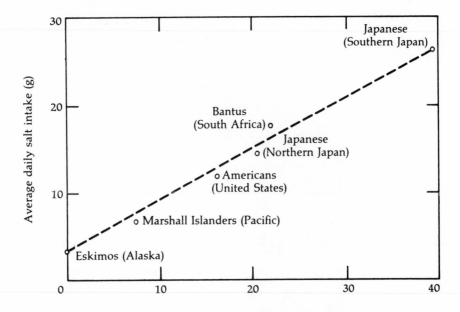

% persons with high blood pressure

Reprinted with permission from *Essentielle Hypertonie, Ein Internationales Symposium* (1960) with permission of Springer-Verlag, Heidelberg, p. 53.

The circle charts that follow will help you to know which foods are high and low in sodium.

What Is Cholesterol?

Cholesterol is waxy. It's not really a fat but acts very much like one. Although cholesterol is used by many parts of the body, a certain amount travels in the serum of the blood.

As cholesterol is carried around in the bloodstream, some of it may stick to the lining of the arteries, the blood vessels that bring blood to all parts of the body. These deposits of cholesterol can build up and make the artery narrower and less flexible. Doctors and nurses call this atherosclerosis (ath'er ō' sklur o' sis). You may also have heard this problem called "hardening of the arteries."

Sometimes an artery can get stopped up completely, and then part of the tissue of the organ it supplies with blood dies. If the artery is bring-

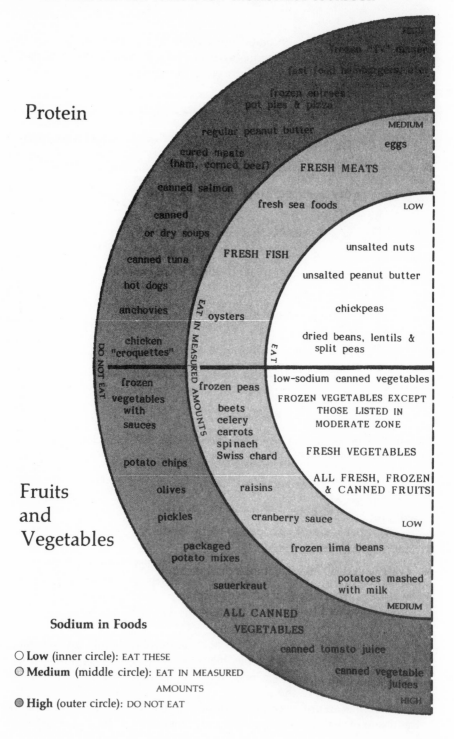

Protein

Fruits
and
Vegetables

fresh
frozen "TV" dinner
fast food hamburgers, etc.
frozen entrees
pot pies & pizza

regular peanut butter

MEDIUM

cured meats
(ham, corned beef)

FRESH MEATS

eggs

canned salmon

fresh sea foods

LOW

canned
or dry soups

canned tuna

FRESH FISH

unsalted nuts

hot dogs

unsalted peanut butter

anchovies

oysters

chickpeas

chicken
"croquettes"

dried beans, lentils &
split peas

frozen
vegetables
with
sauces

frozen peas

beets
celery
carrots
spinach
Swiss chard

low-sodium canned vegetables

FROZEN VEGETABLES EXCEPT
THOSE LISTED IN
MODERATE ZONE

potato chips

FRESH VEGETABLES

olives

raisins

ALL FRESH, FROZEN
& CANNED FRUITS

pickles

cranberry sauce

LOW

packaged
potato mixes

frozen lima beans

sauerkraut

potatoes mashed
with milk

MEDIUM

ALL CANNED
VEGETABLES

canned tomato juice

canned vegetable
juices

HIGH

DO NOT EAT

EAT IN MEASURED AMOUNTS

EAT

Sodium in Foods

○ **Low** (inner circle): EAT THESE
◐ **Medium** (middle circle): EAT IN MEASURED
                                    AMOUNTS
● **High** (outer circle): DO NOT EAT

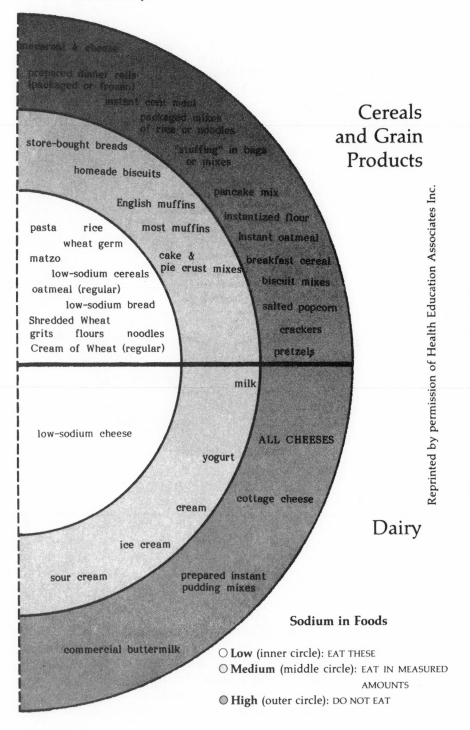

Cereals
and Grain
Products

macaroni & cheese

prepared dinner rolls
(packaged or frozen)

instant corn meal

packaged mixes
of rice or noodles

store-bought breads

"stuffing" in bags
or mixes

homeade biscuits

pancake mix

English muffins

instantized flour

pasta   rice   most muffins

instant oatmeal

wheat germ

matzo   cake &   breakfast cereal
                     pie crust mixes
    low-sodium cereals

biscuit mixes

oatmeal (regular)

low-sodium bread   salted popcorn

Shredded Wheat

grits   flours   noodles   crackers

Cream of Wheat (regular)   pretzels

milk

low-sodium cheese

ALL CHEESES

yogurt

cottage cheese

cream

Dairy

ice cream

sour cream   prepared instant
                            pudding mixes

commercial buttermilk

Sodium in Foods

○ **Low** (inner circle): EAT THESE
○ **Medium** (middle circle): EAT IN MEASURED
AMOUNTS
◉ **High** (outer circle): DO NOT EAT

Reprinted by permission of Health Education Associates Inc.

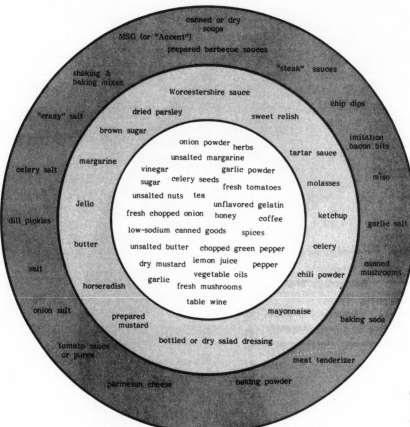

The Sodium Content of Other Foods

○ **Low** (inner circle): USE FREELY
◐ **Medium** (middle circle): USE IN MEASURED
                             AMOUNTS
● **High** (outer circle): DO NOT USE

ing blood to the brain, a stroke can happen. If the artery supplies the heart, a heart attack can happen. If the artery is leading to the leg, gangrene can develop.

• This is the way an artery looks when it's healthy. Notice how smooth the lining is. What you can't see is how flexible this healthy artery is — how easily it can respond to changes in blood flow.

Healthy Artery

• This is the way the same artery looks after plaque starts to build up. You can see that there is less of an opening for the blood to pass through.

Artery with a
beginning build-up
of plaque

• This is the way an artery looks when it has developed the problem of atherosclerosis. What you can't see is how rigid and inflexible the artery now is and how unresponsive it is to changes in blood flow.

Artery with
Atherosclerosis

How Do Artery Walls Get Injured?

One of the questions you may be asking is, "Why does cholesterol get stuck on the walls of arteries?" No one is sure exactly why this happens, but researchers and doctors have some answers.

Cigarette smoking injures the walls of arteries. When people smoke, the smooth linings of arteries get scratched. These scratches attract cholesterol and other particles from blood that is passing by.

High blood pressure damages the walls of arteries. Because high blood pressure pushes the blood more forcefully against the artery walls, fast moving particles in blood, including cholesterol, can damage the walls and stick to them at the sites of injury. More and more plaque ingredients grab onto the same spot, building up the plaque deposit and blocking the blood from flowing through freely.

Just having too much cholesterol in the blood can damage the walls of arteries and begin the formation of plaque.

The cholesterol in the blood comes from two sources:

• fats and cholesterol in the diet

• cholesterol that is made in the body by the liver

The body is always going to be producing a certain amount of its own cholesterol and sending it into the bloodstream. In order to make a change in the amount of blood levels of cholesterol, a person has to change the fats and cholesterol in his diet.

The cholesterol in food is always from animal products—there is none in food that comes from plants. There is a big difference in the amount of cholesterol from one animal product to another.

Of the foods Americans eat, egg yolks, liver, and processed lunch meats have the highest amounts of cholesterol per serving. Fish and poultry have relatively small amounts of cholesterol per serving. Butter, cheese, and whole milk have a lot of cholesterol. But because the body makes its own cholesterol out of fats, the amount of fat and the kind of fat a person eats make a difference in the amount of cholesterol that ends up in the blood.

There Are Different Kinds of Fats

You may have heard people talk about saturated and unsaturated fats. Actually, all food fats are a mixture of saturated and unsaturated fats. When a food is high in saturated fat, however, that's the label that we give to it.

Saturated fats are the kind of fats that make blood cholesterol levels go up. Foods that are high in saturated fats are the ones that persons on cholesterol-lowering diets will have to avoid. Saturated fats are the ones that are generally solid at room temperature. Many foods that are high in saturated fats are also high in cholesterol—for example, butter, lard, beef and lamb, pork, eggs, cheese, and whole milk.

A few oils are high in saturated fats even though they are liquid at room temperature: palm and coconut oils. These are the so-called "tropical oils." Because these oils are relatively inexpensive, they are used widely in processed foods, such as salad dressings and commercially prepared bakery products and mixes. These oils make the product have a longer shelf life. Sometimes the label says "vegetable oil." When you don't know what the vegetable oil is, it may be a tropical oil. Leave the product on the supermarket shelf.

Foods that are high in unsaturated fats are the kind that your doctor would like you to eat, instead of foods that are high in saturated fats. Fats that are mostly unsaturated are usually liquid at room temperature. There are two categories of unsaturated fats: mono-unsaturated fats and poly-unsaturated fats.

Mono-unsaturated fats, such as peanut and olive oil, are liquid at room temperature but become harder when refrigerated.

Poly-unsaturated fats, such as safflower oil, corn oil, soybean oil, and sesame oil, are liquid at room temperature and stay liquid when refrigerated. The unsaturated fats have been found to have a cholesterol-lowering effect.

Hydrogenated oils are vegetable oils that have been modified to be more solid at room temperature. Shortening and margarine are vegetable oils that have been hydrogenated. When you read the label on the box, you might read "hydrogenated soybean oil." The process of hydrogenation changes the oil to be more saturated and more solid at room temperature. The soft margarines in tubs have been less hydrogenated than the sticks of margarine and are therefore less saturated. Tub margarine is also easier to spread and therefore the dieter is able to spread a smaller amount on bread.

Changing over to eating fewer foods that are high in saturated fats and limiting the portion size of fat and fatty foods is one step towards a better diet. Another step is to change over to more foods that are high in mono- and poly-unsaturated fats.

HDLs and LDLs Are Another Factor

When cholesterol circulates in the bloodstream, it is attached to a carrier. Because cholesterol is very much like a fat and blood is watery, cholesterol can move around better when it is attached to a carrier.

There are two important carriers that transport cholesterol. One is the LDLs (low-density lipoproteins) and the other is the HDLs (high-density lipoproteins).

Researchers think that LDL brings cholesterol around to the cells in the body. They think that HDL collects the used cholesterol from the cells, and delivers it to the liver where it is broken down and gotten rid of. The LDLs are called "delivery trucks" and the HDLs, "garbage trucks."

Many doctors and researchers believe that the ratio of LDL to HDL is important. In other words, the difference between the delivery and pickup rates of cholesterol is a determinant of the blood cholesterol levels. An interesting finding has been that people with rather high levels of HDL have fewer heart attacks than other people.

You may be wondering how it is that some people have more or less HDL? Smokers have much less HDL than nonsmokers. Smoking does make a difference, even for young people who smoke. Exercise also makes a difference. People who exercise regularly have high levels of HDL, compared to LDL levels. Your doctor is the best person to advise you on an exercise program.

Diet also seems to make a difference in the amount of HDL a person has. The amounts of cholesterol and saturated fat a person eats seem to influence the ratio of HDL to LDL. High saturated fat, high cholesterol diets increase the LDLs without increasing the HDLs.

The charts that follow will tell you how many calories are in a specific amount of food: 1 cup of whole milk has 150 calories, for example. The chart will also tell you how much total fat that amount of food has: 1 cup of blueberries has 1 gram (a very small amount) of fat. A single avocado has 37 grams (a very large amount) of fat.

You will need to pay attention to the serving size of each food item on the list. At first glance, cheddar cheese (6 grams) seems to be lower in fat than cottage cheese (9 grams). When you check the portion sizes, however, you will see that it was 1 cubic inch of the cheddar cheese and 1 cup of the cottage cheese being referred to.

Another column of the charts helps you to know whether the fat is

DAIRY PRODUCTS

	Calories	Total Fat (gm)	U to S ratio	Cholesterol (mgs)
blue cheese—1 oz	100	8	5:10	30
cheddar—1 cubic inch	70	6	7:10	30
creamed cottage cheese—1 cup	220	9	5:10	32
low-fat (1%) cottage cheese—1 cup	165	2	3:10	10
cream cheese—1 oz	100	10	6:10	31
mozzarella (skim)—1 oz	80	5	6:10	16
American cheese—1 oz	105	9	6:10	27
whole milk—1 cup	150	8	6:10	33
1% fat milk—1 cup	100	3	9:10	10
ice cream—1 cup	270	14	6:10	88
sherbet—1 cup	270	4	7:10	16
fruit yogurt—8 oz container	230	3	7:10	29
egg (1) whole	80	6	25:10	274
egg (white only)	15	Trace	*	0
egg (yolk only)	65	6	25:10	274
butter—1 tablespoon	100	12	7:10	33

unsaturated to saturated fats. With a veal cutlet, the ratio is 12:10 (12 to mostly unsaturated or saturated. The first number represents unsaturated fat, the second, saturated. The number pairs represent the ratios of 10), of unsaturated fat to saturated fats—about even. For salmon, the ratio is 45:10, or more than 4 times as much unsaturated fat. There are no ratios for foods that are low in fat. For these foods, the column has an asterisk.

The last column of the chart tells you how much cholesterol there is in the food. Many doctors tell their patients to limit their cholesterol intake to 300 mgs per day. Some people are told to limit cholesterol intake to 200 mgs per day if the higher limit of 300 mgs does not bring down their serum cholesterol levels.

About Dairy Products

Stick to the ones that are low in fat. There are low-fat versions of milk, cottage cheese, and yogurt. Popular cheeses are becoming more available in lower-fat and low-sodium versions. Remember that the fat is still saturated and the amount still needs to be limited.

Be careful about choosing a substitute for cream in your coffee. "Nondairy" coffee lighteners are often high in saturated fat. Coconut oil or hydrogenated vegetable oil may be one of the ingredients. Your best choice is low-fat milk.

Egg yolks are high in fat and cholesterol, but the whites are not. Frozen egg substitutes that are low in cholesterol are on the market. Many of the recipes in this book call for egg substitute.

Choose Meat Servings Carefully

As there are 16 ounces to the pound, a 3-ounce serving is a little less than one-quarter of a pound of meat. This may be a much smaller serving than you are used to eating.

Start out with four ounces of meat or fish per serving—this will cook down to three ounces.

A hamburger that is three-inches across and one-quarter-inch thick (after cooking) is about three ounces.

Many people limit the number of meat servings to three a week—the rest of the time, chicken, turkey, fish, or vegetarian meals are eaten. Eat larger portions of vegetables. That way you won't feel so deprived.

Remember always to remove all the fat that you can see before you start to cook meat.

Eat More Fish and Poultry

Fish has almost no saturated fat and can be enjoyed often. Poultry is low in saturated fat. When you cook chicken, remove the skin before cooking. In any case, don't eat the skin of turkey or chicken, because the fat is in the skin and just beneath it. Ground turkey meat can be found in the meat departments of most supermarkets. Fat and skin have often been ground in with the meat, making this a high fat food.

PROTEIN FOODS

	Calories	Total Fat (gm)	U to S ratio	Cholesterol (mgs)
Meat				
hamburger—3 oz	185	10	15:10	75
lean roast beef—3 oz	125	7	13:10	66
sirloin steak—3 oz	330	27	14:10	75
lamb chop (visible fat				
removed)—2 oz	120	6	14:10	54
liver—3 oz	195	9	26:10	330
ham—3 oz	245	19	18:10	51
pork chop (visible fat				
removed)—2 oz	150	9	20:10	56
bologna—1 slice	85	8	17:10	16
sausage (1)	70	6	16:10	105
veal cutlet—3 oz	185	9	12:10	138
Poultry				
chicken (½ breast 2.8 oz)	160	5	26:10	66
turkey—1 cup chopped	265	9	26:10	160
Fish				
clams—3 oz	45	1	40:10	57
cooked haddock—3 oz	140	5	24:10	63
canned salmon—3 oz	120	5	45:10	36
Legumes, Nuts & Seeds				
almonds—1 cup	775	70	115:10	0
beans (dry, cooked)—				
1 cup	210	1	*	0
coconut meat—1 cup				
shredded	275	28	Trace: 10	0
lentils—1 cup	210	Trace	*	0
peanut butter—1 tbs	95	8	42:10	0
sunflower seeds—1 cup	810	69	75:10	0
walnuts—1 cup	785	47	110:10	0

Fruits and Vegetables Are Low in Fat

Most fruits and vegetables have little or no fat and are low in calories. They have the advantage of being able to fill your plate and your stomach while you stay on your diet.

An extra bonus is that fruits and vegetables (along with whole grains)

FRUITS & VEGETABLES

	Calories	Total Fat (gm)	U to S ratio	Cholesterol (mgs)
Fruits				
apple—1	80	1	*	0
banana—1	100	Trace	*	0
pear—1	100	Trace	*	0
cherries—10	14	Trace	*	0
cantaloupe—½	80	Trace	*	0
grapes—10	35	Trace	*	0
grapefruit—½	50	Trace	*	0
avocado—1	370	37	30:10	0
blueberries—1 cup	90	1	*	0
orange—1	65	Trace	*	0
peach—1	40	Trace	*	0
Vegetables				
tomato—1	25	Trace	*	0
potato—1	145	Trace	*	0
potato salad—1 cup	250	7	*	0
broccoli—1 cup	40	Trace	*	0
lettuce—3 leaves	Trace	Trace	*	0
onion—1 cup	65	Trace	*	0
corn—1 ear	120	1	*	0
asparagus—1 cup	30	Trace	*	0
green beans—1 cup	30	Trace	*	0
carrots—1 cup	50	Trace	*	0
cucumber—6 slices	5	Trace	*	0
peas—1 cup	150	1	*	0
French fried potatoes (oven heated)—10	110	4	26:10	0

are high in fibre, or bulk. There is evidence that a diet high in fibre may have a special part to play in lowering blood fats, especially cholesterol. There will be more about this later in this chapter.

Fruit juices do not have fibre and often have had extra sugar, and therefore calories, added. Eat a piece of fruit instead of drinking a glass of juice.

Eat More Fibre

Fibre is the newer name for roughage. Dietary fibres come only from plants. Animals foods have no fibre at all. Fibres are parts of the cells of plants. Fibre is not digested as it passes through people's intestines. It

BREADS, GRAINS AND CEREALS

	Calories	Total Fat (gm)	U to S ratio	Cholesterol (mgs)
bagel—1	165	2	*	0
baking powder biscuit—1	105	5	*	0
Italian bread—1 slice	85	Trace	*	0
raisin bread—1 slice	68	2	*	0
rye bread—1 slice	60	Trace	*	0
white bread—1 slice	70	1	*	0
oatmeal—1 cup cooked	130	2	*	0
bran flakes—1 cup	105	1	*	0
corn flakes—1 cup	95	Trace	*	0
egg noodles—1 cup	200	2	*	50
macaroni & cheese—1 cup	430	22	*	42
pancakes—1	60	2	*	20
spaghetti—1 cup	155	Trace	*	0
popcorn (air popped)— 1 cup	25	Trace	*	0
popcorn (popped with oil)—1 cup	40	2	*	0
rice—1 cup	180	Trace	*	0

SNACK FOODS, FATS AND OILS

	Calories	Total Fat (gm)	U to S ratio	Cholesterol (mgs)
vegetable shortening—1 T	110	13	30:10	0
lard—1 T	115	13	15:10	12
margarine—1 T	100	12	48:10	0
corn oil—1 T	120	14	72:10	0
soybean oil—1 T	120	14	60:10	0
olive oil—1 T	120	14	60:10	0
safflower oil—1 T	120	14	98:10	0
butter—1 T	100	12	7:10	33
French dressing—1 T	65	6	90:10	0
low-cal French dressing— 1 T	15	1		0
mayonnaise—1 T	100	11	45:10	10
cupcake with icing—1	130	5	15:10	0

does attract water though, and holds on to it. It makes a person's feces softer and bulkier and easier to pass. That's why fibre is good for constipation.

The waste of a person on a low-fibre diet will remain in the body for a longer time than the waste of a person on a high-fibre diet. More and more water will be reabsorbed the longer the waste material remains in the body. The result will be small, hard-to-pass stools and a longer time between bowel movements. Doctors are concerned that when waste is allowed to remain too long in the colon, it may increase the risk of cancer of the colon. Populations of people who eat diets that are high in fibre have many fewer colon-related problems.

If you have diabetes, colitis, or diverticulitis, don't add more fibre to your diet until you talk to your doctor first.

You can't guess how much fibre is in a food by looking at it. For example, cherries are low in fibre (for a fruit) and strawberries are high. Common sense about cooking doesn't help much either. Would you have thought that cooked carrots have the same amount of fibre as raw carrots? They do. Crunchy French bread is no higher in fibre than soft white bread, because in both cases the bran (loaded with fibre) has been removed. Also, when you toast bread, it gets harder, but toasting doesn't increase the amount of fibre—just as cooking the carrot did not increase the amount of fibre.

Doctors and researchers have found that fibre has a beneficial effect on lowering blood fats, especially cholesterol. This may play an important part in staying healthy.

To increase the amount of fibre in their diets, many people start by adding a little bran (especially oat bran) to soups, casseroles, muffins, pancakes, or spaghetti sauce. But adding bran may not be enough. The kind of fibre in bran is different from the kind of fibre in vegetables. Although they all aid in lessening constipation, the fibre in beans, vegetables, and oat bran seems to be better at helping the body manage fats and cholesterol in a healthy way.

If you don't already eat a high-fibre breakfast cereal, this is a good way to increase the amount of fibre in your diet. High-fibre cereals have 4 to 5 grams of fibre per serving.

Make Sure There Is Soluble Fibre in Your Diet

Fibre is important in everyone's diet, but a cholesterol-lowering diet should be high in soluble fibre. Most high-fibre foods (remember these foods all come from plants) have both soluble and insoluble fibre. These two kinds of fibre together are called "total dietary fibre." Most foods contain more insoluble fibre than the soluble kind, but only soluble fibre has been shown to have a cholesterol-lowering effect.

Volunteers in university studies were put on diets that were planned to be cholesterol-lowering. When some of the subjects ate foods high in soluble fibre, their blood cholesterol levels went down very quickly. And their cholesterol levels stayed down when they continued eating foods high in soluble fibre every day.

What are these foods that are high in soluble fibre? Oat bran and beans are especially high. They are not exotic or hard-to-find foods, but certainly foods that were a larger part of many healthy diets in previous generations.

How Much Fibre Do You Need?

The usual recommendation is at least 4 servings of high-fibre fruits and vegetables, and 2 servings of high-fibre breads and cereals each day. This means that most people will be eating one fruit or vegetable with each meal and another serving of fruit or vegetable as a snack.

When you add fibre to your diet, do so slowly. Many people experience gas or a full, bloated feeling for the first days. If this feeling doesn't disappear, eat slightly less fibre for a day or two and then gradually increase the amount of fibre again. Be sure to increase the amount of liquid you drink as you increase the amount of fibre in your diet. Remember that fibre absorbs water as it goes through the body.

SUPERMARKET STRATEGY: PLAIN TALK ABOUT CLAIMS AND LABELS

WHEN HELEN WENT for a checkup several months ago, her doctor told her that her serum (blood) cholesterol level was too high at 270. He also told her that her blood pressure was a little too high, despite the blood-pressure-lowering medication she had been on for years. The doctor told Helen to watch her diet, both for cholesterol and sodium. Too much sodium could make her blood pressure medication less effective. Helen tried to be careful, but after her most recent checkup, the doctor reported that her blood pressure was still too high and that her cholesterol had gone up even higher, to 290.

What went wrong? We could question the accuracy of one or more lab tests for cholesterol. We could point out that the difference between 270 and 290 is fairly minor. But we might also acknowledge the possibility that Helen's serum cholesterol really is going up. This is not surprising, since Helen is confused about what a cholesterol-lowering diet is all about. Helen has also been snookered by all the misleading claims in TV ads and the misleading labels on products in the supermarket. Helen is avoiding table salt and high-cholesterol foods such as eggs and shrimp, but she's taking in large amounts of sodium and saturated fat.

The label on a can of solid vegetable shortening brags that it has "no cholesterol." But when we read the list of ingredients, we see that it contains palm oil. As you can see from the chart on the next page, palm is one of the worst fats for a person's arteries. Helen has been cooking a lot of her foods in it.

A more honest and helpful label for foods might be "artery-friendly." Artery-friendly would describe a food that does not clog arteries or raise serum cholesterol levels. When you read labels on foods at the supermarket, select foods that have the artery-friendly fats at the beginning of

FATTY ACID COMPOSITION OF OILS & FATS

Saturated	Monounsaturated	Polyunsaturated

Safflower Oil

| 9 | 13 | 78 |

Sunflower Oil

| 11 | 20 | 69 |

Corn Oil

| 13 | 25 | 62 |

Olive Oil

| 14 | 77 | 9 |

Soybean Oil

| 15 | 24 | 61 |

Peanut Oil

| 18 | 48 | 34 |

Sockeye Salmon Oil

| 20 | 55 | 25 |

Cottonseed Oil

| 27 | 19 | 54 |

Lard

| 41 | 47 | 12 |

Palm Oil

| 51 | 39 | 10 |

Beef Tallow

| 52 | 44 | 4 |

Butterfat

| 66 | 30 | 4 |

Palm Kernel Oil

| 86 | 12 | 2 |

Coconut Oil

| 92 | 6 | 2 |

Sources: *Handbook No. 8-4* and Human Nutrition Information Service, U.S.D.A.

the chart. The first five on the list are the most artery-friendly. Buy foods that list these oils: safflower, sunflower, corn, olive or soy. Don't buy any food item whose label lists any of these artery-clogging saturated fats: lard, palm oil, beef tallow, butter, palm kernel oil or coconut oil.

Many many foods are artery-friendly: fruits, vegetables, grains, complex carbohydrates, chicken, turkey, fish. Foods that are less artery-friendly need to be eaten in small amounts: red meats, most dairy products, saturated fats and foods made from saturated fats. That's a fairly short list. We could wonder how Helen managed to eat so many artery-clogging foods. The problem is that modern supermarkets are filled with artery-clogging convenience foods, most of which did not exist when Helen was a young girl.

The giant food companies that make so many convenience foods with saturated fats have planned enormous advertising campaigns. They know that labels such as "no cholesterol" get people such as Helen to buy foods that are actually not health-promoting.

A Walk Down Supermarket Aisles

Let's take a make-believe walk down the aisles of a supermarket and make sense out of all the claims. (We'll skip the pet food and non-food aisles, which make up about one-third of the store.)

To minimize sodium intake, a shopper should *not* buy any product whose label lists salt or sodium (sodium chloride, monosodium glutamate, etc.).

In most supermarkets you come first to the produce section. This is one of the safest aisles in which you can fill up your shopping cart. All fruits, except for coconut, are artery-friendly and very low in sodium. All fresh vegetables are artery-friendly. Avocados are high in fat and need to be consumed in moderation. But at least most of the fat in avocados is the safer, unsaturated type.

Next in the supermarket we come to the aisle with ketchup, mayonnaise, oils, salad dressings, etc. Here you need to do some careful reading of labels before you decide what to put in your shopping cart. By law, ingredients must be listed in order of their prominence by weight. The main ingredients come first. Foods such as mayonnaise, ketchup, relish, etc., are generally safe from the point of view of fat, but they are fairly high in sodium. If you or someone in your family needs to be on strict sodium restriction, you can make these items at home.

The good news is that the new "Lite Ketchup," which is reduced in calories and low-sodium, tastes much better than the older versions of low-sodium ketchup. The bad news is that the label is a bit deceptive. It lists the calories, milligrams of sodium, etc., for one tablespoon. One level tablespoon is a pretty small amount of ketchup, compared to an average serving. An average serving is probably two or three times that amount, so you have to figure you'd get two or three times the amount of calories, sodium, fat, etc.

To read the labels on soy sauce is an excellent learning experience about portion size information. Kikkoman regular soy sauce has 960 mgs of sodium in one tablespoon. The Lite version has 599 mgs of sodium in a tablespoon. But the label states that each serving of Lite has only 85 mgs of sodium (low enough to make it appear to be a low-sodium product). The company makes this claim by listing a serving as half a teaspoon. Who do you know who puts only half a teaspoon of soy sauce on Chinese food? (We have a low-sodium soy sauce substitute on page 62.)

Most commercial mustard is too high in sodium for anyone with a sodium restriction. Homemade mustard (page 57) takes only a few minutes.

Read the labels before you put any commercial salad dressings in your shopping cart. Be realistic about how much you are going to put on your salad, compared to the tiny one-level-tablespoon portion the labels describe. How artery-friendly are the oils in the salad dressings?

Many commercial seasonings are very high in sodium. Leaving off table salt won't accomplish much if you use Shake 'n Bake coating mixes, MSG, tenderizer, etc. Pickles and olives are very high in sodium.

The soda (pop, tonic) aisle may be next. Sodas may not be health foods, but are safe in terms of fat and sodium. Most diet sodas are now made with NutraSweet, rather than sodium saccharin, and so are low in sodium. It's easy to read the label and make sure that the kind you are buying does have NutraSweet.

If you enjoy coffee or tea, you will be glad to know that they are safe in terms of fat or sodium restriction. But be careful about what you add to them. Many powdered, non-dairy creamers or "lighteners" are made from saturated fat, usually from the worst offender—coconut oil. Someone suggested we call them "heavy-eners" rather than lighteners. Like real cream, these products are bad for your arteries. Fortunately, the frozen coffee "creamers" are now made from safer fats, such as soy oil. Some people prefer to drink their coffee black; some have learned to like nonfat milk in their coffee or tea.

There is an exception. The fancy instant coffees, such as Cafe Vienna or Dutch Chocolate Mint, contain a large amount of saturated fat in the form of coconut oil. In Café Français, hydrogenated coconut oil is the first ingredient. (Coffee is the fourth ingredient, after coconut oil, corn syrup solids and sugar.)

You may also like hot cocoa. There is some controversy about the effect of cocoa on serum cholesterol. Although much of the fat in cocoa is saturated, a large portion is stearic acid, which does not seem to increase serum cholesterol the way other saturated fats do. Hot cocoa mixes, however, may contain coconut oil, palm, or palm kernel oils. Read the labels before you buy!

The snack food section is huge in most supermarkets. The healthiest snack is probably plain (unbuttered unsalted) popcorn, popped at home in a hot air popper. None of the commonly available snack foods is healthy: potato chips, corn chips, etc. Just because a label says "no salt" or "no cholesterol" does not make the food good for you. You're better off avoiding the snack food aisle.

Nuts such as peanuts, almonds or walnuts are high in calories and sometimes salt. But at least the fat is more unsaturated than saturated.

Sweet snack foods, such as cupcakes, pies and other lunchbox treats, also get a large amount of shelf space. You can safely assume that they are all high in calories and sugar. You can judge the fat by reading the label. None of them are good for you, but you probably already know that.

Ironically, people think that Mom's homemade apple pie or cupcakes are healthier, because they are homemade and seem to be sacred, like the flag. But Mom's homemade baked goods may be just as bad for you as the commercial ones. Did Mom use solid vegetable oil or lard in her piecrust? Many Moms today use a piecrust mix having either beef fat or lard. Mom's homemade chocolate goodies are not good for you. Cake mixes and frosting mixes (or canned frosting) have a lot of sugar, sodium and fat. Sad to say, solid chocolate is not artery-friendly. Avoid anything made from baking chocolate.

It's ironic too that although donuts are commonly thought of as being unhealthy, muffins have an admirable reputation. Certainly it is entirely possible to make healthy muffins; see pages 220–221. But most muffins eaten by Americans are made from unhealthy ingredients. Muffins from package mixes, that mix up in a jiffy, may have beef fat.

Muffins made by the large donut companies may be tasty, but they're not healthy. The bran muffin of a huge donut chain has 122 calories more than the same company's Bavarian Cream-filled donut covered with chocolate frosting. It also has 35 to 40 percent more fat. Oat bran muffins from another donut company are full of fat, sugar and sodium. It is understandable why people are fooled; the name "oat bran muffin" sounds so healthy. The donut company's oat bran muffins taste and look especially appetizing to anyone who has tried to make homemade oat bran muffins using very little fat. The homemade, hard, flat, dry little pious muffins offer little competition. Try our recipe on page 220 instead.

The bread section in most supermarkets tends to be huge. Commercial bread products may be made from either artery-friendly fats or artery-clogging fats. But it's easy enough to read the fine print. Remember not to be fooled by the big "no cholesterol" labels. Almost all commercial bread products are high in sodium. In fact, there is more sodium in a piece of regular white or wheat bread than in a piece of bacon. For people who need to restrict sodium, homemade breads make sense. See pages 224–239.

In the cereal section, you can find items with many unhealthy ingredients, such as sugar, which may even be the first ingredient. You can also find healthy foods that list oat bran as the first ingredient. There are also many cereals made from regular bran, which is wheat bran. Regular bran is particularly effective in relieving constipation. Oat bran is more effective in dealing with serum cholesterol problems. You may want to buy products with both types of bran.

In the canned goods section, you will need to continue to read the fine print. Canned fruits are safe in fat and sodium, as are tomato paste and "no-salt-added" vegetables. You would be wise not to stock up on the "no-salt-added" vegetables until after you've decided whether or not you like them. Most people find them tasteless and much prefer fresh or frozen vegetables.

Very few people like the low-sodium canned soups. They can make eating seem like a punishment. Be careful in reading the labels on reduced-salt soups; the portion sizes listed may not accurately represent the portions one would eat. The labels on regular canned soups often give nutritional information as if 2¾ persons were to share one small can.

No-salt-added canned tuna is a safe staple to keep on hand. Canned products with meat in them are not artery-friendly.

Meats have little labelling information, so you need to prepare yourself before you face the meat counter. Many doctors recommend that we limit ourselves to three small servings of lean red meat each week. This includes all breakfasts, all lunches and all dinners. Although lean meat is much better than well-marbled (i.e., fatty) meat, it still has considerable saturated fat and cholesterol. It's important to be accurate about portion size.

A serving of cooked meat is about three ounces. This is the size of the smallest, thinnest hamburger patty at McDonald's. It is much smaller than the average U.S. portion, which is about 8 ounces. Some restaurants brag that they serve 16 or even 32 ounces of steak—king-size portions. When you buy red meat (beef, pork, lamb), buy about 4 ounces of raw meat per person.

While you are at the meat counter, choose more chicken and turkey. For the sake of your arteries, don't buy any bacon, sausage, hot dogs, bologna, etc. Pass the deli counter without buying any cold cuts. Turkey bologna and turkey or chicken hot dogs are lower (but not low) in fat, but are very high in sodium. Ground turkey has had fat added to it.

You should plan more meals around fish, although this is more difficult for people who live in areas where good fresh fish is rare. Fairly recently it has been found that fatty fishes contain substances that seem to protect people against heart disease. The substances are called omega-3 fatty acids. This may explain why Greenland Eskimos have had almost no heart disease, despite their fatty diets. We would all be wise to eat more tuna, swordfish, salmon, rainbow trout and low-cholesterol shellfish such as oysters and scallops. We would be especially wise to eat these foods broiled or baked, rather than deep-fat fried.

There is some confusion about shellfish and cholesterol. It's true that shrimp are high in cholesterol; a 3½-ounce serving has 152 mgs of cholesterol. For comparison, consider that a single egg yolk has 274 mgs of cholesterol. A 3-ounce (tiny) serving of lean beef has 100 mgs. So shrimp is like many high-cholesterol foods. You need to eat it in moderate amounts, and you need to consider how much saturated fat is in these same foods.

Actually, shellfish have an advantage over eggs, meat and cheese. The following quote is from the *Tufts University Diet & Nutrition Letter* (Vol. 5, no. 5, June 1987):

Seafood lovers who avoid shellfish may be doing themselves a double disservice, for *researchers have discovered that much of what they formerly took to be cholesterol in mollusks is really a composite of several different types of sterols and these noncholesterol sterols may actually inhibit cholesterol absorption.* Scientists recently reporting in the journal *Metabolism* have found that volunteers who were fed diets containing oysters and clams absorbed 25 percent less cholesterol than when they ate crab, which is classified as a crustacean rather than a mollusk. That's not to say that crustaceans are bad and mollusks are good. On the contrary, *most shellfish*—mollusks *and* crustaceans—are actually fairly low in cholesterol. A 1½-pound Maine lobster contains only about 140 milligrams. Ten small clams have just 30 to 31 milligrams. And Alaska king crab contributes a scant 42 milligrams per 3½-ounce serving. Moreover, *all* shellfish are extremely low in fat as well as calories. In fact, only about 0.5 to 2 percent of shellfish is fat, says Jacob Exler, PhD, who is currently preparing a "handbook 8" on shellfish for the U.S. Department of Agriculture. And much of the fat in these sea foods is omega-3 fatty acids.

When you look at foods in the store's freezer cases, be sure to read the fine print. You will probably decide to pass up nearly all items. The frozen entrees are very high in sodium and often contain artery-clogging fats. Ice cream is unfortunately not artery-friendly, although there are many safe substitutes. Fruit sorbets, sherbet and frozen yogurt often are very low in fat.

Plain frozen vegetables are fine, but you need to avoid those with fancy (high-fat high-sodium) sauces. The label on a product such as broccoli with cheese sauce lists the sodium, calorie and fat content as if six people were sharing that one small box. In real life, two people often share a box of frozen vegetables, and so, each gets three times the amount of calories, sodium and fat as the label describes.

In the large dairy case at the supermarket, there are very few artery-friendly choices: nonfat yogurt and nonfat or skim milk. The American Dairy Association has spent millions of dollars trying to convince us that milk and cheese are foods we should all eat every day. Although they're a good source of protein and calcium, they are not at all artery-friendly. Most cheeses have more fat than fatty beef and it's largely artery-clogging saturated fat. Many people find cheese to be the most difficult fatty food to give up. It will be much easier for you to give it up if you don't put it in your shopping cart.

There are an increasing number of lower-fat and low-sodium cheeses on the market. Because they still have some saturated fat, it's wise not to overdo. A lower-fat cheese has about 4–7 grams of fat per ounce, compared to about 10 grams per ounce for a regular cheese. It may have about 15 mgs of cholesterol per ounce, compared to 30 grams of cholesterol per ounce in a regular cheese. When you add lower-fat low-sodium cheese to a dish such as lasagne, grate it and spread a thin layer. To be honest with you, lower-fat low-sodium cheeses are rather tasteless. It does not take a great deal of willpower to go easy on them.

The differences in the amounts of fat in different types of milk may surprise you. Whole milk, which is often called homogenized milk, has 3.3 percent fat, but this figure is based on weight. Most of the weight in milk is the water content. If you count only those parts of the milk that contain calories, the fat in whole milk represents 74 out of every 150 calories per cup. In other words, whole milk is 49 percent fat, and much of this fat is saturated fat. With low-fat (2 percent) milk, 35 percent of the calories come from fat. In nonfat milk, only 5 percent of the calories come from fat.

Labels on other dairy products can also be misleading. "Light" cream cheese may have only half the fat of regular cream cheese, but it's still very high in fat. In fact, 75 percent of the calories in "light" cream cheese come from fat.

Butter has more saturated fat than lard or beef tallow, neither of which you would probably choose to eat. The ads on TV that state that butter has no more calories than margarine are accurate, but misleading. Butter is bad for you and your arteries because of the large amount of cholesterol and saturated fat, not because of the calories.

In selecting a margarine or "spread," pick one whose first ingredient is liquid safflower, sunflower or corn oil. Soft margarines in tubs are a good choice.

Why Helen's Cholesterol and Blood Pressure Are Up

Helen had not understood the basic principles of a cholesterol-lowering diet. If someone were to ask her what she had to eat yesterday, her answer would have sounded fine, superficially. Helen would tell us that she had granola, an oat bran muffin, cottage cheese, lean beef, chicken, broccoli and potato.

When we look more closely at what Helen ate, we begin to see why Helen's serum cholesterol is going up. For breakfast, Helen stayed away from bacon and eggs. Instead she had granola (made from coconut oil) and whole milk (49 percent fat). She put "light" (75 percent fat) cream cheese on her white bread toast (high in sodium). She put a non-dairy creamer (with coconut oil) in her coffee.

While she was out doing errands, Helen stopped for a snack. Even though the donut shop was the only place to stop for a cup of coffee, Helen avoided donuts. Instead she had an oat bran muffin (which was mostly flour, sugar and coconut oil, plus a very small amount of oat bran). She put coffee creamer (coconut oil) in her coffee.

For lunch Helen ordered the "diet plate" at the restaurant. It had cottage cheese (high in salt and fat), plus a 6-ounce hamburger patty. Helen had a glass of milk (49 percent fat). Her roll and butter added quite a bit of sodium and fat.

For dinner, Helen avoided high-cholesterol foods such as shrimp. She had (high-sodium) Shake 'n Bake chicken. She has been told to take off the skin, but she doesn't because that would make the chicken too dry. Helen makes homemade potatoes au gratin (from a package mix) and heats up a broccoli-with-cheese-sauce concoction. She heats up some dinner rolls from a can (they're made from beef fat). For dessert, Helen serves homemade apple pie. (The crust was made from a mix and contains lard.) People at Helen's house drink big (16-ounce) glasses of whole milk (49 percent) and ask for seconds. Coffee with coconut oil creamer completes the meal. While watching TV, Helen nibbled a few cookies (the label lists palm kernel oil).

Poor Helen took in enough saturated fat for her serum cholesterol to go up and enough sodium to interfere with the effectiveness of her blood-pressure-lowering medication.

The moral for all of us is: Avoid the temptation to guess how much fat or sodium is in any food item. Common sense is of very little help. Who could guess that bread has more sodium than bacon, or that granola could be worse than eggs?

You need to make a study of foods before you buy them. When you look at a food label that does contain nutrition information, but no cholesterol information, it is fairly safe to assume that the product is high in cholesterol. There are charts about fat in Chapter One. For sodium, see the charts at the end of this book.

One problem with many meal plans is that they assume that people eat most of their foods at "meals," with an occasional snack. Surveys show that this is not true for many people. They eat between meals or they eat casually instead of having formal meals, yet people tend to overlook foods eaten informally when they're reporting what they ate. Dr. Paul A. Fine reported to the American Medical Association that the average family in the United States does *not* eat three square meals a day, even though people in the family may believe that this is the case. Rather, the average family actually engages in 20 "food contacts," although people are reluctant to admit this, even to themselves. You need to look at the way *you* actually eat. When you eat matters less than *what* you eat. Even if you are eating at an "informal contact," the food item needs to be low in sodium.

MAKING HEALTHY EATING REASONABLY CONVENIENT

MANY PEOPLE MAKE an attempt at healthier eating and soon give it up. They find it's not convenient, so they make excuses for not eating the way they know they should. It's up to you. To greatly increase the odds that you will stick with healthy eating, you need to make it reasonably convenient.

This chapter is designed to give you some practical help in making the transition to healthier eating easier. This chapter is a collection of hints that have worked for other people.

1. Take an Honest Look at the Food That's in Your Kitchen Now

If your kitchen is now stocked with canned hash and canned soups, packaged mixes, butter and tenderizer, you may have a problem. Ask yourself or your spouse: "What are we going to do with all those unhealthy foods?" Use them up to be thrifty? Unhealthy foods used for noble motives (like thrift) are just as bad for you as any other unhealthy food. You could give or throw them away.

When you first start to plan healthier cooking on a regular basis, it's easy to imagine what you won't be using: salt, MSG, and butter. But you also need to buy some items that you may never have bought. Low-sodium products are an obvious first thought. But we advise you to buy *only one* of each new item and taste it to see if you find the food palatable. It makes sense to stock up on items that you know your family likes, such as uncooked spaghetti, fruits, and so forth. If your spice cupboard is rather bare, buy some fresh ones. We recommend basil, cinnamon, dill, pepper, dry mustard, paprika, garlic powder, and onion powder (see Seasonings, page 52).

Wine is a favorite ingredient for people who take pride in making low-fat, low-sodium dishes taste as good as any without restrictions. All the alcohol cooks away, but a nice flavor is left. But do not use cooking wines that have added salt. (This is an old-time practice to discourage the cook from drinking it.) If you want to try just one bottle, we recommend that you buy a bottle of dry vermouth. Because the flavor is fairly "strong," it adds a lot of flavor. With plain food, such as chicken soup, leaving out the salt makes a very bland dish until you add the vermouth and let it cook. Adding wine or vermouth does *not* make the food taste like wine. If your unsalted cooking tastes bland, try it. If you prefer not to use wine, substitute fresh or frozen lemon juice. Substitute half as much lemon juice as the amount of wine called for in the recipe.

2. Make Healthy Substitutions

Experienced cooks often modify recipes and substitute one ingredient for another. Following are some suggestions for healthy substitutions.

Instead of using eggs, use egg substitutes, such as Egg Beaters or Scramblers. You'll find these in the freezer case at the store. You can also choose to use just egg whites, as commercial egg substitutes are made largely from egg whites. You can save money by separating eggs at home and discarding the cholesterol-filled yolks. The egg whites are fine, health-wise, and will look a little more "eggy" if you add a drop of yellow food coloring. Egg white salad (discard the yolk after hard-boiling) looks authentic with a little yellow mustard. Chopped chives or dill adds a nice flavor to help make up for the missing salt.

For whole or low-fat milk, substitute skim milk. (Nonfat dry milk is perfectly fine from the point of view of health. It is palatable in cooking, but very few people like to drink it.)

Yogurt cheese makes a very good substitute for sour cream or cream cheese. Regular yogurt is too watery to make an appetizing substitute. The recipe for yogurt cheese is on page 88.

To achieve a substitute bacony flavor, you can use Liquid Hickory Smoke flavoring, which is sold with the spices at most supermarkets. To add a bacony flavor to a sandwich, mix ⅛ of a teaspoon of Liquid Hickory Smoke with mayonnaise or margarine and spread on bread. You can add a teaspoon of Liquid Hickory Smoke to a pot of soup.

A healthier substitute for sausage can be made by flavoring *lean* ground beef, as with the pizza topping on page 155.

For any kind of a tomato sauce, use diluted, plain tomato paste. Be sure that the brand of tomato paste you buy does not have added salt. The contrast in the sodium content is unbelievable. Fresh tomatoes would add only 28 mgs of sodium, but may be out of season. For many months of the year, the only available fresh tomatoes are hard and tasteless, plus very expensive. Tomato paste has only 69 mgs of sodium in a small can. A medium-size can of stewed tomatoes has about 1,303 mgs of sodium. A can of whole tomatoes has 900 mgs of sodium. Tomato puree has 1,701 mgs of sodium. A can of tomato sauce has 2,130 mgs of sodium.

For canned vegetables, substitute fresh or frozen.

For ice cream, substitute frozen yogurt, which is usually sold in the same freezer case at the store.

To make a healthier substitute for baking chocolate, use 3 tablespoons of cocoa plus 1 tablespoon of margarine for each one-ounce square of baking chocolate called for in the recipe.

Baking soda and baking powder are both high in sodium. If you are on a restricted diet it would be very unwise to allot your few milligrams of sodium to baking soda, which has 821 mgs in a teaspoon (5 mL). Unfortunately, baking soda (sodium bicarbonate) has no commonly available low-sodium replacement. You may have read that potassium bicarbonate can be bought at pharmacies and used as a substitute, but the pharmacies we checked no longer stock it.

Baking *powder* has fewer mgs of sodium—339 per teaspoon (5 mL). Low-sodium baking powders have less than 1 mg in each teaspoon (5 mL). The instructions on the low-sodium baking powders advise the cook to use 1½ times the amount the recipe calls for when replacing regular baking powder. We had the best results when we shook the jar *every time* before measuring. We found that low-sodium baking powder was most successful in pancakes, waffles and muffins, but did not work in cakes or quick breads such as banana bread. You may want to consider using regular baking powder in recipes that don't work with low-sodium baking powder.

You need to accept the fact that some recipes really cannot be converted to healthier versions. A cheese soufflé is normally made from eggs, butter, and cheese. A soufflé made from egg substitute, unsalted margarine, and low-fat low-sodium cheese is likely to be so tasteless that no one would want to eat it. There is no yummy substitute for chocolate cream pie with whipped cream.

Dishes that depend primarily on salt for the traditional flavor taste pretty awful in unsalted versions. There is no recipe for bread stuffing in this book, because the real flavor is salt. Even with sage or savory, unsalted stuffing tastes like wet bread.

3. Stay with Healthy Eating and You'll Adjust Faster

The evidence that soluble fibre is healthy is pretty overwhelming. Many people start to add oat bran and dried beans to their diet, but they soon stop eating oat bran or beans because of problem with flatulence or gas. But if you start with relatively small amounts and if you *continue* to eat such foods, your body will adjust. After several weeks of eating beans, most people have much much less gas than they had at first. So give foods with soluble fibre a real try.

When you first start eating unsalted and low-sodium foods, many foods seem rather tasteless. But the good news is that this reaction does not last. After about 2 to 3 weeks of being on a true low-sodium diet, most people find that their taste sense starts to adjust. They no longer miss the instantaneous flavor of salt; they detect and enjoy the subtle flavors that are found in various foods. Fresh unsalted vegetables, for example, taste better because you become more aware of the vegetables' natural flavors. But remember, it takes a little while on a low-sodium intake before this change takes place.

When a food has salt on or in it, you notice the taste as soon as it is in your mouth. Unsalted food does *not* give you that quick zap of instant flavor recognition; it is simply slower. When you put a piece of salted steak into your mouth, you taste the salt instantly and then you notice the taste of the meat. With unsalted meat, there is no instantaneous zap—only the slower appreciation of the flavor of the meat itself. If you keep this in mind, you won't be looking for an instant zap of flavor from unsalted foods.

Another thing that happens after a few weeks of low-sodium eating is a reaction to sodium itself. You begin to detect sodium or a "salty" taste in products that *used to* seem OK. For example, dry cereals or packaged frosting mixes begin to taste objectionably salty. This change is actually a good thing. Instead of craving salty foods, you will begin to enjoy low-sodium foods much more than you did at first. This change has been noticed by many people who give up all high-sodium foods. But it does *not* happen to people who give up *only* table salt. You can use this taste readjustment to your advantage. If you stay on a low-sodium diet day after day, you will automatically begin to enjoy the many flavors of different foods. But this also means that it is particularly foolish to "cheat" on a low-sodium diet. If you go back to eating foods with a lot of sodium, your perception of saltiness may change, and low-sodium foods will seem too bland again, as they did in the first days of low-sodium eating.

Let's be realistic—if you have enjoyed salting your food all your life, you're going to miss the salt, especially at first. But if you switch back and forth between low- and high-sodium eating, you are making the change harder on yourself, because you won't get the physical readjustment in taste. So the hint is to stay with low-sodium eating on a regular basis.

4. Add Lots of Other Seasonings and Make the Meal Look Appealing

If you learn to make food taste delicious, you and other people in your family are not so likely to get discouraged and reach for the salt shaker. In cooking, fresh vegetables, herbs and spices add flavor, as do table wine and lemon juice. Instead of putting the salt shaker on the table, put out lots of other seasonings. Treat yourself to a nice pepper mill. Try lemon juice, vinegar, onion powder, or any herb or spice that you like. Put out the Unsalt Shaker (recipes, pages 52).

Low-fat low-sodium cookbooks have been accused of relying too heavily on garlic, tomato paste, wine or onions. The reason healthy recipes do this, though, becomes clear when you try doing some cooking. When you leave out the salt, you really do need to add something with flavor—onions, green peppers, mushrooms, spices, herbs, garlic or wine. If you dislike garlic, or do not want wine, you will certainly leave them out. But, if you leave out the garlic and the wine and the mushrooms and the peppers, you're going to end up with a very bland dish. Use the flavors that you and your family like.

Foods that traditionally have little flavor *except salt* (such as commercially prepared chicken soup or chicken pie) are the ones that are most difficult to make into delicious low-salt versions. It may be wise to wait a few weeks or until your taste has really readjusted to low-salt eating before you expect unsalted chicken pie to seem tasty. You will *not* find a recipe for chicken pie in this book, because frankly, we could not come up with a tasty low-salt version. But making a tasty low-salt Chicken Cacciatore (page 170) is fairly easy, because the usual flavors—tomato and onion—are there to add taste.

In this book, portions are figured for a person who needs to cut down on salt (or fat or calories). For meat, the portion size is 4 ounces (120 g) of raw meat. This will cook down to approximately 3 ounces (90 g) when cooked; you may be surprised at how small this looks. The best way to know meat weight is to buy a kitchen scale. Since a 3-ounce (90 g) cooked serving of meat or fish looks small, it helps to fill the dinner plate with other foods. A generous serving of rice, noodles, pasta, potatoes or vegetables can help. Or serve one green and one yellow vegetable.

Attractive garnishes help, too—Corn Relish, Five-Minute Chutney (pages 63 and 64). Low-sodium Mustard (page 57) can help eye and taste appeal. You can put Low-sodium Ketchup (page 55) in a squeeze bottle if you want it to look like familiar old ketchup.

5. Make Extra to Freeze

Is that a piece of advice you've heard again and again? It's here because freezing healthy foods helps to make them convenient. Having delicious foods on hand will make it easier to stay on your diet. Some foods freeze well and are delicious when defrosted and reheated. Other foods dry out and are not as tasty as when cooked fresh and just served. You will find out what works for you as you go along.

Cooked dried beans are a wonderfully healthful substitute for meat, but are not very convenient. It makes sense to soak and then cook up a large batch, for example two bags of fried beans. Then you can freeze them in amounts that would be convenient for your family.

As a general rule, it's a good idea to freeze the amount that you will want to serve. For example, you might make two meat loaves: one for a family meal and the other to freeze for sandwiches. It makes sense to slice the second meat loaf and wrap each slice before freezing. That way you have a convenient low-sodium sandwich filling. Try slicing bread before freezing, too. You can freeze the loaf of bread wrapped in one piece and take out slices as needed. Plan ahead for freezing: Use freezer quality plastic bags, freezer paper, or aluminum foil for wrapping; glass canning jars with screw tops are ideal for freezing soups and sauces; plastic freezer containers are easy to buy and use. Keep your freezing equipment on hand so you can make another convenient meal.

Remember, liquids expand as they freeze; don't overfill your containers. Leave some room when freezing soups and sauces in glass or plastic containers. When freezing food in plastic bags, you need to leave room for expansion; don't put the tie down too close to the food. Cover foods tightly; freezers, especially the frost-free type, rob foods of moisture. Take care to be sure that, when it's defrosted, your food will still be delicious.

Keep ingredients such as chicken stock handy in the freezer. Home-made low-sodium chicken stock is such a delicious addition to a recipe, it's worth the extra effort to make it ahead to have on hand.

Freeze leftover tomato sauce in ice cube trays. The metal ice cube trays seem to work better than the plastic ice cube trays. Put your leftover sauce in the ice cube tray after dinner and freeze overnight. The next day, remove the metal divider and dump the frozen cubes into a plastic freezer bag. Use the cubes to flavor sauces and to toss over noodles or pasta.

Defrost frozen foods in a hurry by running hot water around the outside of the container. Run the water until the block of food is loose and you can dump it into the top of a double boiler. Then heat the food over medium heat until it's defrosted and hot. Although the double-boiler method is easy, it's not nearly as fast as using a microwave oven. A microwave oven is a relatively expensive kitchen tool, but it makes low-sodium low-fat eating more convenient. If there is a way to afford it, give serious thought to buying a microwave oven. The combination of freezing in serving-sized portions, then defrosting and heating food in a microwave shortens meal preparation time.

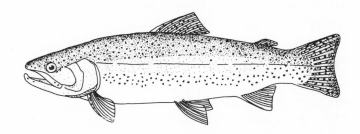

6. Buy and Use the Right Equipment

Many people have gotten into the habit of using lots of convenience foods, which require very little food preparation. If—for the sake of your health—you decide to give up frozen entrees, Shake 'n Bake, canned soups, etc., then you will have to go back to real cooking. For this you'll need a good sharp kitchen knife and a good vegetable peeler.

Cooking is more convenient if your kitchen is stocked with the tools you need, such as a frying pan with a flat bottom, small and large saucepans with lids, a soup pot, a wire whisk, a mixing bowl or two, a sharp kitchen knife, a vegetable peeler, a big stirring spoon, either wood or metal, and a vegetable steamer.

7. Try to Get a Friend or Family Member to Go Along with Healthier Eating

Having the moral support of a friend or family member can help when you feel discouraged. But don't make the mistake of turning the responsibility over to someone else. Other people can be a help, but you are the one who decides what food to put in your mouth. For example, since you know that pickles are high in sodium, you can avoid putting them on the plate. People who get involved in planning their own diets are more likely to stay with them. If you aren't the cook at your house, you can still read labels and make positive suggestions.

Shopping, meal planning and cooking will be more convenient if you don't make separate high- and low-sodium meals. The major reason for not preparing two separate meals, however, is the realization that this procedure usually results in one tasty high-sodium high-fat meal and one tasteless low-sodium low-fat meal.

Other family members can add a little salt at the table. But they would be well advised to salt lightly. The offspring of people with high blood pressure are fairly likely to develop this condition when they are older, especially if they eat high-sodium foods. You can do family members a tremendous favor if you teach them to enjoy foods that are delicious without being high in sodium or saturated fat.

8. Don't Fall into the Trap of Making Excuses for Eating Unhealthy Foods

If you hear yourself making these excuses, stop:

"It's only a little piece of ham, so it's okay."

"The recipe won't be traditional without——"

"The label says it has no cholesterol."

Another kind of excuse for staying on a high-sodium diet is an intellectual statement in defense of salt: "The need for salt is so inborn that animals made long treks to salt licks!" But you can point out that human beings were not among the trekkers. Only herbivores did this. (Herbivores are animals that eat only plants and thus get a diet that is rich in potassium and deficient in sodium.) Herbivores can have a true salt craving that makes them go in search of salt licks. Omnivores and carnivores might have gone to salt licks too, but in search of herbivores, not in search of salt.

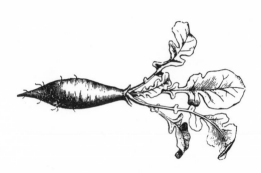

9. Start to Plan Each Meal Around a Food That's Good For You

When you first switch to healthier eating, it seems as if all you can think about is what you can't eat. It's more productive to start with the foods you can eat. Think of all the foods that are rich in complex carbohydrates.

Let's say you need to think of seven dinner menus for the next week. Let's say that you will serve red meats at three meals. For the other four, you can plan around one chicken, one fish, one pasta and one bean dish. If you are feeling more inclined to give up red meat, you could have only two meals per week with it, and two with chicken. Or you could have one meal per week with red meat, two with chicken, two with pasta, etc. In many families the bean choices are less familiar. So each week, you can try one new bean recipe. This cookbook can give you lots of suggestions.

Plan breakfasts around good sources of soluble fibre, especially oat bran. You can serve it as a hot cereal, with skim milk and fruit. When you do this, add some toast with margarine and jelly. Otherwise, the oat bran/skim milk/fruit is so free of fat that you may have trouble making it until lunch time. Some people mix oat bran with regular oatmeal. Plain oatmeal is a healthy choice. There are many healthy cold cereals. Homemade muffins or French toast or pancakes are other options.

Some lunches can be planned around split pea or bean soup. Tacos with bean filling are rich in soluble fibre. Lunch at home can be beans and corn bread. Brown bagged lunches can have soup or a leftover casserole in a thermos. See page 95 for healthy sandwich fillings.

10. Use This Book to Help You Get Used to Healthier Cooking

By using recipes in this book, you get used to this type of cooking and will be ready to evaluate other recipes. Each time you look at a new or old recipe, think about *each ingredient* for a minute and ask yourself if it is OK for healthy eating. If it's not, you can leave it out (salt, tenderizer), or you can substitute something that is healthier (low-sodium tuna for regular tuna, yogurt cheese for sour cream).

Most of the recipes in this book are planned to serve four people. But on the other hand, these four servings are an approximation. The recipes would not serve four teenage boys or others with large appetites. Alice B. Toklas was once asked how many people a recipe would serve. She answered, "How should I know how many it serves? It depends on their appetites, what else they have for dinner, whether they like it or not."

A few recipes state that they will serve more or fewer persons. With a recipe for baked bread, for example, it's not feasible to make bread that just serves four.

Following most of the recipes, a sodium and calorie count is given. These numbers were calculated from tables provided by the United States Department of Agriculture (USDA).

In some recipes in this book, no sodium or calorie content is given. Recipes such as tacos have so many different possibilities of combinations that selecting one version would be arbitrary. A taco with bean filling or meat? With or without cheese? What kind of cheese? In other cases it is impossible to know what the yield is. Let's say that a carrot is cut up and used to flavor a chicken stock, but is removed from the stock. How would you know how much of the sodium or calories were removed and how much stays in the stock?

11. Be Careful When You're Eating Away from Home

Americans, on the average, eat 33 percent of their meals away from home. The more restrictive your diet is, the harder it is to choose items from standard menus. Most restaurants today make extensive use of prepared frozen foods, which are sometimes just reheated in a microwave oven. Such foods are high in fat and sodium. This is especially true of restaurant chains; the practice is *not* at all limited to fast-food restaurants.

Although it's not commonly recognized, many regular restaurants have also switched over to the use of prepared food items. The majority of restaurants today buy prepared entrees—something like "TV dinners"—and keep them in freezers. That way they can offer a varied menu without needing a well-trained chef.

The fact that a restaurant uses prepared food is likely to be a well-kept secret. If you want to learn more about the state of the art of restaurant food, you owe it to yourself to take a look at one of the many trade journals written for restaurant managers. Large public libraries have copies of them.

In these trade journals a company that sells cooking oil brags that its oil can be re-used for frying 2,948 servings while the other company's oil can be re-used for *only* 2,734 servings. A company that sells Italian food based an advertising campaign for restaurant managers on the notion that its food comes so ready that the restaurant can hire untrained people instead of cooks: "Teach him to boil water and you've got it made."

There are TV-dinner-type choices for seafood, chicken, meat, vegetables, appetizers and desserts. The meats often come partially pre-cooked with the grill marks burnt in. The flavor may have been rubbed or even injected into the food. These frozen entrees are highly salted—that's why you feel thirsty after eating out. The large amount of salt is also likely to make you retain fluid and make you think you've gained weight and ruined your diet. Such entrees are often made from unhealthy saturated fats such as coconut oil.

When telephone surveyors have asked restaurants about the use of pre-fixed foods, the results have, unfortunately, not shown universal honesty. Unfortunately, 80 percent of those who denied using any pre-fixed foods in the first telephone survey changed their position when the caller in the second telephone survey pretended to be a sales representative of a company with a better price on pre-fixed restaurant food. Some restaurants, of course, do cook raw foods from scratch. These are the ones you want to locate.

There is a reason why you need to be aware of the wide use of pre-fixed foods. You have to make the effort to find one or more restaurants that still cook their own food. Otherwise, you may end up in a restaurant that buys all of its chicken as prepared entrees. Then you would be kidding yourself if you thought that they could broil some plain raw chicken for you.

Do all restaurants sell TV-dinner-style food? The answer is no. Some restaurants—especially those that are individually owned and run—pride themselves on real home cooking. There are a few expensive restaurants that make all their own food from scratch. There are also quite a few family-operated restaurants that pride themselves on making their own food; try to find one in your area.

When you eat out, be prepared to order plain foods such as a baked potato and a broiled piece of meat without sauces—foods that do not need to be cooked in advance with sauces. Be prepared to politely ask your waitress or waiter which food items are *not* the preassembled ones that need only reheating. Ask which entrees are cooked from raw foods. Be prepared to ask that no fatty or salty ingredients be added to your food. If you don't speak up, you may be surprised to find soy sauce on your prime rib, as we did. Learn to be cautious about some of the things you are told. In an attempt to please a potential customer, your waiter or waitress may even offer you false reassurance about the supposedly healthy content of the food.

Most fast-food restaurants will prepare their food items for you as you request. You can order *unsalted* french fries. You can order a plain hamburger, and ask that they hold the pickles, cheese, ketchup, mayonnaise, salt and any special sauce. Ask for extra onion, lettuce and tomato, if you wish. You can order fried chicken, then remove the skin before you eat the chicken.

Some fast-food chains have salad bars where you can make healthy choices. Usually this means no premixed dressing (you can bring your own), no beans, bacon bits, croutons or cheeses. The salad bar probably has containers of oil and vinegar that you can use.

When you go to regular restaurants, open the menu with realistic expectations. There will probably be fewer healthy choices than you thought.

Breakfast—a few tips:
Fruits, fruit juices, coffee and tea are all low in sodium and fat.

Cold cereals that are low in sodium include shredded wheat and puffed rice. (Since they are not popular, many restaurants do not carry them.) The other cold cereals are high in sodium; you may want to carry a plastic bag of low-sodium cereal if you are eating breakfast in a restaurant. You can ask the waitress if she has any of the cold cereals that are on your diet. If there are none available, explain that you have your own. Order a bowl and milk. You can order fruit too, if you like. You can offer to pay for the cereal that would have come with the bowl. Some restaurants offer oatmeal for breakfast. Because interest in healthy eating has increased, more and more restaurants offer choices approved by the Heart Association. Some restaurants offer breakfast entrees made from egg substitutes.

Lunch—if you don't carry your own:
Many luncheon choices are high in fat and sodium: cold cuts (bologna, pastrami, ham, salami), commercial bread and rolls, potato chips, dill pickles, coleslaw, tuna, chicken salad, cheese, and soup. Salad can be a good choice. Mix an oil and vinegar dressing yourself. Leave off the high-sodium salad ingredients, blue cheese dressing, etc.

Dinner—needs planning:
For dinner, it's a good idea to choose a restaurant that specializes in plain foods rather than casseroles and foods with gravies and sauces. Chinese and other oriental restaurants use soy sauce and MSG (monosodium glutamate), which make their foods very high in sodium.

Fruit cocktail, fruit and fruit juices are all low in sodium and fat.

Salad can be low in sodium if you leave out the high-sodium fixings.

Baked potatoes are low in sodium. Request that your baked potato be brought to you *unopened.* (You may want to bring your own unsalted margarine if your diet is very restricted.) Ask if they have any plain boiled pasta or rice, as opposed to pre-mixed rice or pasta side dishes.

Ask if the restaurant has any fresh fish that could be broiled for you without fatty sauces.

Roast beef, prime rib and turkey are often served covered with high sodium sauces or gravies, but you can ask if they have plain meat (with *no* sauce or gravy). An inside slice of a roast should be fairly low in sodium.

Coffee, tea, soda, wine, beer and liquor are all low in sodium and fat.

Pack a bag with unsalted margarine, your favorite unsalted salad dressing, some good unsalted bread, bread sticks, a roll or a matzo. You can quietly take such items out of your bag to go with the meal.

If you are having dessert, fruit gelatin or sherbet is the best choice. If you skipped the fresh fruit as an appetizer, consider having it as a refreshing end to your meal.

More Tips When Eating Out

In interviewing people for this book, we learned that many people eat only breakfast at home. People who eat most of their other meals in restaurants tend to be busy married couples whose children are grown, or single people who hate to cook for one person and usually have high incomes. Less affluent people simply cannot afford to eat out twice a day. In addition to their comfortable income levels, many of the eating out subgroup have high blood pressure or other medical problems that have led their doctors to recommend healthier diets. How can they cut down on sodium and still eat out? In addition to the suggestions for breakfast, lunch and dinner, if you eat out occasionally, here are more suggestions:

• Consider bringing a *lunch* from home, since low-sodium lunches are very difficult to find in restaurants.

• Avoid Chinese restaurants, delicatessens, and restaurants that heat prepackaged foods.

- Find one or more good restaurants that care enough about you and other discriminating customers to go along with your special requests (for example, allowing you to bring your own salad dressing).

- Get in the habit of never even looking at the choices in the foods that are always high in sodium: soups, breads, dishes with fancy sauces, barbecue sauces, especially.

Eating in Airplanes

You can ask your travel agent to request low-cholesterol or low-sodium menus. Be sure to order them at least 24 hours in advance. But, in our extensive travelling experience (since 1981), special meals were not available 90 percent of the time. A major problem: Special choices are available only for full meals, such as dinner. Much of the time, an airline considers what it serves to be a "snack" and there are no special choices available for "snack" lunches.

When the airline is serving a full meal, special dishes are available. But even when our travel agent had requested special dinners, the special meals failed to arrive 50 percent of the time. One flight attendant told us that, in his seven years of flying, special meals—low-sodium, kosher, vegetarian—were unavailable 80 percent of the time. Flight attendants from two other airlines told us that special meals almost never arrive. If you do get a "low-sodium" meal, it may not really be low-sodium. We have been served sausages, salted salad dressing, salami, salt and salted butter as part of "low-sodium" meals.

According to flight attendants, fish is now the "in" choice for almost all special airline meals. The fish we were served was so unpleasantly strong and "fishy" that we found it painful to sit with it in front of us. And we love fresh fish.

When you are travelling, you may want to bring along a kit of your own foods—just in case available foods are inappropriate when you are hungry.

Visiting

When invited to eat at someone's home, it's a good idea to think about ways to handle your diet. If it is a large party where no one notices what you eat or whether you eat at all, you can eat before you go to the party— if you're afraid that the cheese tray or other fatty, salty foods will be too tempting.

At an intimate dinner where food is the high point of the evening— the main focus of the social occasion—you will want to tell your hostess in advance about your diet. Together, you can work out arrangements. Perhaps a low-fat low-sodium choice can be included in her plans.

SEASONINGS, CONDIMENTS AND RELISHES

Low-sodium food can be bland—a real problem. If you or your family feel that way, don't just sit there—do something. Make and use flavorful, low-sodium condiments.

Some popular condiments are naturally low in sodium: jams and jellies—3 mgs in 1 tablespoon (15 mL); mint jelly—3 mgs in 1 tablespoon (15 mL); cranberry orange relish—12 mgs in ½ cup (125 mL); applesauce—3 mgs in ½ cup (125 mL).

When beginning low-sodium cooking, you will be grateful for products such as commercial low-sodium ketchup even when they lack the flavor you would prefer. The new unsalted ketchups made by the large food companies, luckily, taste much better than some of the older ones. If you can't find any that you like, try one or both of these homemade ketchups.

This chapter includes zesty seasonings to liven your dishes, popular condiments, and also marinades to flavor food—and each recipe needs only five or ten minutes to whip up. You'll find sauces in other chapters as well; check the index.

Seasonings
The Unsalt Shaker

If you find it hard *not* to pick up the salt shaker and "shake" when you sit down to eat, you can make up an *unsalt shaker*. Try using different blends on various foods. A few shakes of any combination adds just a trace of sodium. Enjoy shaking the Unsalt Shaker! Empty the salt out of a shaker, wash and dry it. Mix some spices together in a bowl. Spoon the mixture into the clean shaker. Add a few grains of uncooked rice to prevent it from caking.

World Favorite

5 t.	onion powder	25 mL
1 T.	garlic powder	15 mL
1 T.	paprika	15 mL
1 T.	dry mustard	15 mL
1 t.	thyme	5 mL
½ t.	white pepper	2 mL
½ t.	celery seeds	2 mL

Exotic Blend

1 T.	dry mustard	15 mL
1½ t.	white pepper	6 mL
1 t.	curry powder	5 mL
3 T.	onion powder	45 mL
½ t.	garlic powder	2 mL

Gentle Italian

2 T.	onion powder	30 mL
1 t.	powdered oregano (leaf oregano may clog up the shaker)	5 mL
1 t.	celery seed	5 mL

Classic Blend

½ t.	white pepper	2 mL
½ t.	celery seed	2 mL
5 t.	onion powder	25 mL
2 t.	garlic powder	10 mL
2½ t.	dry mustard	12 mL

Herb Blend (use a shaker with large holes)

1 t.	thyme	5 mL
1 t.	marjoram	5 mL
1 t.	sage	5 mL
1 t.	powdered basil	5 mL
1 t.	lemon peel	5 mL

Salt-free Chili Powder

Ideal for seasoning chili beans, beef tacos, burritos—any "spicy" food.

2 T.	*Durkee's paprika*	*30 mL*
2 t.	*Durkee's imported oregano*	*10 mL*
1¼ t.	*Durkee's ground cumin*	*6 mL*
1¼ t.	*Durkee's garlic powder*	*6 mL*
¾ t.	*Durkee's ground red pepper*	*3 mL*
¾ t.	*Durkee's onion powder*	*3 mL*

Mix all ingredients thoroughly. Store in *airtight* container. Use as desired.

Makes 4 tablespoons. (60 mL)
About .59 mgs sodium per teaspoon (5 mL)

Note: Commercial chili powder varies in sodium content from brand to brand. Don't assume that the brand on your shelf is low in sodium until you *find out* for yourself (by calling or writing to the manufacturer). Since most brands do have salt, you may need to figure that each teaspoon (5 mL) of a brand with salt adds approximately 31 mgs.

Reprinted by permission of Durkee Famous Foods, Westlake, Ohio

Hot Peppers or Chilies and Hot Sauce

Using hot peppers or chilies can be a natural part of low-sodium cooking. Chilies are naturally low in sodium with only a few milligrams per pepper. And they counteract the bane of low-sodium cooking—"It's tasteless."

Use fresh chilies with skins removed: To remove skins, broil a few inches from the heat, turning frequently for about 5 minutes or until the skins blister on all sides. Pop the blistered chilies into a closed plastic bag for 15 minutes. Then the skins will easily tear off. Or, if in a hurry, hold with a tong the heated chili under running water; peel and remove seeds. Use fresh, or freeze for another day.

Avoid hot peppers commercially packed in oil, since they have some added salt. Brands range from 10 to 138 mgs per tablespoon. To learn the exact amount of added salt, write to the manufacturer *whose brand you like.*

Tabasco sauce and Louisiana red hot sauce are liquid hot pepper seasonings. Using a sauce from a bottle is much more convenient, but these products do contain salt—in small amounts. McIlhenny-brand Tabasco sauce, distributed in most countries, is lower in sodium and may be a wiser choice for people on low-sodium diets.

Roll and Bake Coating Mix

Make up a batch to keep on hand to bread your chicken, fish or pork chops!

1 box (8 oz.)	low-sodium cornflakes	1 box (227 g size)
⅔ c.	flour	180 mL
2 t.	paprika	10 mL
2 t.	onion powder	10 mL
1½ t.	garlic powder	7 mL
¾ t.	fresh ground pepper	3 mL
1½ T.	safflower oil	22 mL
1½ T.	sugar	22 mL

Crush the cornflakes *very fine* using a blender or food processor; or crush flakes in a plastic bag with a rolling pin. Mix cornflake crumbs in a bowl with remaining ingredients (clean fingers work as well as anything). Store in a covered container in a cool, dry place; it keeps for weeks.

Makes 9 cups (2¼ L)
Sodium, 1 tablespoon (15 mL): trace
Calories: 12

Condiments

Ketchup

1	medium onion, coarsely chopped	1
½ c.	water	125 mL
12 oz.	no-salt-added tomato paste	340 mL
¼ c.	sugar	60 mL
¾ c.	vinegar	190 mL
¼ t.	cinnamon	1 mL
½ t.	dry mustard	2 mL

Whip onion and water in blender at high speed until onion is liquefied. In a small saucepan, combine the onion–water mixture with remaining ingredients; stir with a wire whisk. Cook over low heat for about 10 minutes. Cool. Store in the refrigerator in a covered container (preferably a plastic squeeze bottle).

Makes 3 cups (750 mL)
Sodium, 1 tablespoon (15 mL): 3 mgs
Calories: 12

Peach Ketchup

A sweeter version.

12 oz.	no-salt-added tomato paste	340 mL
½ c.	water	125 mL
1 t.	onion powder	5 mL
2 T.	corn syrup	30 mL
2 T.	sugar	30 mL
¾ c.	vinegar	190 mL
1 t.	dry mustard	5 mL
¼ t.	cinnamon	1 mL
1 small jar	baby food peaches	1 small jar
¼ t.	liquid hickory smoke (optional)	1 mL

Combine all ingredients in a saucepan. Over medium heat, stir with a wire whisk for two minutes or until the sugar has dissolved and the mixture is smooth. Store, covered, in refrigerator.

Makes 2½ cups (625 mL)
Sodium, 1 tablespoon (15 mL): 5 mgs
Calories: 15

Mayonnaise

This delicious mayonnaise is so easy to whip up in a blender or food processor—much better than commercial low-sodium mayonnaise. Remember, homemade mayonnaise does not keep as well as the commercial ones. Make each batch when needed. (Egg substitute does not work in blender mayonnaise, but one tablespoon of this mayonnaise contains only the cholesterol in ¹/₂₄ of an egg.)

1	egg	1
2 T.	fresh lemon juice	30 mL
½ t.	dry mustard	2 mL
1 c.	safflower oil	250 mL

Combine egg, lemon juice, mustard and ¼ of the oil in blender or food processor. Mix on low speed and quickly add remaining oil in a steady stream; beat for 20 seconds. Spoon into a jar and store, covered, in the refrigerator.

Makes about 1-1½ cups (375 mL)
Sodium, 1 tablespoon (15 mL): 3 mgs
Calories: 84

Hot Mustard

¼ c.	flour	60 mL
¼ c.	dry mustard	60 mL
1 t.	sugar	5 mL
½ t.	unsalted margarine	2 mL
⅓ c.	water, boiling	90 mL
¼ c.	vinegar, boiling	60 mL

Mix first 4 ingredients in a small bowl. Add the boiling water and stir to make a stiff dough. Gradually add boiling vinegar and mix to a desired consistency.

Makes ½ cup (125 mL)
Sodium, 1 tablespoon (15 mL): Trace
Calories: 35

Mild Mustard

3 T.	flour	45 mL
2 T.	dry mustard	30 mL
2 t.	sugar	10 mL
¼ t.	turmeric	1 mL
½ t.	unsalted margarine	2 mL
¼ c.	water, boiling	60 mL
1 T.	white wine (op-tional)	15 mL
2 T.	cider vinegar, boiling	30 mL

Mix the first 5 ingredients together in a small bowl. Add the boiling water and mix. Then add the wine, if using, and the boiling vinegar.

Makes ½ cup (125 mL)
Sodium, 1 tablespoon (15 mL): trace
Calories: 33

Horseradish

Buy a horseradish root the right size to make one cup (250 mL) of chunks. (Horseradish root has an unusual, gnarled appearance.) If the fresh horseradish you bought yields more than one cup, use it all and add more vinegar—as long as there is about ¾ as much vinegar as horseradish. Since fresh horseradish root is not always available, you may want to make extra horseradish and freeze it in small batches. One tablespoon (15 mL) of commercially prepared horseradish has about 200 mgs of sodium.

| 1 piece (8 oz.) | horseradish root | 1 piece (226 g) |
| ¾ c. | white vinegar | 190 mL |

Wash and peel horseradish root using a vegetable peeler; cut into large chunks. Place about 1 cup (250 mL) in a blender or food processor. Add the vinegar. Blend until mixture is fairly smooth. Drain any excess vinegar by placing the horseradish in a colander or mesh strainer and discard the liquid. Store horseradish, covered, in the refrigerator.

Makes 1 cup (250 mL)
Sodium, 1 tablespoon (15 mL): trace
Calories: 12

Horseradish Gravy

Serve with broiled fish or meat. Add more horseradish for a "hot" taste.

2 T.	unsalted margarine	30 mL
2 T.	flour	30 mL
¾ c.	skim milk	190 mL
3 T.	Horseradish (above)	45 mL
1 t.	vinegar	5 mL
1 t.	sugar	5 mL

Melt margarine in a small saucepan. Add flour, stir and cook for a minute or so. Add the milk, stirring with a wire whisk over medium heat until the mixture thickens; remove from heat. Stir in the horseradish, vinegar and sugar.

Makes 1 cup (250 mL)
Sodium, 1 tablespoon (15 mL): 7 mgs
Calories: 22

Barbecue Sauce

As good a barbecue sauce as any in a restaurant, and *better* than bottled barbecue sauces. If you're cutting down on meat, but love the flavor of barbecue, try this sauce over cooked navy or great northern beans.

1 T.	*unsalted margarine*	*15 mL*
¼ c.	*low-sodium ketchup*	*60 mL*
½ c.	*cider vinegar*	*125 mL*
3 T.	*molasses*	*45 mL*
2 T.	*sugar*	*30 mL*
¼ t.	*paprika*	*1 mL*
dash	*Tabasco sauce*	*dash*
1 small jar	*baby food peaches*	*1 small jar*
½ t.	*dry mustard*	*2 mL*
½ t.	*ginger*	*2 mL*
¼ t.	*liquid hickory smoke (optional)*	*1 mL*

Combine all the ingredients in a saucepan and cook gently for 15 minutes.

Makes 1½ cups (375 mL)
Sodium, 1 tablespoon (15 mL): 2 mgs
Calories: 20

Chili Sauce

If you find a brand of chili powder with *no salt* listed on the ingredient list, you will avoid 31 mgs of sodium. To make your own, try Salt-free Chili Powder (page 54).

1 c.	*Ketchup (homemade, page 55)*	*250 mL*
2 dashes	*Tabasco sauce (more if you like it "hotter")*	*2 dashes*
1 t.	*onion powder*	*5 mL*
1 T.	*sugar*	*15 mL*
2 T.	*vinegar*	*30 mL*
½ t.	*no-salt-added chili powder*	*3 mL*

Combine all ingredients. Store in refrigerator.

Makes 1 cup (250 mL)
Sodium, 1 tablespoon (15 mL): 3 mgs
Calories: 16

Hamburger Sauce

If you love fast-food style hamburgers, make up this sauce for your own homemade hamburgers (pages 102 and 103).

¾ c.	Mayonnaise (page 56)	190 mL
2 T.	Ketchup (page 55)	30 mL
2 T.	Sweet Relish (page 62)	30 mL
2 t.	sugar	10 mL
2 t.	vinegar	10 mL
¼ t.	dry mustard	1 mL

Stir together all ingredients. Store, covered, in refrigerator.

Makes 1 cup (250 mL)
Sodium, 1 tablespoon (15 mL): 2 mgs
Calories: 67

Hot Cocktail Sauce

⅓ c.	Ketchup (page 55)	90 mL
1 T.	Horseradish, less for a milder flavor, (page 58)	15 mL
2 dashes	Tabasco sauce	2 dashes

Combine ketchup, horseradish and Tabasco sauce in a small bowl.

Makes 6 tablespoons (90 mL)
Sodium, 1 tablespoon (15 mL): 3 mgs
Calories: 9

Tartar Sauce

3 T.	Mayonnaise (page 56)	45 mL
1 T.	Sweet Relish, drained (page 62)	15 mL

Combine mayonnaise and relish in a small bowl. Serve immediately or refrigerate, covered, until mealtime.

Makes ¼ cup (60 mL)
Sodium, 1 tablespoon (15 mL): 3 mgs
Calories 65

Sweet-and-Sour Pineapple Sauce

This sauce can be cooked with chicken or pork or served with vegetable, fish and grain dishes.

½ c.	*water*	*125 mL*
1 c.	*drained crushed pineapple*	*250 mL*
½ c.	*juice drained from pineapple can*	*125 mL*
1 T.	*molasses*	*15 mL*
3 T.	*sugar*	*45 mL*
½ t.	*ginger*	*2 mL*
½ c.	*vinegar*	*125 mL*
3 T.	*cornstarch*	*45 mL*

Stir all ingredients in a saucepan over medium heat until mixture boils. Reduce heat and cook gently for about 10 minutes.

Makes 2¼ cups (560 mL)
Sodium, 1 tablespoon (15 mL): trace
Calories: 9

Chinese Peach Sauce

½ c.	*peach preserves*	*125 mL*
2 T.	*cider vinegar is best*	*30 mL*
⅛ t.	*ground ginger*	*.5 mL*
⅛ t.	*garlic powder*	*.5 mL*

Combine all the ingredients* in a small saucepan over low heat and cook for one minute. Store extra sauce in a covered container in the refrigerator. Serve hot or cold.

* Double the amount for the 96 Egg Roll Hors d'Oeuvres (page 93).

Makes ¾ cup (185 mL)
Sodium, 1 tablespoon (15 mL): 1 mg
Calories: 37

Soy Sauce Substitute

Use as a soy sauce substitute. No, it doesn't taste just like soy sauce, because soy sauce tastes very salty. In fact, there are 1,319 mgs of sodium in one tablespoon (15 mL) of soy sauce—a clue that it is mainly salt.*

½ c.	cola drink	125 mL
2 t.	cornstarch	10 mL
2 t.	molasses	10 mL
2 T.	lemon juice	30 mL
⅛ t.	ginger	1 mL
¼ t.	Angostura bitters	1 mL
1 T.	sherry (not cooking sherry)	15 mL

In a small saucepan, stir all of the ingredients over low heat. Cook for a minute or less. Using a funnel, pour into a container such as a bottle with a shaker top. If you save, wash and reuse a soy sauce bottle with a shaker top, the sauce will seem more "authentic." Store in the refrigerator.

* New commercial soy sauces continually appear on grocery shelves. These are lower in sodium, but they are *not* low-sodium; it will be necessary to read the labels.

Makes ⅔ of a cup (180 mL)
Sodium, 1 tablespoon (15 mL): 1 mg
Calories: 13

Relishes

Sweet Relish

4	sweet green peppers	4
1	medium onion	1
⅓ c.	sugar	90 mL
½ t.	celery seed	2 mL
1 t.	mustard seed	5 mL
dash	cinnamon	dash
dash	allspice	dash
¾ c.	vinegar	185 mL

Chop peppers and onion using a food grinder or food processor or chop with sharp knife on cutting board. Transfer pepper-onion mixture to saucepan; stir in ½ c. (125 mL) of the vinegar. Cook over medium heat for 10 minutes, stirring often. Drain vegetables and discard liquid. Return the vegetables to the pan. Add the spices and the remaining ¼ c. (60 mL) vinegar. Cook gently about 5 minutes. Cool. Store in a covered container or glass jar in the refrigerator.

Makes about 1¾ cups (435 mL)
Sodium, 1 tablespoon (15 mL): 2 mgs
Calories: 7

Corn Relish

Easy and delicious. Serve corn relish with baked beans to help round out the protein. Or serve as a garnish to any "plain" meal.

⅔ c.	cider vinegar	180 mL
2 T.	cornstarch	30 mL
1 t.	pickling spice	5 mL
¼ t.	cinnamon	1 mL
⅓ c.	sugar	90 mL
10 oz.	frozen corn	300 g
½	red or green pepper, finely diced	½

Combine the vinegar, cornstarch, pickling spice, cinnamon and sugar in a saucepan. Simmer for 15 minutes, stirring occasionally. Meanwhile, cook frozen corn as directed on label (but leave out the salt); drain. Mix with chopped pepper in a bowl. Pour the sauce over the corn and peppers (or you can strain and discard spices). Refrigerate overnight to blend flavors.

Makes 2½ cups (625 mL)
Sodium, ¼ cup (60 mL): 1 mg
Calories: 59

Five-Minute Chutney

A tasty accompaniment for curry and easy to make. Try chutney on no-salt cheese, meat, chicken, or tuna sandwiches instead of butter or mayonnaise.

1 jar (7¾ oz)	junior baby food apricots	1 jar (200 g)
¼ c.	apricot preserves	60 mL
¼ c.	cider vinegar	60 mL
1 T.	brown sugar	15 mL
¼ t.	onion powder	1 mL
2 pinches	cayenne red pepper	2 pinches
1 pinch	allspice	1 pinch
1 t.	ginger (use less if you want a milder taste)	5 mL
1 T.	cornstarch	15 mL

Combine all of the ingredients except the cornstarch in a saucepan. Heat gently and stir until the brown sugar dissolves. Spoon the cornstarch into a bowl. Using a whisk or spoon, gradually stir in about ½ cup (125 mL) of the fruit mixture. Add the cornstarch–fruit mixture to the saucepan; heat gently and stir until thickened.

Makes 1 cup (250 mL)
Sodium, 1 tablespoon (15 mL): 2
Calories: 27

DRESSINGS, MARINADES AND SAUCES

Dressings

Good and Good for You Dressing

1 c.	water	250 mL
¼ c.	sugar	60 mL
¼ c.	lemon juice	60 mL
¼ c.	vinegar	60 mL
1 T.	safflower oil	15 mL
½ c.	low-sodium ket-chup	125 mL
1	clove garlic	1
2 t.	celery seeds	10 mL
1	small onion, grated	1
grind	black pepper	grind

Put all ingredients together in a jar. Shake well. Chill before using. Store in refrigerator. Shake well before serving.

Makes 2½ cups (625 mL)
Sodium, 1 tablespoon (15 mL): less than 1 mg
Calories: 12

Oil-and-Vinegar Dressing

⅔ c.	safflower oil	180 mL
⅓ c.	tarragon vinegar, other vinegar or lemon juice	90 mL
dash	pepper	dash
1	clove garlic, peeled	1
½ t.	dry mustard	2 mL
dash	Tabasco sauce	dash
½ t.	paprika	2 mL
1½ T.	sugar	22 mL
½ t.	basil, dill, or other herb that you like	2 mL

Shake all the ingredients in a covered container. Store in the refrigerator.

Makes 1 cup (250 mL)
Sodium, 1 tablespoon (15 mL): trace
Calories: 85

Tangy Red Dressing

Delicious and attractive, this dressing is great even on plain lettuce.

½ c.	low-sodium ketchup	125 mL
¼ c.	safflower oil	60 mL
¼ c.	water	60 mL
½ c.	sugar	125 mL
⅓ c.	lemon juice	90 mL
¼ t.	onion powder	1 mL
grind	pepper	grind
½ c.	vinegar	125 mL
1	clove garlic, peeled	1

Shake all ingredients in a covered jar. Store in the refrigerator. Shake before each use.

Makes 1½ cups (375 mL)
Sodium, 1 tablespoon (15 mL): 1 mg
Calories: 42

Low-Calorie Italian Dressing

It's best to make several hours before serving so that the flavors blend.

½ c.	vinegar	125 mL
2 T.	safflower oil	30 mL
1 T.	cornstarch	15 mL
½ c. + 1 T.	water	125 mL + 15 mL
¼ t.	paprika	1 mL
¼ t.	dry mustard	1 mL
½ t.	celery seed	2 mL
¼ t.	oregano	1 mL
1	medium clove garlic, pressed	1
¼ t.	basil	2 mL
1 T.	sugar	15 mL

Stir vinegar, oil and ½ (125 mL) cup water in a small saucepan until it boils. Mix cornstarch and 1 tablespoon (15 mL) water in a small dish. Add the cornstarch mixture to the saucepan and continue cooking over low heat. When mixture boils again, remove from heat; add other ingredients. Pour the dressing into a container, cover tightly, and refrigerate.

Makes 1 cup (250 mL)
Sodium, 1 tablespoon (15 mL): trace
Calories: 23

Light 'n Easy Cucumber Dressing

¼ c.	low-fat yogurt	60 mL
1	medium cucumber, peeled and cubed	1
½	green pepper, seeded and sliced	½
1	clove garlic	1
2 dashes	white pepper	2 dashes
2 dashes	onion powder	2 dashes
¼ c.	Mayonnaise (page 56)	60 mL

Combine everything except mayonnaise in the blender. Blend and pour into a storage container. Stir in mayonnaise. Cover tightly and refrigerate.

Makes 2 cups (500 mL)
Sodium, 1 tablespoon (15 mL): 2 mgs
Calories: 13

Creamy Italian Dressing

Wonderful and easy.

1 c.	Mayonnaise (page 56)	250 mL
½ t.	garlic powder	2 mL
½ t.	onion powder	2 mL
½ t.	crushed dried red pepper	2 mL
¼ c.	cider vinegar	60 mL
1 t.	sugar	5 mL
3 T.	Sweet Relish (page 62)	45 mL
grind	pepper	grind

Mix all of the ingredients together. Store in a tightly covered container in the refrigerator. Mix again before serving.

Makes 1¼ cups (310 mL)
Sodium, 1 tablespoon (15 mL): 3 mgs
Calories: 71

Russian Dressing

(If you add some chopped low-sodium pickles, you'll have a thousand island dressing. You could also add diced green pepper or cucumber.)

4 T.	Mayonnaise (page 56)	60 mL
2 T.	Ketchup (page 55)	30 mL

Mix the mayonnaise and ketchup just before serving. Store in the refrigerator.

Makes 6 tablespoons (90 mL)
Sodium, 1 tablespoon (15 mL): 3 mgs
Calories: 65

Fruit Dressings

Honey Dressing

This dressing is especially nice with fruit salads.

¼ c.	honey	60 mL
¼ c.	vinegar	60 mL
2 T.	safflower oil	30 mL
2 T.	water	30 mL

Combine all ingredients in a covered container and shake. For best flavor, keep chilled until you're ready to use it. Store in the refrigerator.

Makes ¾ cup (190 mL)
Sodium, 1 tablespoon (15 mL): trace
Calories: 43

Spicy Dressing

Good on fruit salads any time of year.

½ c.	Mayonnaise (page 56)	125 mL
2 T.	lemon juice	30 mL
2 T.	skim milk	30 mL
½ t.	celery seed	2 mL
⅛ t.	cinnamon	1 mL
dash	ginger	dash
1 T.	sugar	15 mL

Combine all the ingredients in a small bowl. Store in a covered container in the refrigerator. Shake before using.

Makes ¾ cup (190 mL)
Sodium, 1 tablespoon (15 mL): 3 mgs
Calories: 47

Marinades

Marinades add flavor to foods and also help to tenderize tougher meat cuts. To marinate: Place the food in a nonmetal container; cover with the marinade for at least one hour, or preferably longer (all day or overnight), in refrigerator.

Plan ahead. When you are thinking about serving a meat, place it in a marinade instead of just leaving it in the wrapping paper. It's difficult to calculate how much of the marinade or sauce is absorbed by each piece of meat, so we can't be sure how much sodium and how many calories are added to any meat.

All the recipes for marinades in this book are *very low* in sodium. If you are marinating a very tough cut of meat, you may want to add a little *unsalted* tenderizer to the marinade. Meat tenderizer is so high in sodium—5,490 mgs in one tablespoon (15 mL)—that it should *not* be used by anyone who needs to cut down on salt.

Lemony Marinade

Brush marinade on raw chicken parts before broiling for a great chicken dish.

6 T.	lemon juice	90 mL
4 T.	unsalted margarine	60 mL
4 T.	low-sodium ketchup	60 mL

In a saucepan stir all ingredients and simmer over low heat for 10 minutes.

Makes ¾ cup (190 mL)
Sodium, 1 tablespoon (15 mL): 1 mg
Calories: 32

Sweet-and-Sour Marinade

The pineapple sweetens chicken or pork, especially.

¼ c.	cider vinegar	60 mL
½ c.	crushed pineapple (unsweetened)	125 mL
2 T.	honey	30 mL
1 T.	low-sodium ketchup	15 mL

Stir together all the ingredients to make the marinade.

Makes 1 cup (250 mL)
Sodium, 1 tablespoon (15 mL): less than 1 mg
Calories: 12

White Wine Marinade

Good for chicken, pork, or lamb.

1 c.	white wine such as Chablis	250 mL
¼ c.	lemon juice	60 mL
2 T.	honey	30 mL
¼ t.	garlic powder	1 mL
¼ t.	dry mustard	1 mL
2 T.	safflower oil	30 mL

In a small saucepan stir all of the ingredients. Heat gently until dissolved.

Makes 1½ cups (375 mL)
Sodium, 1 tablespoon (15 mL): trace
Calories: 23

Tomato-Wine Marinade

Adds a powerful flavor to beef.

1 c.	red wine, such as Burgundy	250 mL
2	cloves garlic, finely minced	2
6 oz.	no-salt-added tomato paste	170 mL
½ t.	basil	2 mL

Whisk together all of the ingredients.

Makes 1½ cups (375 mL)
Sodium, 1 tablespoon (15 mL): 1 mg
Calories: 15

Orange Juice Marinade

Good on chicken.

⅓ c.	orange juice	90 mL
1 T.	safflower oil	15 mL
¼ c.	vinegar	60 mL
1	clove garlic, finely chopped	1
1	small onion, finely chopped	1
½ t.	dry mustard	2 mL
1 t.	cinnamon	5 mL

Combine all ingredients in a bowl to make the marinade.

Makes ¾ cup (190 mL)
Sodium, 1 tablespoon (15 mL): trace
Calories: 22

Burgundy Marinade

This robust marinade is terrific for tenderizing tough cuts of beef, such as round.

2 T.	olive oil	30 mL
1	medium onion, sliced very thin	1
1	garlic clove, crushed	1
¼ c.	red wine vinegar	60 mL
½ c.	Burgundy or other dry red wine	125 mL
¼ c.	water	60 mL
1 t.	thyme	5 mL
grind	black pepper	grind
1	bay leaf	1

Heat the oil in a small saucepan and stir in the onion; cook over moderate heat until onion is soft and yellow. Add the garlic and cook for a minute or two. Add the wine vinegar, stir for 3 minutes more; then add remaining ingredients and cook 5 minutes. Cool.

Makes 1½ cups (375 mL)
Sodium, 1 tablespoon (15 mL): 3 mgs
Calories: 22

Herb Marinade

Good for tenderizing and adding flavor to tougher cuts of lamb or beef.

3 T.	lemon juice	45 mL
2 T.	safflower oil	30 mL
1	clove garlic, minced	1
¼ t.	thyme	1 mL
¼ t.	oregano	1 mL
½ t.	rosemary	2 mL
1	medium onion, thinly sliced	1
grind	black pepper	grind

In a nonmetal container with a cover, shake all ingredients.

Makes ½ cup (125 mL)
Sodium, 1 tablespoon (15 mL): 1 mg
Calories: 37

Sauces

Fresh Tomato Sauce

This *pomodori crudi* is a wonderful way to serve summer tomatoes. Serve over pasta, such as small shaped macaroni, ziti, rotelle or little shells. For a hotter version, try Fresh Tomato Sauce with Chili (page 208).

2 lb.	*very ripe fresh tomatoes*	900 g
2	*cloves garlic, minced*	2
¼ t.	*oregano*	1 mL
1 T.	*fresh parsley, chopped*	15 mL
⅓ c.	*olive oil*	90 mL
¼ lb.	*no-salt-added Swiss cheese*	110 g

Place tomatoes in a pot of boiling water for a minute or so until their skins break open. Scoop the tomatoes out of the boiling water. Peel off the tomato skin, scoop out the seeds. Save as much juice as you can. Cut the tomatoes into chunks. Mix the tomatoes with their juice, the garlic, oregano, parsley, oil and cheese in a bowl. Let stand at room temperature for at least an hour, to let flavors blend. Just before serving, cook pasta according to package directions, *except* leave out the salt. Drain. Toss with tomato sauce. Serve while hot.

Serves 4
Sodium per serving: 15 mgs
Calories: 319

Meat Sauce

If you want to make a meat sauce, saute ½ lb. (225 g) of very lean ground beef in a separate pan. After it is cooked, drain off the fat and add meat to Tomato Sauce (page 74). Simmer to combine the flavors.

Tomato Sauce

This easy sauce can be used on pizza,* on spaghetti or can be used in other recipes. There is no fat added to this recipe. You can add Italian meatballs. Cook the meatballs separately using the recipe in the red meat chapter. Drain off the fat and add the meatballs to the tomato sauce. Simmer to combine the flavors.

12 oz.	no-salt-added tomato paste	340 g
1 t.	basil	5 mL
1 t.	oregano	5 mL
⅛ t.	pepper	1 mL
1 t.	onion powder	5 mL
½ t.	garlic powder	2 mL
2 T.	sugar	30 mL
2 c.	water	500 mL
2 T.	vinegar	30 mL

Put all ingredients in a large saucepan. Stir with a whisk to combine. Simmer for at least 20 minutes.

* Make *half* this recipe for Pizza (page 154) and simmer while preparing the dough, or freeze in small amounts for quick use.

Makes about 3 cups (750 mL); a serving is one-half cup (125 mL)
Sodium per serving: 23 mgs
Calories per serving: 58

Tomato Sauce with Peppers and Mushrooms

Add 1 cup (250 mL) of sliced mushrooms and ½ of a green pepper, finely chopped. Simmer until the vegetables are as tender as you like.

Sodium, 1 serving: 22 mgs
Calories: 45

Mama's Sauce

Vermouth adds a snappy flavor to this variation of Tomato Sauce (above). Add 2 medium onions, finely chopped, and simmer until soft. Stir in ½ c. (125 mL) vermouth and continue simmering until the alcohol cooks away.

Sodium, 1 serving: 23 mgs
Calories: 95

BREAKFAST

OUR CHANGES IN attitude towards food may show up the most in what we consider a "good" breakfast. Bacon and eggs are out, being much too high in saturated fat and cholesterol. Oat bran is very in, because it is such an excellent source of soluble fibre. Just two tablespoons per day can make a difference! Many people find that the easiest way to get their oat bran is by eating it as a hot cereal with skim milk and fruit. Plain oat bran is healthier than the oat bran cereals, which have more calories from the sugar and fats added. Many people microwave their hot oat bran. Oat bran muffins (page 220) are another good way to add soluble fibre to the diet.

Fruit and Fruit Juice

If you like to start breakfast with juice or fruit, you can choose *any* pure juice. The sodium and calorie contents are given on the beverage list in the Appendix (page 269). Avoid tomato juice and V-8 vegetable juice, which have more than 800 mgs of sodium in one cup (250 mL)—obviously much too high for anyone on any kind of a sodium restriction. Low-sodium tomato and blended vegetable juices are available; try a small can to see if you like the taste *before* you stock up.

Juice drinks are slightly higher in sodium than pure juices. But there is an even more compelling reason not to buy them—they contain mostly water with a small amount of juice (about 5–10 percent), plus coloring agents and sugar. Considering that the price is almost as high as the price of pure juices, you are not getting much for your money.

Whole fresh fruits are not only naturally low in sodium—they also provide more filling food than juices with the same calories and vitamins. Adding a piece of fruit to breakfast is a real morale booster. Seasonal fruits are not too expensive—grapefruit in the winter and melon in the summer, for example. Hot broiled grapefruit is almost as easy as chilled grapefruit and makes a special treat on a cold morning.

Broiled Grapefruit

After cutting the grapefruit in half, sprinkle on a little sugar or honey. Broil for about 5–10 minutes, or until it is hot and bubbly.

Sodium, half grapefruit: 1 mg
Calories: 40

Cold Cereals

Cold cereals are standard breakfast dishes in many homes. Although the grains from which all cereals are made contain just a trace of sodium, many manufacturers *add* large amounts. Unfortunately, cereals that are advertised claiming "good nutrition" tend to be among the highest in sodium. In one ounce (30 g) there are sodium mgs: All-Bran, 287; cornflakes, 291; Special K, 218; Total, 375; Wheaties, 393.

Luckily, most low-sodium cold cereals list the sodium contents on the label. These are available: Sovex fruit and nut granola, Sovex unprocessed wheat bran, Quaker unprocessed bran, Puffa Puffa rice, puffed rice (not the fancy ones), puffed wheat, plain shredded wheat (Spoon Size shredded wheat is the same), frosted Mini-Wheats, and toasted wheat germ.

Familia Swiss Birchermuesli, a combination of grains and fruits, is available in many markets. There are several different versions, so select the one with *no*-added-salt. Look for the red box.

Also, you may want to try to see if you like low-sodium cereals, such as cornflakes. Use them as a substitute for bread crumbs in recipes. (See Roll and Bake Coating Mix, page 55.)

If you have been a cereal eater, you should be able to find one low in sodium that you like. A half cup (125 mL) of milk adds about 63 mgs of sodium plus valuable calcium. And the complete protein in the milk complements the incomplete protein in the cereal.

Hot Cereals

If you like hot cereal, you are lucky—all of the popular ones are naturally low in sodium (1 to 3 milligrams in a serving): oatmeal, Cream of Rice, Cream of Wheat, farina, Maltex, Malt-O-Meal, Wheatena.

Although the *long* cooking cereals are all *low* in sodium, instant and quick cooking types vary considerably: regular and "quick" oats, 1 mg per serving; Quaker "instant" oats, 400 mgs; Nabisco "instant" Cream of Wheat, 10 mgs. Manufacturers change the formulas for their products. Read the labels every time you shop.

Cereals cook just as well when you leave out the salt. For more flavor, try adding cinnamon, nutmeg, and a little sugar or honey. Be careful with brown sugar; there are 4 mgs sodium in a level tablespoon (15 mL). Or slice a banana or peach on your cereal.

Granola

Granola has become a popular breakfast cereal. But commercial granolas are loaded with sodium *and* calories. If you're interested, just check the boxes. This granola recipe, on the other hand, is surprisingly low in calories.

3 c.	oatmeal (regular)	750 mL
½ c.	wheat germ	125 mL
⅔ c.	sliced unsalted almonds or other unsalted nuts	180 mL
1 T.	safflower oil	15 mL
¼ c.	honey	60 mL
2 T.	molasses	30 mL
¼ c.	apple juice	60 mL

Mix oatmeal, wheat germ and almonds in a flat lasagne or jelly roll pan. In a saucepan combine and heat the oil, honey, molasses, and apple juice. Drizzle over the oatmeal mixture; use a spatula to push the mixture around in the pan. Bake in 325°F (165°C) oven for about 30 minutes. Then, mix again and bake 10 minutes. (The longer you cook it, the crunchier it gets.)

Makes 4½ cups or 9 one-half cup (1.1 L) servings
Sodium per half-cup serving: 3 mgs
Calories: 231

Special Breakfast or Brunch

For a low-sodium breakfast or brunch with an informal flair, arrange the waffle iron, waffle batter and toppings on the buffet. These toppings also create a special waffle dessert:

Strawberry: Defrost frozen strawberries and fill an attractive serving dish for guests to spoon over waffles.
Applesauce: Heat applesauce in a saucepan, adding a dash of cinnamon or nutmeg.
Pineapple: Crushed pineapple is tasty.

Pancake and Waffle Batter

For a change in the morning, you might want to make pancakes,* waffles or French Toast.

Making pancakes from the following recipe takes about one minute longer than commercial pancake mix, which is *very* high in sodium.

Low-sodium baking powder works well in this recipe. For toppings, maple and pancake syrups are fairly low in sodium but high in calories. So if you're watching calories, try applesauce.

¾ c.	skim milk	190 mL
1½ T.	safflower oil	22 mL
1	egg or egg substitute	1
1 T.	low-sodium baking powder (shake and stir before measuring)	15 mL
3 T.	sugar	45 mL
1 c.	flour	250 mL

In a large bowl, combine the milk, oil and egg or egg substitute. Stir in the baking powder, sugar and flour. Mix just enough to moisten flour; do not overmix. (The batter will still have small lumps.) Griddle according to directions that follow.

* Mix a scant cup (240 mL) of fresh or frozen whole blueberries to your pancake batter or chopped apples to your waffle batter for flavor. The fruits add a very small amount of sodium.

Makes 16 small pancakes
Sodium per pancake (with egg): 10 mgs
Calories: 62

Pancakes

Preheat a lightly oiled griddle or frying pan *while mixing the batter.* Griddle must be hot—drops of water will sizzle and "dance" when dropped on it. Pour about ¼ cup (60 mL) or less for each pancake onto the griddle or frying pan. With a spatula turn pancakes when bubbly and edges are cooked. Serve hot. To freeze, cool and wrap in freezer wrap. To reheat, use toaster, oven, or microwave oven.

Waffles

Preheat waffle iron when mixing your batter. Test the waffle iron by sprinkling a drop of water on it. If the water "dances," the iron is hot enough. To prevent sticking, brush waffle iron with oil, or spray with a vegetable coating spray. Pour in about ⅓ of a cup (90 mL) for each waffle. When there is less steam escaping from the corners of the waffle iron, the waffles are done. If you like crispy waffles, continue cooking until almost no steam escapes. Serve hot. To freeze and reheat, read under Pancakes above.

Toast

Toast is a favorite breakfast food and low-sodium breads are increasingly available in the freezer department of grocery stores. Especially, homemade low-sodium breads make wonderful toast. Try making some when you feel ambitious (Breads, page 219). If your sodium intake is highly restricted, be careful about making toast from regular commercial bread; there are about 228 mgs in 2 slices.

French Toast

Serve French Toast with maple or pancake syrup or try lower calorie applesauce for a delicious change. Leftover slices of any kind of bread can be used.

1 t.	*unsalted margarine*	*5 mL*
¼ c.	*skim milk*	*60 mL*
1	*egg or egg substitute*	*1*
4 slices	*low-sodium bread*	*4 slices*

Preheat a frying pan or griddle over medium heat. Melt the margarine in the pan. Using a fork, in a bowl combine the milk and egg or egg substitute. Dip both sides of the bread into this mixture. Fry on both sides until browned.

Makes 2 servings
Sodium per serving (with egg): 60 mgs
Calories: 195

Breakfast Meats and Other Dishes

All traditional breakfast meats are too high in sodium. If you need convincing, look at the sodium content: bacon—274 mgs in 2 slices; ham—1,114 mgs in 3 ounces (90 g); sausage—812 mgs in 3 ounces (90 g).

When you serve an egg without the meat and the plate does look very empty, try breakfast potatoes as a substitution. Hash browns or cottage fries have made "diner" breakfasts very popular. Plan ahead. When you're boiling or baking potatoes for dinner, cook a few extras for the next day's breakfast and store them in the refrigerator. As you prepare breakfast, you can cook potatoes quickly. Just add cold diced potatoes to the skillet, sprinkle with paprika, then add the egg (or egg substitute).

English Muffins

Commercial English muffins are packed with added sodium—from 225 to 600 mgs per muffin. Brands vary a great deal; check before you buy. You may have to write to the manufacturer to get this information.

Homemade English muffins are delicious, although, admittedly, it does take time for the dough to rise. But the muffins are not hard to make. If you make up a batch when you are going to be home anyhow, it won't seem like much trouble at all.

These muffins are cooked on a griddle the old-fashioned way! And they freeze well.

¼ c.	warm water (water used with packaged yeast should feel warm, but not hot, to the touch)	60 mL
1 T.	sugar	15 mL
1 pkg.	dry yeast	1 pkg.
½ c.	skim milk	125 mL
2 T.	safflower oil	30 mL
2 T.	unsalted margarine	30 mL
¼ c.	cool water	60 mL
3 c.	flour, more if necessary	750 mL
2 T.	corn meal	30 mL

Pour the warm water into a mixing bowl, stir in the sugar, and sprinkle the yeast on top. Wait a minute then stir and set aside until yeast bubbles up, about 10 minutes. Meanwhile, heat milk in small pan, add oil and margarine. Stir and heat until margarine melts, add the cool water and remove from heat. Pour in large bowl; cool to lukewarm. Add yeast mixture and all but half cup (125 mL) of the flour. Mix by hand or wooden spoon until flour is absorbed. Sprinkle half of the remaining flour on a working surface. Knead, adding more flour if the dough is sticky, until smooth and elastic. Place dough in mixing bowl, cover with clean cloth. Put bowl in a warm place away from drafts; let rise until doubled, about 1 hour.

Punch dough down; divide into 12 parts and shape with hands into muffins about 3½" (9 cm) in diameter. Dust a cookie sheet lightly with cornmeal. Place muffins on the cookie sheet and lightly dust the tops with cornmeal. Cover with a clean cloth and let rise for about 1 hour. Heat an ungreased griddle or cast-iron frying pan until moderately hot. Cook muffins for 9 minutes on each side until golden brown. Regulate the heat so that the muffins cook through but don't burn. Cool muffins before splitting. Store in refrigerator or freezer.

Makes 12 muffins
Sodium per muffin: 6 mgs
Calories: 176

Quick Biscuits

Self-rising flour, often used for biscuits, is outrageously high in sodium. All-purpose flour works well with low-sodium baking powder in this recipe. You can use unsalted margarine or honey or jelly on your biscuits—very low in sodium, but high in calories. For more quick breads see Breads (page 219).

1 c.	flour	250 mL
2½ t.	low-sodium baking powder (shake or stir before using)	12 mL
1 t.	sugar	5 mL
2 T.	unsalted margarine	30 mL
⅓ c.	skim milk	90 mL

Sift the flour, baking powder and sugar together twice into a mixing bowl. Using fork or pastry blender, cut the margarine into the flour mixture until it has the consistency of coarse cornmeal. Add milk and stir just enough to moisten. Shape the dough into a ball. Sprinkle flour on a work surface. Using a rolling pin, roll the dough until ½ in. (1 cm) thick. Cut with a 2-in. (5-cm) biscuit cutter to make approximately 6 biscuits. If you do not have a biscuit cutter, use any round top. Spray a cookie sheet with a vegetable coating spray. Place biscuits on the cookie sheet. Bake in 450°F (230°C) oven about 10 minutes.

Makes 6 large biscuits
Sodium per biscuit: 8 mgs
Calories per biscuit: 127

Eggs and Egg Substitutes

Your doctor can tell you how many eggs per week you should eat. For a person cutting down on cholesterol, the egg yolk is the thing to avoid, and the white is OK; for a person who needs to cut down on sodium, the yolk is OK, while the white is not. The yolk has about 9 mgs of sodium and the white about 50.

When you can enjoy an egg, the traditional cooking styles are fine, and by using a non-stick frying pan, you will avoid using fats. Chopped chives or minced onion perk up scrambled eggs or omelettes.

Egg substitutes, such as Fleischmann's Egg Beaters, available in the frozen food section of grocery stores, are somewhat higher in sodium; the equivalent to one egg, ¼ cup (60 mL) of Egg Beaters has 90 mgs of sodium. But egg substitutes contain no cholesterol. If you are cutting down on cholesterol, you may want to try egg substitutes to make scrambled "eggs," French toast or pancakes. Unsalted scrambled egg substitute will need your most creative seasoning for anything close to a delicious breakfast. Check the label for the sodium content of new brands.

Home Fries

You can also add a small amount of chopped onion.

2 T.	safflower oil	30 mL
1 T.	paprika	15 mL
4	medium potatoes, cooked, peeled, and diced	4

Heat oil in frying pan. Sprinkle paprika over the potato pieces. Drop potatoes into the frying pan and fry over medium heat for a few minutes, stirring frequently.

Makes 4 servings
Sodium per serving: 6 mgs
Calories: 169

SNACKS
AND
APPETIZERS

Snacking may be frowned on but eating small amounts of food throughout the day is healthier than eating three very large meals a day. The problem is that "snack foods" are often very salty or less nutritious than they could be. So if the snack is a good one, there is no reason to give up snacking. Just remember to count the total number of calories and the total number of milligrams of sodium per day. Even foods you eat standing up count!

Sometimes you may want a snack that is convenient and no trouble to fix. When you've invited guests to your home who need to cut down on sodium, you may not mind going to a little more trouble. Guests will be grateful if you serve delicious low-sodium snacks and will probably ask you for the recipe.

Unsalted nuts (peanuts, almonds, walnuts, etc.) are available in most stores and the potato chip companies are chipping away at the unsalted snack-food business—somewhat bland but not bad-tasting at all.

Raw fruits and vegetables are always excellent choices for snacking. Try cutting them into little cubes, and serve them on toothpicks (you may dip fruit into lemon juice to prevent darkening). Keep fruits in your home "snack" places. And homemade popcorn satisfies the urge to munch with very few calories, no fat, and no sodium. The type of corn popper that uses hot air (without oil) is a good gift for someone who loves to munch while losing weight. Season with the Unsalt Shaker (page 52).

Crudités

Crudités is a French word meaning "raw." Served as hors d'oeuvres, crudités are very popular at fancy restaurants and parties. Serve crudités with a dipping sauce from this chapter, or any of the salad dressing recipes (pages 65 to 69). If salad dressing is made up in advance, preparing crudités will be quick. Cut up seasonal vegetables that your family likes. Nibbling raw vegetables satisfies the snacking urge with very few calories.

These popular raw vegetable choices are all low in calories and sodium: chunks of zucchini; cherry tomatoes; sections of broccoli; carrot sticks; cucumber slices; small mushrooms; scallions or green onions; cubes of green pepper.

Yogurt Dip for Crudités

1 (8 oz.)	container of yogurt	1 (240 g)
2 T.	Mild Mustard (page 57)	30 mL

Combine with a wire whisk.

Serves 4
Sodium, 1 tablespoon (15 mL): 6 mgs
Calories: 11

Fruits for Dipping

Cut up pieces of fruit and toss them with a little lemon, pineapple or grapefruit juice to keep the fruit from turning brown. Try fruits like apples, pears, plums, nectarines. Dip with Spicy Dressing and Honey Dressing (page 69).

Onion Dip

This onion dip does *not* taste like the popular dip made from sour cream and dry onion soup mix. We hope you won't be disappointed and will appreciate this one on its own merits (*much* lower sodium). It's best made ahead so that the flavors blend.

1 T.	olive oil	15 mL
1	large onion, finely diced or grated	1
2 T.	cornstarch	30 mL
½ c.	skim milk	125 mL
¼ t.	onion powder	1 mL
½ t.	liquid hickory smoke	2 mL
½ t.	dry mustard	2 mL
dash	Tabasco sauce (more if you like it hotter)	dash
1 (8 oz.)	container of yogurt	1 (240 g)

Warm the oil in a skillet and cook onion over medium heat for approximately 10 minutes until lightly browned. Add the cornstarch and stir with a wire whisk for a couple of minutes. Add the milk and seasonings and stir with a wire whisk, simmering until the mixture is smooth and thick. Pour into a small bowl and cool slightly. Fold the yogurt into the onion mixture.

Makes 1½ cups (375 mL)
Sodium, 1 tablespoon (15 mL): 8 mgs
Calories: 17

Other Ideas for Dips

Many salad dressings can be used as dipping sauces. We recommend that you try: Good and Good for You Dressing (page 65); Creamy Italian Dressing (page 68); Light 'n Easy Cucumber (page 67); Russian Dressing (page 68). Recipes from the condiment section also make good dipping sauces: Hot Cocktail Sauce (page 60); Barbecue Sauce (page 59).

Pinto Bean Dip

This recipe is a natural for everyone on low-sodium, low-cholesterol diets. If you can't find a low-sodium, low-cholesterol cheese, simply omit the cheese. The recipe will still be flavorful. You can substitute other kinds of beans.

1 T.	olive oil	15 mL
1	medium onion, diced	1
1	clove garlic, minced	1
dash	liquid hickory smoke	dash
1 t.	no-salt chili powder	5 mL
dash	Tabasco sauce	dash
2 c.	pinto beans, cooked without salt	500 mL
2 oz.	no-salt-added cheese	60 g
2 T.	vinegar (cider is best)	30 mL
1 T.	sugar	15 mL

Heat the oil in a skillet over medium heat and sauté onion and garlic for a few minutes until soft. Add the hickory smoke, chili powder, and Tabasco sauce. Grate the cheese and stir into the beans with the vinegar and sugar. Whip all together in a food processor or blender until the dip is smooth. Add more Tabasco if you like a "hotter" flavor. Store, covered, in the refrigerator.

Makes 1½ cups (375 mL)
Sodium, 1 tablespoon (15 mL): 4 mgs
Calories: 35

Red Bean Dip

Taco shells with no added sodium, broken into small pieces, make ideal dippers. Cold crisp vegetables are even better—try cherry tomatoes, cucumber sticks, pieces of green pepper, and other crudités.

¼ c.	low-sodium ketchup	60 mL
2 T.	cider vinegar	30 mL
dash	Tabasco sauce (more if you like it hotter)	dash
¼ t.	liquid hickory smoke	1 mL
1 t.	garlic powder	5 mL
3 c.	kidney beans, cooked without salt	750 mL

Measure all ingredients into a blender or food processor and blend until smooth. Scrape into small jars or bowls and chill. At serving time, garnish with parsley, cucumber slices, scallions, cherry tomatoes, or whatever vegetables are in season.

Makes 3 cups (750 mL)
Sodium, 1 tablespoon (15 mL): 1 mg
Calories: 15

Guacamole Dip

Never bought an avocado? Try this dip as your first avocado dish. Serve fresh, since avocado does not keep well. An avocado is ripe when the flesh yields to gentle pressure.

1	large avocado, soft and ripe	1
1 T.	onion, minced	15 mL
1	large ripe tomato	1
1 T.	lemon juice	15 mL
¼ t.	ground black pepper	1 mL
dash	Tabasco sauce (optional)	dash

Cut the avocado in half, lengthwise. Discard the large pit and scoop the avocado into a bowl (save the skins to refill, if you like). Peel and dice the tomato and add to the avocado with the seasonings; mash, using a fork, potato masher or the plastic blade of a food processor. Serve immediately or chill before serving.

Makes 1¼ cups (310 mL)
Sodium, 1 tablespoon (15 mL): trace
Calories: 21

Yogurt Cheese

Nonfat yogurt is now available in supermarkets. It contains valuable calcium and protein and is quite low in fat and moderately low in sodium. It can be used in cooking but may break down and become watery. For cooking the use of "yogurt cheese" is much more satisfactory.

The idea is to allow yogurt to drip through cheesecloth or a funnel overnight. Start by placing several layers of cheesecloth inside a funnel or colander. (We have also used coffee filter paper and the plastic or ceramic coffee filter system, and they worked beautifully.) Place this funnel or colander over a bowl or large mug. Then spoon 2 cups of nonfat yogurt into the funnel. Let the whole thing sit in the refrigerator overnight. Later discard the watery whey that has collected in the bottom part. The "yogurt cheese" that remains in the top section is now ready to use in many different ways. The longer you allow the mixture to drip in the refrigerator, the more solid the yogurt cheese becomes. After 8 hours, it is like sour cream. After 24 hours, it is more like cream cheese.

You can use it as a substitute for sour cream or cream cheese in recipes for dips. You can mix it with chopped chives to put on baked potatoes. You can mix it with other salad dressing ingredients to make a "creamy" dressing. You can use it in equal parts with mayonnaise to cut down on the number of calories.

Curried Tuna Canapés

Curry provides an interesting flavor. Leftover cooked chicken can be used in place of the tuna.

7 oz.	low-sodium tuna	198 g
⅓ c.	low-sodium mayonnaise	90 mL
¼ t.	onion powder	1 mL
½ t.	curry powder	2 mL
	Five-Minute Chutney (page 64) (optional)	
50	small matzo crackers (or unsalted melba toast)	50

Drain the tuna, discard liquid, and mash tuna in a bowl. Add the mayonnaise, onion powder and curry powder. Stir until well mixed and tuna is flaky. Spoon curried tuna on each cracker. Spread a layer of Five-Minute Chutney on the crackers, if using. Broil for a minute or two before serving.

Makes 50 canapés
Sodium, each canapé: 3 mgs
Calories: 30

Exotic Dip

1 c.	Yogurt Cheese (page 88)	250 mL
2 T.	Five-Minute Chutney (page 64)	30 mL
¼ t.	curry powder (more if you like it "hotter")	1 mL

Mix the ingredients together and refrigerate until serving time. Serve with carrot sticks, green and red pepper wedges and cauliflower and broccoli florettes.

Makes 1 cup (250 mL)
Sodium, 1 tablespoon (15 mL): 10 mgs
Calories: 14

Shredded Wheat Snacks

A fantastic idea for low-sodium snacking—easy to mix and eat. It's faster to make than popcorn.

⅓ c.	unsalted margarine	90 mL
½ t.	curry powder	2 mL
½ t.	onion powder	2 mL
⅛ t.	ginger	1 mL
3 c.	Spoon Size shredded wheat	750 mL

Melt margarine in a large frying pan and stir in the curry powder, onion powder and ginger. Toss the shredded wheat in the seasoned margarine and stir while heating for 5 more minutes.

Makes 3 cups (750 mL)
Sodium, ½ cup (125 mL): 2 mgs
Calories: 179

Marinated Mushrooms

These are worth the effort and keep well in the refrigerator. By comparison, a pound of canned mushrooms contains about 2,000 mgs of sodium.

1 lb.	*fresh small mushrooms*	*450 g*
¼ c.	*dry vermouth*	*60 mL*
½ c.	*water*	*125 mL*
2 T.	*olive oil*	*30 mL*
1 T.	*vinegar*	*15 mL*
2 T.	*fresh parsley, finely chopped*	*30 mL*
3	*cloves garlic, minced*	*3*

Wash the mushrooms, trim the stems and drop into a saucepan. Add the vermouth and water and simmer for 5 minutes. Ladle the mushrooms and the liquid into a bowl. Stir in the oil, vinegar, parsley and garlic and refrigerate.

Makes about 100 mushrooms
Sodium, each mushroom: 1 mg
Calories: 5

Mushroom Roll Ups

Great to make ahead of time and heat up before serving.

3 T.	*unsalted margarine, at room temperature*	*45 mL*
½ lb.	*mushrooms, chopped*	*225 g*
2 T.	*onion, finely chopped*	*30 mL*
14 slices	*low-sodium bread*	*14 slices*

Melt 1 tablespoon (15 mL) of the margarine in a frying pan. Add the mushrooms and onion and cook gently for about 5 minutes; cool. Trim the crusts from the bread and flatten each slice with a rolling pin. Spread remaining margarine on the bread. Divide the filling on the bread. Roll up each slice like a jelly roll and place on a cookie sheet, seam side down. Without cutting all the way through, with a sharp knife make 4 small slashes across each roll. (Wrap and freeze until needed, if you like.) Just before serving, bake in a 350° F (175° C) oven until brown, about 10 minutes.

Makes 14 roll ups
Sodium, 1 roll up: 10 mgs
Calories: 97

Sautéed Chicken Tidbits

We suggest serving these party tidbits with little bowls of your favorite condiments.*

⅓ c.	*flour*	*90 mL*
dash	*white or black pepper*	*dash*
1¼ lb.	*boneless chicken breast cutlets*	*600 g*
1 T.	*unsalted margarine*	*15 mL*
1 T.	*olive oil*	*15 mL*

Mix the flour and pepper together in a bowl. Cut the cutlets into bite-size pieces. Coat the chicken by shaking the chicken and flour in a closed paper bag. Heat margarine with the oil in a large frying pan. Add the pieces of chicken and cook over medium high heat until they are just cooked through and golden brown. Turn the pieces while cooking so that they brown evenly. Cutlets cook fairly quickly, so be careful not to overcook. Serve with toothpicks to dunk the chicken.

* Try Sweet-and-Sour Sauce (page 61); Five-Minute Chutney (page 64); Barbecue Sauce (page 59); Mustard (mild or hot) thinned with a little water and vinegar (page 57). For memories of fast-food chicken pieces (Chicken McNuggets), try honey, too.

Makes 8 snack-size servings
Sodium per serving: 37 mgs
Calories: 126

Baked Potato Skins

These are the latest in fancy restaurant hors d'oeuvres. Sodium content and calories are quite low.

4	*baking potatoes, baked in their skins*	4
2 T.	*unsalted margarine*	*30 mL*
½ t.	*onion powder*	*2 mL*
½ t.	*garlic powder*	*2 mL*
½ t.	*paprika*	*2 mL*

Cut baked potatoes in half lengthwise and scoop out the insides, leaving a layer of potato near the skin. (You might like to make Home Fries [page 82] with the part you scoop out.) Melt the margarine in a saucepan and mix in the onion powder, garlic powder and paprika. Arrange the potato skins, insides up, on a cookie sheet. Brush potatoes with the flavored mixture. Bake in 400°F (205°C) oven 15–20 minutes, or until lightly browned. You can add a filling and return the potatoes to the oven for a few minutes.* Or, put out dishes of sauces and let your friends choose their own toppings.

*There are many good fillings: Sweet Relish (page 62); Hot Cocktail Sauce (page 60); Ketchup (page 55); Mustard (page 57); Barbecue Sauce (page 59); Sweet-and-Sour Sauce (page 61)

Makes 8 servings
Sodium: Low
Calories: Low

Party Pizzas

Terrific for low sodium snacks!

Make Pizza Dough (page 154) and Tomato Sauce (page 74). Prepare cookie sheets by dusting with a fine layer of cornmeal. After the dough has been mixed, break off small amounts of dough, each about the size of a walnut. With your hands, shape each piece of dough into a ball and then flatten it into a circle about 2½ inches (6 cm) across. Place circles on a cookie sheet. Spoon on a little pizza sauce and top with a little grated low-fat low-sodium cheese. If you want extras on your pizzas, try thin slices of sautéed mushroom, green pepper or onion. Or try ground beef cooked with fennel (page 155)—a topping that tastes like sausage. Bake in 450°F (230°C) oven for about 10 minutes.

Makes 16, 2½-inch (6-cm) pizzas

Egg Roll Hors d'Oeuvre

For cute and delicious party appetizers, adapt Egg Rolls (page 216). Just cut each egg roll wrapper into quarters. Place one teaspoon (5 mL) of filling in each wrapper; roll and fry as in the basic recipe. You need 24 egg roll wrappers to make 96. Make them in advance and keep in a warm oven or on a special warming tray.

Vegetable Tempura or Onion Rings

A special snack for special get-togethers, such as watching the big game. Use available vegetables: zucchini, cauliflower florets, broccoli florets, sliced broccoli stems and green beans. Onion rings are always the favorites.

2	*large onions, sliced* or	2
4 c.	*fresh vegetables in bite-size pieces*	1 L
4 T.	*flour*	60 mL
1 T.	*cornstarch*	15 mL
½ t.	*low-sodium baking powder*	2 mL
¼ c.	*water*	60 mL
1 T.	*egg substitute*	15 mL
	oil for frying	

Combine 3 tablespoons flour, cornstarch, baking powder, water and egg substitute in a bowl. Beat with a wire whisk until the batter is smooth and foamy. Steam vegetables for approximately 5 minutes or less time if you like the vegetables crispy. Put the remaining tablespoon flour into a paper bag and add the onions or vegetable pieces. Shake well to coat lightly. Drop the onions or vegetables into the batter. Turn each piece over and over in the batter to coat well.

Pour the oil into a frying pan and heat to 375° F (190° C). (An electric frying pan is best.) Slip each vegetable segment into oil. Using a long-handled spoon to turn, cook for approximately 5 minutes until golden brown. Drain on paper towels. Serve at once.

Makes 8 servings
Sodium per serving (with cauliflower): 6 mgs
Calories: 64

Party Spareribs

A finger-licking snack for special get-togethers!

3 lb.	spareribs	1.4 kg
1 T.	unsalted margarine	15 mL
¼ c.	low-sodium ketchup	60 mL
½ c.	cider vinegar	125 mL
3 T.	molasses	45 mL
2 T.	sugar	30 mL
¼ t.	paprika	1 mL
dash	Tabasco sauce	dash
1 small jar	baby food peaches	1 small jar
½ t.	dry mustard	2 mL
½ t.	ginger	2 mL
¼ t.	liquid hickory smoke (optional)	1 mL

Cut the spareribs between the bones. To remove excess fat, parboil for about 5 minutes. Drain ribs in a colander. Refill the pot with cold water, plunge ribs in cold water to firm; drain. While the ribs are cooking, make the sauce by mixing remaining ingredients in a saucepan. Cook gently for 15 minutes. (If it's more convenient to finish the recipe later, put the ribs in a bowl, cover with the sauce and refrigerate.) When ready to cook, arrange the ribs on the rack of a broiler pan. Brush with sauce. Bake in 450° F (230° C) oven for 15 minutes. Turn on oven broiler. Brush ribs with more sauce and broil for a minute or two. Turn, brush with sauce, and broil on other side. Serve with plenty of napkins!

Makes 8 small servings
Calories: Impossible to estimate

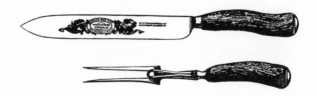

SANDWICHES

Recipes and advice about sandwiches and other foods that you can take with you are found in this chapter. You can also keep these sandwich ideas in mind for meals at home. When busy or tired, many people prefer a light soup and sandwich meal.

Popular sandwich fillings—cold cuts, hotdogs, turkey roll or breast, chicken loaf—are taboo for healthy eating.

Companies that make cold cuts, in some instances, have started making unsalted cold cuts—turkey breast, etc. You may have to write to the manufacturer to find out how much sodium cold cuts actually contain.

There are quite a few other healthy sandwich fillings. No one needs a recipe for peanut butter and jelly. Fortunately, all jams and jellies are naturally low in sodium. Unsalted peanut butter is available in nearly all large grocery stores; health food stores sell it also. Try peanut butter on apple, pear or banana slices, for a change.

Other sandwich ideas include low-sodium tuna salad, egg white salad or thin slices of leftover chicken, turkey or beef, with cranberry sauce for extra flavor.

Try restaurant favorites at home—Meatball Sandwiches (page 101) or Tacos (page 211)—easy and delicious.

Adding Hot Items to a Cold Lunch

A widemouthed Thermos insulated container is terrific for packing hot soup or a serving of a casserole for lunch to carry out from home. To make sure that the food is still hot several hours after it's packed, pour boiling water into the Thermos, put on the cover, and let it sit. At the same time, put the soup or other food into a saucepan and heat until it's very hot. Then dump out the boiling water and add the hot food and cover the Thermos. This method works well for all of the hot soups (pages 106 to 115). You might find it most convenient to make up batches of soup and freeze the extra soup in the amount that will be used in the Thermos.

Steak Sandwich

1 T.	*safflower oil (optional)*	15 mL
1	*medium onion, thinly sliced (optional)*	1
1 lb.	*no-salt-added meat for steak sand-wiches (usually available in freezer cases—check label)*	450 g
4	*Soft Rolls (page 232) shaped long*	4

Heat oil in a skillet or griddle over medium high heat and sauté onions, if using. Add the meat and heat briefly on each side.

Serves 4
Sodium per serving (without options): 68 mgs
Calories (without options): 411

Submarine, Hero, Hoagie, Grinder, Po'boy . . .

Make long rolls and pack a submarine sandwich (also called a grinder, a hoagie, a po'boy, etc.).* The secret to the special taste: Prepare the sliced onion ahead of time so that the seasonings are absorbed.

1 T.	*olive oil*	15 mL
2 T.	*cider vinegar*	30 mL
1 t.	*oregano*	5 mL
1	*small onion, sliced thinly*	1
1	*Soft Roll (page 232)*	1
2 oz.	*unsalted tuna*	60 g
	tomato, thinly sliced	
	lettuce, finely shredded	

Whisk the olive oil, vinegar and oregano in a bowl. Add the onion slices and cover the bowl. Marinate for at least 3 hours. Slice and open the roll. (Some people like to pull the roll open and remove part of the inside to make room for the filling.) Add the tuna, tomato slices and lettuce; drain the onion and add to the filling. Drizzle with the flavored marinade. To pack for lunch, wrap with plastic wrap. If you prefer your sandwich hot, wrap it in aluminum foil and heat in a 325°F (165°C) oven for approximately 10 minutes, or wrap it with plastic wrap and heat briefly in a microwave oven.

*If you like hot peppers, buy fresh ones, cut them in half and discard the seeds before adding to the sandwich. Hot peppers that come in jars are more convenient but have added salt.

Makes 1 sandwich
Sodium per sandwich: 31 mgs
Calories: 560

Old New England Favorite

½ c.   *Baked Beans (page 203)*   *120 mL*
1   *Pita bread or 2 slices of bread*

Sandwiches made from cold, leftover baked beans were once a tradition in New England. Often, relish or ketchup or horseradish was added. It's less traditional, but tidier, to put the beans in pita bread. Some people like to put in slices of onion or tomato. Beans and wheat are complementary proteins, so you get complete protein with almost no fat. You also get a good serving of soluble fibre in a particularly delicious form.

Rachel Sandwich

If you are on a low-sodium diet you can't eat a Reuben—grilled corned beef, Swiss cheese and sauerkraut on rye—with 2,317 mgs of sodium! Have you ever heard of a Rachel? Rachels are almost as popular as Reubens in some delicatessens. Serve with hot or mild mustard (page 57).

2 oz.	*lean trimmed roast beef, thinly sliced*	*60 g*
1 oz.	*no-salt low-fat cheese*	*30 g*
2 T.	*Russian Dressing (page 68)*	*30 mL*
2 slices	*low-sodium bread, preferably rye (page 237)*	*2*
1 t.	*unsalted margarine, softened*	*5 mL*

Preheat your skillet or griddle over medium-high heat. Meanwhile, spread the meat, cheese and dressing on one slice of bread. Cover with the other piece of bread. Spread a thin layer of margarine on the outside of both slices of bread. Cook until nicely browned on both sides.

Makes 1 sandwich
Sodium per sandwich: 64 mgs
Calories: 555

Hot Open-Faced Sandwiches

Hot open-faced sandwiches are popular for quick meals. For instance, you can mix low-sodium tuna with low-sodium mayonnaise. Spread on a piece of bread and broil a few inches from the heat for approximately 5 minutes.

Cold Pita Sandwiches

You can vary your pita sandwiches. Use Pita Pocket-Bread (page 238) and fill the pocket with the tasty combinations that follow.

Stuff a little lettuce into the bottom of the pocket. Add Chicken Salad, (page 104), tuna salad (made with low-sodium tuna), thinly sliced roast beef, or leftover ground beef. Top with a slice of fresh tomato, chopped onion, bean or alfalfa sprouts, slivered celery, carrots or other vegetables, if you like. Just wrap the sandwich and you're ready to go.

Zesty Cheese Filling

Use this filling in a pita or roll. For zestier fillings, try Meat Filling for Tacos or Burritos (page 211) or Chicken Filling for Tacos (page 212).

2 oz.	low-sodium cheese	60 g
2 T.	olive oil	30 mL
1 T.	cider vinegar	15 mL
¼ t.	oregano	1 mL
grind	pepper	grind
¼ t.	garlic powder (optional)	1 mL
1	Pita Pocket-Bread (page 238) or 1	1
	Soft Roll (page 232)	

Cube the cheese. Combine all the other ingredients in a small bowl. Add the cheese cubes; marinate 30 minutes. Slice pita or roll and fill with marinated cheese.

Serves 1
Sodium per recipe: 23 mgs
Calories: 584

Hot Pita Sandwiches

Hot pita sandwiches make a delicious change for lunch at home or a quick dinner. Stuff your pocket sandwich with either of the fillings that follow.

Steak Filling

1 T.	safflower oil	15 mL
½	medium green pepper, cut into small chunks	½
¼ c.	mushrooms, sliced	60 mL
1	medium onion, cut into small chunks	1
2 oz.	frozen sandwich steaks, 100 percent beef, no-salt-added	60 g
1	medium pita bread, sliced in half	1

Heat the oil in a skillet. Add the green pepper, mushrooms and onion; stir and cook gently until the vegetables are soft and the onion is golden. Add the sandwich steaks; cook on one side about 45 seconds, then turn and cook on the other side until brown. Scoop the steaks and vegetables into the pita bread. Serve hot.

Serves 1
Sodium per recipe: 56 mgs
Calories: 458

Vegetarian Filling

1 T.	safflower oil	15 mL
½	medium onion, cut into small chunks	½
½	medium green pepper, cut into small chunks	½
¼ c.	mushrooms, sliced	60 mL
1 oz.	no-salt cheese, thinly sliced	30 g
1	Pita Pocket-Bread (page 238)	1

Heat the oil in a skillet and add the vegetables. Stir-fry until the vegetables are soft. Lay the cheese slices on top of the vegetables. Cook for one minute until the cheese begins to melt. Slice the pita and scoop the melting cheese and vegetables into the bread. Serve hot.

Makes 1 serving
Sodium per sandwich: 22 mgs
Calories: 387

Grilled Cheese Sandwich

This popular sandwich will be delicious if you are able to find a source of delicious low-sodium cheese. If your favorite low-sodium cheese does not yet come presliced, slice it at home.

2 slices	*low-sodium bread*	2 slices
1 oz.	*no-salt cheese such as Swiss*	30 g
1 t.	*unsalted margarine*	5 mL
	thin slices of onion, tomato and	
	tuna (optional)	

Preheat a griddle or frying pan over medium heat. Slice the cheese very thin and place it with onion, tomato and any extras you want on the bread. Close it up like a sandwich. Spread the margarine on both sides of the bread. Grill on both sides until bread is toasted and cheese melts.

Makes 1 sandwich
Sodium per sandwich (without options): 22 mgs
Calories: 213

Peanut Butter and . . .

Peanuts are a good source of fibre as well as a very popular food. The kind of peanut butter that is commonly available in supermarkets is very smooth and creamy because it contains hydrogenated vegetable oil. It also contains salt and sugar. Many stores also sell "natural" peanut butter, which is a better choice. With this type, the oil will separate and you will need to stir the mixture before you spread it on your bread. When you are reading labels to see whether or not peanut butter has been hydrogenated, also check to see that no salt or sugar has been added.

Peanut butter and jelly is a popular combination, as is peanut butter with slices of banana. Peanut butter and applesauce is fine. Some people like to cut an apple into sections and spread a layer of peanut butter directly on the apple slices.

Cheese Dreams

1 T.	safflower oil	15 mL
⅛ t.	liquid hickory smoke	.5 mL
1	large tomato	1
6 oz.	low-sodium cheese	180 g
4 slices	low-sodium bread	4 slices

Combine the oil and hickory smoke in a small shallow bowl. Slice the tomato into thin slices and dip into the flavored oil. Slice the cheese thinly and cover the bread. Spread tomato slices on top. Place on a broiler pan and broil a few inches from the heat for approximately 5 minutes.

Makes 4 sandwiches
Sodium per sandwich: 21 mgs
Calories: 324

Meatball Sandwich

Cook extra meatballs when you're making them for dinner. Use the leftovers for sandwiches. Freeze in small packs with the sauce so that you have enough for one sandwich.

¼ lb.	Italian Meatballs (page 188)	120 g
⅓ c.	Tomato Sauce (page 74)	90 mL
1	Soft Roll (page 232)	1

If the meatballs are large, slice them in half. Heat the meatballs and sauce in a saucepan. If eating at home, arrange meatballs in the roll and serve. If packing a lunch, be sure that the meatballs and sauce are very hot. Wrap the roll and pack it separately.

Makes 1 sandwich
Sodium per sandwich: 102 mgs
Calories: 523

Hamburger

Hamburgers can be grilled, broiled, fried or charcoal-broiled. You probably have ideas about what tastes good on a hamburger. If you add a thin slice of low-sodium cheese, you'll have a low-sodium cheeseburger.

Popular hamburger toppings include: ketchup, Barbecue Sauce or Chili Sauce (page 59); a slice of tomato; lettuce; thin onion slices; sliced or diced onion, sautéed in a small amount of unsalted margarine; sautéed green pepper slices; sautéed mushroom slices; Russian Dressing (page 68).

Fast-Food-Style Hamburgers

Arguments over which is better—McDonald's "Big Mac" or Burger King's "Whopper"—may continue to rage among people who admit to being fast-food fanatics. Someone in your family may be fond of fast-food-style hamburgers—they have sold *billions*, after all. If so, you can make low-sodium versions at home, which are pretty good substitutes for the Big Mac (which has 1,060 sodium mgs) or the Whopper (which has 990 mgs sodium).

1 lb.	*very lean ground beef*	450 g
2 oz. (optional)	*low-sodium cheese, sliced very thin*	60 g
4	*Soft Rolls (page 232)*	4

Garnishes, Whopper Style

¼ c.	*shredded lettuce*	60 mL
1	*medium onion, thinly sliced*	1
1	*tomato, thinly sliced*	1
4 T.	*low-sodium mayonnaise*	60 mL
1	*low-sodium pickle, thinly sliced.*	1
	Low-sodium pickles are available at some health food stores. If you can't find them, just omit this ingredient. Do not substitute a regular pickle.	

Garnishes, Big Mac Style

¼ c.	shredded lettuce	60 mL
4 T.	Hamburger Sauce (page 60)	60 mL
1	small onion, diced	1
1	low-sodium pickle, thinly sliced*	1

Divide the meat into 4 or 8* patties. Broil or grill over medium-high heat until done as desired (rare, medium or well-done). After you turn the patties over to the second side, add a very small piece of low-sodium cheese, if desired.

To assemble a "Big Mac" hamburger, cut each roll across two times to make three pieces. Put one patty on each of the two bottom pieces. Top with desired garnishes.

To assemble a "Whopper" hamburger, cut across each roll in half; fill with hamburger and garnishes.

* You may want to make one large patty out of the ¼ pound of meat per person. Or if you want to make Big Mac-style hamburgers, divide each ¼ pound in half and cook two very thin patties per person.

Makes 4 Whopper- or Big Mac-style hamburgers

Chili Burger

¼ lb.	very lean ground beef	120 g
¼ c.	Chili con Carne (page 214)	60 mL
1	Soft Roll (page 232)	1

Form the beef into a patty and pan-fry in a skillet, or broil on a broiler pan. While the hamburger is cooking, heat the Chili con Carne in a saucepan. Set the burger on half of the roll and add the chili. Serve hot.

Makes 1 chili burger
Sodium per serving: 91 mgs
Calories: 642

Club Sandwich

3 slices	low-sodium bread	3 slices
⅛ t.	liquid hickory smoke	.5 mL
1 T.	low-sodium mayonnaise	15 mL
1½ oz.	cooked chicken or turkey, thinly sliced	45 g
1	small tomato, sliced	1
1	leaf of lettuce	1

Toast the bread. Mix liquid smoke and mayonnaise in a small bowl and spread thinly on one side of 3 pieces of toast. Place the chicken on the mayonnaise side of one piece of toast. Cover with a second piece of toast. Put the tomato slices and lettuce on the second piece of toast. Cover with the last piece of toast. Cut sandwich on the diagonal and then across again to make 4 triangles. Spear with a toothpick, if desired, to hold it together.

Chicken Salad

If chicken salad with unsalted mayonnaise seems bland, spice it with a low-sodium salad dressing such as Creamy Italian, Light 'n Easy Cucumber, or Good and Good for You (pages 65 to 68). Add celery seeds, paprika or curry powder to the mayonnaise before mixing it with chicken.

12 oz.	cooked, diced chicken	360 g
3 T.	low-sodium mayonnaise	45 mL
	celery, chopped	
	onion, chopped (optional)	

Mix chicken in a bowl with mayonnaise until the chicken is coated. Add chopped onion and a small amount of chopped celery, if desired. Stir to combine.

Makes filling for 4 sandwiches
Sodium, filling per sandwich: 57 mgs
Calories: 118

Sloppy Joes

A favorite food with young people. This low-sodium version is tasty enough to please even people who are not used to low-sodium food. It can also be frozen in small portions, for later defrosting, to make a quick meal or sandwich. If you made Sloppy Joes with a commercial seasoning mix, there would be more than 3,500 mgs of sodium per sandwich.

1 lb.	very lean ground beef	450 g
6 oz.	no-salt-added tomato paste	170 g
1¼ c.	water	310 mL
2 t.	cornstarch	10 mL
½ t.	onion powder	2 mL
¼ t.	garlic powder	1 mL
½ t.	celery seed	2 mL
½ t.	Salt-free Chili Powder (page 54)	2 mL
½ t.	dry mustard	2 mL
1½ T.	sugar	22 mL
dash	Tabasco sauce (more if you like it hot)	dash
¼ c.	wine vinegar	60 mL
1	small onion, finely chopped	1
½	green pepper, finely chopped	½

Brown the ground beef in a frying pan, mashing the meat with a fork as it cooks. Combine remaining ingredients in a saucepan. Stir and cook over low heat. Skim off any fat and add the browned meat to the sauce; stir. Serve on toasted low-sodium bread (7 mgs each); or if you have some homemade rolls in the freezer, this is a logical choice.

Serves 4
Sodium per serving (without roll): 84 mgs
Calories (without roll): 260

SOUPS

PEOPLE WHO EAT SOUP take in fewer calories than those who do not eat soup.[1] It may be that people feel more satisfied. Soup takes longer to eat. Soup is also a good choice for someone who is having problems chewing or who is not feeling up to eating a full meal. Whether you're feeling sick or well, soup is always comforting.

Regular canned soups are very convenient. But with a sodium content of 1,810 to 2,475 mgs *per can*, forget them! Canned low-sodium soups are just as convenient and available although more expensive per serving. To be honest with you, none of the people who taste-tested foods for us found the commercial low-sodium soups delicious or even acceptable. Both of the canned low-sodium chicken soups tested by *Consumer Reports* were rated "poor in sensory quality."[2]

Homemade low-sodium soups, if well-seasoned, are better than commercial ones. Some people who do not have the time or inclination to make soup may want to try flavoring the canned soups.

Plan ahead and keep chicken stock in the freezer. For 15 minutes of work you will create delicious soup to satisfy you for hours. If you are not home during the day, make soup on a weekend or in the evening. And if you have a microwave oven, you can defrost and heat homemade soup as quickly and easily as you would heat a can of soup. In other words, low-sodium cooking can be convenient.

We have a tip for you if your family has been used to canned soup: Cut the vegetables into very small pieces so that the soup will have more of a familiar look. Especially, be careful about which vegetables you add to soup, since the sodium does go into the *liquid*. That's why carrots and celery are called for in small amounts. Check sodium content in Appendix (page 269).

Do you like croutons in your soup? Unfortunately, commercial croutons are extremely high in sodium and homemade croutons made with low-sodium bread and unsalted margarine bear little resemblance to the store-bought ones. You might be surprised at what a nice crunchiness plain popcorn adds when sprinkled on top of soup. Try it with Split Pea Soup (page 112) and Senate Bean Soup (page 113).

Chicken Stock

Soups and other recipes often call for homemade chicken stock. Homemade unsalted chicken stock is very helpful for low-sodium cooking because the other choices (milk or regular bouillon) are high in sodium. There are low-sodium, dry packaged instant broths available. We tried them and, frankly, did not like the potassium chloride aftertaste. Try this recipe and you may never need to try commercial ones again.

1 T.	olive oil	15 mL
1 pkg.	soup greens*	1 pkg
	package of "greens" usually contains:	
2	carrots	2
2 stalks	celery	2 stalks
1	medium onion	1
1	yellow turnip	1
1	parsnip	1
¼ c.	parsley	60 mL
2 lb.	chicken breasts, bone in, skin removed	900 g
1	bay leaf	1
2 qt.	water (If it takes more water than this to cover the ingredients, your cooking pot is too wide.)	2 L
⅓ c.	vermouth	90 mL
dash	cayenne pepper	dash
dash	black or white pepper	dash

Heat the oil in a soup pot and pan-fry the peeled and diced vegetables over medium heat; a good way to do this is to get one vegetable ready at a time and add to the warm oil. Keep cooking and preparing until all the vegetables have been added. Add remaining ingredients. Turn the heat to high and bring to a boil, turn down heat and simmer for about 2½ hours. Strain over a bowl. Use the chicken for Curry (page 207), Chicken Salad (page 104), etc., and freeze the stock in one-meal quantities.

* If your store does not sell soup greens, you can just buy separate vegetables. Don't overlook vegetables such as turnips or parsnips; they add a lot of flavor to the liquid.

Makes about 6 cups (1.5 L)
Sodium, cup (250 mL): 43 mgs
Calories: 44

Mushroom-Barley Soup

This hearty soup freezes well.

1 T.	unsalted margarine	15 mL
1 T.	safflower oil	15 mL
1	small onion, chopped fine	1
4 c.	Chicken Stock (page 107)	1 L
½ lb.	fresh mushrooms, diced	225 g
¼ t.	onion powder	1 mL
1	bay leaf	1
2 T.	chopped parsley	30 mL
¼ t.	white pepper	1 mL
3 T.	barley	45 mL
2 T.	cornstarch	30 mL
1 c.	skim milk	250 mL
¼ c.	sherry (not cooking sherry)	60 mL

Melt margarine in a soup pot; add the oil and onion and sauté for about 5 minutes. Add the chicken stock, mushrooms, onion powder, bay leaf, parsley, white pepper, and barley; cook over low heat for 45 minutes, stirring occasionally. In a small bowl, mix the cornstarch and the milk, stirring with a wire whisk until smooth. Add to the soup pot. Reduce heat and cook gently for 2 to 3 minutes until thickened, stirring constantly; remove bay leaf. Before serving, stir in the sherry.

Makes about 5 cups (1.3 L)
Sodium, 1 cup (250 mL): 65 mgs
Calories: 180

Chicken Noodle Soup

A popular canned chicken noodle soup has 960 mgs of sodium per 1 cup (250 mL) serving (only ⅓ of the can of soup since *a can is theoretically figured to have 2.69 servings*). Campbell's chicken noodle soup contains 2,580 mgs of sodium.

6 c.	Chicken Stock (*page 107*)	1.5 L
1 c.	thin noodles, cooked and drained	250 mL

Cook chicken stock and use tongs to remove chicken; leave the vegetables in the soup, but discard bay leaf. When chicken is cool enough to handle, discard bones and cut chicken into bite-size pieces. Add chicken and noodles. Serve hot.

Makes about 6 cups (1.5 L)

Onion Soup

A simple and tasty recipe.* You may want to freeze part of the recipe in portions. A cup of soup made from a mix would contain almost 1,000 mgs of sodium.

4 T.	unsalted margarine	60 mL
2 T.	safflower oil	30 mL
4	large onions, thinly sliced	4
3 T.	flour	45 mL
6 c.	Chicken Stock (*page 107*)	1.5 L
grind	black pepper	grind
¼ c.	white wine	60 mL

Use a large cooking pot. Heat the margarine and oil and sauté the onions over *low* heat for about 20 minutes, until the onions are golden and soft. Stir occasionally and do not let the onions brown. Sprinkle the flour over the onion. Stir occasionally to avoid burning and cook for 2 minutes. Stir in the chicken stock, wine, and black pepper. Simmer over low heat for 20 to 30 minutes. Serve hot.

* To serve French style, ladle a serving of soup into an ovenproof bowl. Toast bread (low-sodium for strict dieters or French bread) and rub each piece of toast with a cut garlic clove. Sprinkle grated low-sodium cheese on top of the toast. Broil until the cheese has melted and is golden. Serve hot.

Makes 6 cups (1.5 L)
Sodium, 1 cup (250 mL) without toast: 50 mgs
Calories: 206

Beef Stock

Use vegetables you have on hand, but *small* amounts of the vegetables that are fairly high in sodium (spinach, beets, celery, carrots).

2 lb.	*marrow bones or other soup bones*	900 g
1 t.	*olive oil*	5 mL
2 c.	*vegetables to add flavor, such as 1 carrot, 1 yellow turnip, 1 onion, 1 stalk celery, small handful parsley*	500 mL
8 c.	*water*	2 L
grind	*pepper*	grind
dash	*Tabasco sauce*	dash
1	*bay leaf*	1
½ t.	*dry mustard*	2 mL
1 t.	*basil*	5 mL
½ c.	*red wine, such as Burgundy*	125 mL
2 T.	*no-salt-added tomato paste*	30 mL
1 c.	*small noodles or ABC macaroni (optional)*	250 mL

Brown the marrow bones in warm oil in a large soup pot. Coarsely chop the vegetables and add, stirring occasionally with a wooden spoon. Add the water and remaining ingredients. Simmer for at least 2 hours. Cool and refrigerate overnight. The next day, remove and discard the layer of fat and bones. If you prefer clear stock, strain to remove the vegetables and bones. Or leave the vegetables in the soup. You can also cook separately a cup of small noodles or half cup of ABC macaroni to thicken the vegetable soup. Store in small portions in the freezer. (An ice cube tray works for very small amounts. Freeze and pop out; store in a freezer bag. Use stock cubes to flavor unsalted rice and gravy.)

Makes 5 cups (1.3 L)
Sodium, 1 cup (250 mL): 48 mgs
Calories: 65

Vegetable-Beef Soup

1 t.	*safflower oil*	5 mL
¾ lb.	*very lean beef, cubed*	338 g
1 pkg.	*"soup greens," diced (see note* under Chicken Stock, page 107)*	1 pkg
2 qt.	*water*	2 L
1	*bay leaf*	1
good grind	*pepper*	good grind

½ t.	basil	2 mL
3 T.	no-salt added tomato paste	45 mL
½ c.	vermouth	125 mL
1 c.	small thin noodles or	250 mL
½ c.	macaroni, such as ABC	125 mL

Heat the safflower oil in a large soup pot and brown the beef. Add the diced vegetables to the pot, stir and add remaining ingredients. Simmer for 2 to 2½ hours. Skim off foam every hour; stir occasionally. To remove fat, cool and refrigerate overnight. Skim off fat layer and reheat. Or, if in a hurry, place paper towel on top to remove fat. Cook noodles or macaroni separately and add to the soup.

Makes 7 cups (1.8 L)
Sodium, 1 cup (250 mL): 52 mgs
Calories: 145

Ground Beef and Vegetable Soup

1½ lb.	very lean ground beef	675 g
8 c.	water	2 L
6 oz.	no-salt-added tomato paste	170 mL
2 T.	cider vinegar	30 mL
2 t.	basil	10 mL
1 t.	dry mustard	5 mL
2 t.	dill	10 mL
1 t.	garlic powder	5 mL
⅛ to ¼ t.	black pepper, or to taste	1 mL
½ c.	vermouth	125 mL
1	bay leaf	1
¼ c.	chopped parsley	60 mL
2	carrots, finely diced	2
2 c.	finely chopped cabbage	500 mL
1	yellow turnip, finely diced	1
1	parsnip, finely diced	1
10 oz.	frozen corn	300 g
9 oz.	frozen green beans	270 g

Brown the meat in a soup pot. Drain off the fat, wipe the pan and drain meat on a paper towel. Return the meat to the pot. Add all remaining ingredients and simmer over low heat for approximately 2 hours.

Makes 11 cups (2.9 L)
Sodium, 1 cup (250 mL): 52 mgs
Calories: 172

Split Pea Soup

You might like to try this soup with the optional liquid smoke for a smoky flavor without added sodium. It almost makes up for the missing ham bone.

1 lb.	green or yellow split peas	450 g
1	stalk celery, diced	1
2	small carrots, diced	2
2	medium onions, diced	2
8 c.	water	2 L
1	bay leaf	1
½ t.	thyme	2 mL
¼ t.	white or black pepper	1 mL
1 t.	hickory liquid smoke (optional)	5 mL
2 T.	sherry (not cooking sherry) (optional)	30 mL
1 c.	skim milk	250 mL

Wash and pick out any discolored peas and combine with the vegetables in a soup pot. Add the water and the seasonings. Simmer until the peas are soft, about 2 hours. Remove the bay leaf. In a food mill or blender, puree the soup 2 cups (500 mL) at a time. If you like your soup lumpy, do not blend it all. Stir in the sherry, if using, the milk, and any additional water needed for a thinner consistency. Serve hot.

Makes 7 cups (1.8 L)
Sodium, 1 cup (250 mL) without the optional sherry: 48 mgs
Calories: 264

Quick Lentil-Barley Soup

Good on a cold day for a brown bag lunch. Try freezing this soup in one-cup portions for easy reheating.

1	small onion, chopped	1
¼ c.	safflower oil	60 mL
9 c.	water	2.3 L
12 oz.	no-salt-added tomato paste	340 g
½ t.	celery seed	2 mL
½ c.	dry lentils	125 mL
⅓ c.	whole barley	90 mL
¼ t.	black pepper	1 mL
⅛ t.	rosemary	1 mL
¾ t.	basil	3 mL

In a large soup pot, sauté onion in oil until soft, stirring with a wooden spoon. Add remaining ingredients. Cover and cook gently for about 45 minutes, stirring occasionally.

Makes 8 cups (2 L)
Sodium, 1 cup (250 mL): 22 mgs
Calories: 151

Senate Bean Soup

As this recipe calls for mashed potatoes, it's convenient to think of making it when you are having mashed potatoes for dinner.

1 lb.	dry beans, such as great northern, pea, or marrow beans	450 g
4.5 qt.	water	4.5 L
2 t.	liquid hickory smoke	10 mL
2	bay leaves	2
¼ t.	white pepper	1 mL
2	medium onions, finely chopped	2
2	carrots, finely chopped	2
2	stalks celery, finely chopped	2
2	cloves garlic, minced	2
1 c.	mashed potatoes	250 mL

Cover beans with cold water and soak overnight. The next day, drain off the soaking water. In a soup pot, combine the soaked beans, water, liquid smoke, bay leaves and white pepper. Bring to a boil, turn down heat and simmer until beans are tender, about 2 to 2½ hours. Stir in the chopped vegetables and mashed potatoes. Cook for an additional 30 minutes. Remove the bay leaf. The soup can be served as is, or pureed in a food mill, blender or food processor.

Makes 12 cups (3 L)
Sodium, 1 cup (250 mL): 20 mgs
Calories: 110

Corn Chowder

It's the long cooking and browning of the onion that adds the flavor. Double the recipe if you want more than three servings. A great recipe to serve people who don't drink milk and need calcium!

2 T.	unsalted margarine	30 mL
1	medium onion, finely chopped	1
2	medium potatoes, peeled and cut into cubes	2
2 c.	skim milk	500 mL
10 oz.	frozen corn*	300 g
⅛ t.	fresh pepper	1 mL

In a skillet melt the margarine over medium heat. Cook the onion until the pieces are *browned*. Mix onions, potato cubes, and milk in a saucepan. Simmer over medium low heat for 20 minutes, but do not let it boil. Add the corn and pepper. Simmer for another 5 minutes.

* If you like thicker corn chowder, subtitute a can of no-salt-added cream-style corn.

Makes 2¾ cups (690 mL)
Sodium, 1 cup (250 mL): 101 mgs
Calories: 297

Potato Leek Soup

Make this delicious soup whenever your supermarket has leeks.

2 T.	unsalted margarine	30 mL
4	medium leeks	4
2 lb.	potatoes (about 6 medium)	900 g
2 c.	water	500 mL
¾ c.	skim milk	190 mL

Melt the margarine in a soup pot. Thinly slice the white part of the leeks. Cook leeks gently in the melted margarine for 10 minutes or so until they are soft. Meanwhile, peel and dice the potatoes and add to the soup pot with the leeks. Add the water, cover the pot, and simmer until the potatoes are tender, about 30 minutes. Remove some of the potato pieces to a bowl, depending on how "chunky" you like your soup. Put the remainder of the soup through a sieve or mash it with a potato masher. Add the milk and reserved potatoes. Heat over low heat, but be careful not to let it boil.

Makes 5 cups (1.3 L)
Sodium, 1 cup (250 mL): 29 mgs
Calories: 203

Cream of Broccoli Soup

10 oz.	*frozen chopped broccoli**	*300 g*
¾ c.	*water*	*190 mL*
2 T.	*unsalted margarine*	*30 mL*
1	*small onion, diced*	*1*
5 T.	*flour*	*75 mL*
2 c.	*skim milk*	*500 mL*
⅛ t.	*white pepper*	*1 mL*
dash	*allspice* or	*dash*
2 T.	*sherry (not cooking sherry)*	*30 mL*

Cook the broccoli in the water, covered, for 4 or 5 minutes. Meanwhile, melt the margarine in a soup pot, add the onion and sauté for 5 minutes. Sprinkle flour over the onions, stir and cook over low heat for a minute or so. Add the broccoli *and* its cooking water; stir. Add the milk and white pepper. Simmer but **do not boil.** Stir in the sherry or allspice. Cook gently a few minutes more. Serve warm or cold.

* You can substitute 2 cups of fresh broccoli. We have also used a package of frozen broccoli and cauliflower with red peppers—a colorful variation.

Makes about 4 cups (1 L)
Sodium, 1 cup (250 mL) with allspice (not sherry): 73 mgs
Calories: 156

Gazpacho

This cold vegetable soup is luscious when tomatoes are in season—juicy and low in cost.

Gazpacho is usually served with side dishes of chopped onion, tomato, green pepper and cucumber for guests to sprinkle the toppings they like best.

1	medium cucumber, peeled and coarsely chopped	1
2	large fresh tomatoes, chopped	2
1	medium onion, chopped	1
½	green pepper, seeded and chopped	½
1	clove garlic, chopped	1
4 slices	low-sodium bread, trimmed of crusts and crumbled (if you want a thick gazpacho)	4
1 c.	water	250 mL
2 T.	red wine vinegar	30 mL
1 T.	olive oil	15 mL
¼ c.	no-salt-added tomato paste	60 mL

Mix all the ingredients in a large bowl. Blend small amounts at a time in a blender until you have a smooth puree. Chill several hours before serving.

Makes 4 cups (1 L)
Sodium, 1 cup (250 mL): 23 mgs
Calories: 160

Cold Cantaloupe Soup

An elegant first course and less work than fresh fruit cocktail.

1	ripe cantaloupe, seeded	1
½ t.	cinnamon	2 mL
1 T.	lemon juice	15 mL
2 c.	orange juice	500 mL

Scoop out the cantaloupe and beat in a blender or food processor. Add the cinnamon and lemon juice. Blend until the mixture is smooth. In a serving bowl, stir the cantaloupe and orange juice. Chill at least 2 hours before serving.

Makes 6 cups (1.5 L)
Sodium, 1 cup (250 mL): 12 mgs
Calories: 50

SALADS

ALL YOUR LIFE you've probably heard that raw fruits and vegetables are good for you. They are! But surveys at popular salad bars have an interesting twist. People interviewed were asked why they choose the salad bar over other foods. Most replied that they were trying to lose weight. With generous salads smothered in salad dressing, these "low-calorie" lunches averaged 1,000 calories! Many salad dressings pack 100 calories per level tablespoon (15 mL). A person who spoons or pours on a generous layer of salad dressing may be inadvertently adding one to two thousand calories.

Whether you're making a salad at home or choosing items from a restaurant salad bar, you need to avoid the items that are high in sodium. **Avoid** these: canned chickpeas (garbanzo beans), croutons, olives, three bean salad, cottage cheese, cheese, pickled beets, pickles, bacon-flavored bits, canned items such as onion rings, bottled or dry prepared salad dressings.

Moderately high in sodium, these vegetables should only be eaten in moderate amounts: spinach, celery, carrots.

There are many low-sodium salad ingredients. **Eat all you like of these:** lettuce, tomatoes, green pepper slices, cucumber slices, onion slices, radishes, mushroom slices, canned or fresh fruit, oil, vinegar, lemon juice, salad dressings from this book (pages 65 to 69).

Tomato and Cucumber Salad

2	*medium garden-ripe tomatoes*	2
1	*medium cucumber*	1
1 c.	*Good and Good for You Dressing*	250 mL
	(page 65)	

Cut out the stem ends of the tomatoes and slice into chunks. Peel the cucumber and cut into chunks; mix the vegetables in a bowl, preferably glass. Pour the salad dressing over the vegetables. Cover and refrigerate an hour or two. Serve chilled.

Serves 4
Sodium per serving: 15 mgs
Calories: 74

Macaroni Salad

Best made well in advance.

4 oz.	*dry macaroni*	120 g
2 T.	*water*	30 mL
⅓ c.	*Mayonnaise (page 56)*	90 mL
1	*small onion or scallion (optional)*	1
3 T.	*cider vinegar*	45 mL
2 t.	*celery seed*	10 mL
2 t.	*dry mustard (less for milder flavor)*	10 mL
1 T.	*sugar*	15 mL
6 T.	*green or red pepper, finely diced*	90 mL
dash	*white pepper*	dash
¼ t.	*onion powder*	1 mL

Cook macaroni as directed on the box without the salt; drain, rinse with water and drain again. Mix macaroni in a bowl with all remaining ingredients. Chill. Serve on lettuce leaves, if desired.

Serves 4 (side dish or 2 medium-size servings)
Sodium per serving: 11 mgs
Calories: 245

Classic Cucumbers in Vinegar

A traditional summertime favorite. Good at a cookout. Make it ahead to blend the flavors.

1	*medium cucumber, peeled and sliced thin*	1
1 c.	*vinegar*	250 mL
1½ T.	*sugar*	22 mL

Combine the ingredients in a nonmetal bowl; cover and refrigerate. The vinegar mixture may be reused several times.

Serves 4
Sodium per serving: 3 mgs
Calories: 25

Macaroni Salad, Italian style

A curly macaroni such as *rotelle* or *fusilli* makes an attractive salad.

½ lb.	*macaroni*	240 g
3 T.	*olive oil*	45 mL
½	*green pepper, diced*	½
½	*medium onion, diced*	½
2 T.	*vinegar*	30 mL
3 T.	*pimientos, chopped*	45 mL
½ t.	*garlic powder*	2 mL
1 t.	*onion powder*	5 mL
¼ t.	*white pepper*	1 mL

Cook macaroni in boiling water according to package directions *except* leave out the salt; drain. Heat the olive oil in a frying pan and sauté the green pepper and onion until soft. Toss the macaroni with the green pepper and onion. Add the seasonings and toss again. Cover and refrigerate. Let sit at least an hour to blend the flavors.

Serves 4 or 8
Sodium per serving (one-eighth of the salad): 7 mgs
Calories: 310

Quick Potato Salad

If this unsalted version seems a little bland to you, sprinkle on a season-ing your family likes, such as garlic powder or dill, or use the Unsalt Shaker. Nice served on lettuce leaves.*

4	medium potatoes, peeled and quar-tered	4
1	bay leaf	1
½ t.	onion powder	2 mL
2 T.	vinegar	30 mL
¼ c.	boiling water	60 mL
1 T.	safflower oil	15 mL
¼ c.	Mayonnaise (page 56)	60 mL
¾ t.	dry mustard	3 mL
	chopped parsley, chopped onion, celery seed (optional)	
	paprika (optional)	

Pour enough water to cover potatoes in a large pan; add bay leaf and onion powder. Cook until potatoes are tender, about 20 minutes or longer; drain. When cool enough to handle, peel and dice or slice into a bowl. Combine the vinegar, the boiling water and oil. Pour over potatoes and toss well. (Potatoes that are coated in this way will be moist without too much mayonnaise.) Cool. Combine mayonnaise and desired seasonings and add to potatoes. Sprinkle top with paprika, if desired.

* You can also add strips of cold leftover meat or drained low-sodium tuna for a main course salad. Also, you can cook potatoes in their jackets a day in advance; peel when ready to make the salad.

Serves 4
Sodium per serving: 13 mgs
Calories: 276

Marinated Bean Salad

Make this salad year round.* Canned unsalted vegetables would work well here. If these are not available, you can use frozen green beans. If you're not familiar with cooking dry beans, see Beans (page 203).

2 c.	*fresh, frozen or canned unsalted green beans or part green and part wax beans*	500 mL
1 c.	*dry kidney beans, cooked without salt*	250 mL
1	*small onion, chopped*	1
½ c.	*cider vinegar*	125 mL
¼ c.	*safflower oil*	60 mL
¼ c.	*sugar*	60 mL

Mix all ingredients; refrigerate several hours or overnight to blend the flavors.

* Or try with only kidney beans and some diced celery and green pepper. Sodium and calorie contents will be slightly higher, however.

Makes 6 half-cup (125-mL) servings
Sodium per serving: 4 mgs
Calories: 129

Coleslaw

This coleslaw is good as a side dish or as a sandwich ingredient. You can double the recipe and use an average-size cabbage.

1 lb.	*small head cabbage, shredded,*	*450 g*
	about 3½ c. (875 mL)	
1	*carrot*	*1*
1	*small onion*	*1*
½ c.	*Mayonnaise (page 56)*	*125 mL*
1 T.	*sugar*	*15 mL*
1 T.	*cider vinegar*	*15 mL*
good grind	*pepper*	*good grind*
¼–½ t.	*celery seed (optional)*	*1–2 mL*

Shred the cabbage and carrot using a food processor, a blender or a hand grater. Dice the onion. Mix the cabbage, carrot and onion in a large bowl. In a small bowl combine the mayonnaise, sugar, vinegar and pepper. Toss with shredded vegetables. Refrigerate until you are ready to serve. It tastes better if you make it a few hours before serving.

Makes 7 half-cup (125-mL) servings
Sodium per serving: 16 mgs
Calories: 128

Pineapple Coleslaw

You can make this ahead and allow the flavors to blend for a delicious variation. Omit the carrot, onion and sugar in coleslaw (above). Add 8 oz. (225g) crushed pineapple.

Makes 8 half-cup (125-mL) servings
Sodium per serving: 14 mgs
Calories: 68

Fruit Salads

You really don't need formal recipes for making fruit salads—just combine fresh available fruits with different colors and textures. Frozen or canned fruits, all naturally low in sodium, can also be used. A fruit salad looks special when served on a few leaves of lettuce or other green. Chopped walnuts on top are also nice.

Try these salad ideas: banana slices, orange sections, seedless green grapes, unsalted nuts; orange slices, pineapple chunks; pear or peach slices sprinkled with lightly toasted unsalted almond slivers; sweet grapes and pear slices; pineapple chunks with fresh berries (blueberries, raspberries, strawberries); apples and grapes with melon balls; melon balls with cherries and grapes.

Slice apples, pears and peaches with a stainless steel knife to keep them from turning brown. Also, toss the fruit with a sprinkling of lemon, grapefruit or pineapple juice to prevent browning on the cut surfaces.

Waldorf Salad

This pretty salad can be served on lettuce leaves.

2	large firm ripe apples	2
2 t.	lemon juice	10 mL
2 T.	Mayonnaise (page 56)	30 mL
2 T.	walnuts, coarsely chopped	30 mL

Wash, quarter and core the apples. Dice with peel *on*. Toss in bowl with lemon juice. Add mayonnaise, toss to coat the apples; mix in the walnuts. Store in covered container in refrigerator until serving time.

Serves 4
Sodium per serving: 3 mgs
Calories: 115

Gelatin Salads

If your family likes gelatin salads, you can either use plain unflavored gelatin (such as Knox, which has only a trace of sodium) or flavored gelatin (such as Jell-O, which has about 270 mgs of sodium in a 3-ounce (90-g) package). If you use flavored gelatin, you must count the milligrams of sodium in the person's daily total. You can figure about 55 mgs in each ½ cup (125 mL). Dietetic gelatin (D-Zerta brand) has only 6 mgs in a small serving. This does have the brightly colored dye already in it—good if your family expects gelatins to be bright-colored. But D-Zerta contains saccharin, a disadvantage for people who do not want to ingest artificial dyes or saccharin.

Or make gelatins from scratch, just as easy as using a mix. Of course there are more ingredients to get together, but the steps are just about the same—hot water, cold water and so on. The moulded gelatin salads that follow include vegetable and fruit versions to start you off. When you begin to use unflavored gelatin you will certainly create your own combinations. All fresh, frozen or canned fruits work well *except* fresh pineapple.

Seasonal Fruit Gelatin Salad

2 env.	unflavored gelatin	2 env.
¼ c.	cold water	60 mL
½ c.	boiling water	125 mL
⅓ c.	sugar	90 mL
1 c.	apple, orange or cranberry juice	250 mL
2 drops	food coloring if desired (optional)	2 drops
2 T.	lemon juice	30 mL
2 c.	small pieces of fruit such as fresh or frozen cantaloupe balls, seedless grapes, apple, canned pineapple chunks	500 mL

Stir the gelatin into cold water to soften. Add the boiling water and stir until the gelatin dissolves. Add the sugar, juice and food coloring, if desired; stir. To be sure that the pieces of fruit will be evenly distributed, chill the mixture until it is as thick as unbeaten egg white, about 30 to 45 minutes. Fold in the fruit and put into a lightly oiled or sprayed mould. To unmould, see Vegetable-Pineapple Gelatin Salad (page 125).

Serves 4
Sodium per serving: 13 mgs
Calories: 131

Vegetable-Pineapple Gelatin Salad

2	carrots, grated	2
1 c.	cabbage, grated	250 mL
20 oz.	crushed pineapple and juice from can	600 g
small amount	water	small amount
2 env.	unflavored gelatin	2 env.
¼ c.	sugar	60 mL
1 c.	ice water	250 mL
2 T.	lemon juice	30 mL
2 drops	yellow food coloring (optional)	2 drops

Combine the grated carrots and cabbage in a bowl. Drain and reserve the juice from can of pineapple and add the drained pineapple to the carrots and cabbage. Combine the reserved pineapple juice with enough water to make 2 cups (500 mL). Pour this liquid into a saucepan; bring to a boil. Add the gelatin and sugar and stir until dissolved. Stir in 1 cup of ice water, the lemon juice and optional food coloring. To be sure the pieces do not sink to the bottom, chill this mixture until it is slightly thicker than an unbeaten egg white, about 45 minutes. Fold in the pineapple and grated vegetables and pour into a prepared mould. (To be sure gelatin will un-mould without sticking, you can spray the mould with a vegetable coating spray such as Pam.)

To unmould a gelatin salad, fill a large bowl with hot water. Hold the mould in the water for about 20 seconds so that it is immersed to the rim. Remove the mould from the water and hold the serving plate upside down over the mould. With the mould and plate held firmly together, flip the whole thing over so that the serving plate is on the bottom. Still holding the mould and the plate together, give the mould a little shake. When you feel the gelatin dropping onto the plate, lift off the mould.

Serves 4
Sodium per serving: 27 mgs
Calories: 141

VEGETABLES

LOW-SODIUM DIETERS who have been advised to limit their meat portions to 3 ounces (90 g) of cooked meat begin to enjoy and appreciate the vegetables that fill their dinner plates. Leafy vegetables, potatoes and squashes can round out a meal and prevent the low-sodium dieter from feeling deprived. Fortunately, these foods are all naturally low in sodium.

Another reason to eat more vegetables in addition to filling up the dinner plate? Vegetables (and fruits, too) are good sources of vitamins and potassium. Some doctors and researchers have pointed out that a high potassium intake, like a low sodium intake, is salutary.

This chapter offers you low-sodium recipes for old favorites as well as some new ideas—all using fresh vegetables. When substituting frozen vegetables, *never* add salt to cooking water.

Choosing Vegetables

All regular canned vegetables are very high in sodium. Repeated rinsings in fresh water can remove quite a lot of the salt that was added in the canning process. But after all the effort in rinsing them, you won't end up with a very tasty food.

Canned unsalted vegetables, increasingly made by the large food companies, are just as convenient as the regular ones, but unfortunately are also rather tasteless. The special dietetic low-sodium canned vegetables are available but quite expensive. Some brands have added potassium chloride (which leaves an unpleasant aftertaste) while others do not; the label will advise you. Try just one can to see if you like the taste.

The good news is that fresh and frozen vegetables retain vegetables' natural taste and most are unsalted. Frozen vegetables retain more freshness, flavor and nutrients than canned ones. Frozen peas and lima beans are higher in sodium than fresh ones since they are soaked in a salty solution before freezing to keep them plump. Vegetables frozen with added salt, butter or fancy sauces are also high in sodium, *too high* for anyone on a restricted diet. Be sure the read the labels before you buy.

Reading Sodium Numbers
on Convenience Foods

When you are trying to decide which foods are low enough in sodium to buy, be very careful. Manufacturers' nutrition information is often figured on the basis of very *small* servings. For example, a 3-ounce (90-g) serving of a vegetable, such as peas or green beans, is only 6 T. (90 mL)—slightly more than half of the smallest jar of baby food peas. An average serving for an adult is closer to 1 cup (250 mL). A 1-cup (250-mL) serving of Green Giant small onions in a creamy cheese-flavored sauce has 725 mgs of sodium.

So if you read on a package of Birds Eye small onions with cream sauce that a 3-ounce (90-g) serving has only 355 mgs, do not be falsely reassured that the product is moderately low in sodium. The entire package contains 1,065 mgs of sodium.

Vegetables That Are Good Sources of Calcium

If you need to keep your sodium intake low, you may not be eating large amounts of dairy products with necessary calcium. One logical solution is to eat more of the vegetables that are good sources of calcium; these include: broccoli, spinach, kale, turnip greens, beet greens, collards.

Choose Wisely: Fresh Vegetables
Are Worth the Effort

To help you choose vegetables wisely to cut down on sodium, we gave you the sodium content of common vegetables for 1 cup (250 mL) of each. We arranged vegetables in alphabetical order, rather than an arrangement based on the sodium content, because it will be much easier for the cook to find the desired vegetable.

If the cook wants to cook turnips, for example, she or he can find it quickly in an alphabetical list. But in a list by sodium content, she or he would have to look at white turnip in the high group and yellow turnip in the low group.

Also, the differences in sodium are **minor** when vegetables are put in perspective with all foods. Certainly carrots and celery are higher in sodium, but this does **not** mean that people ought to give them up and miss out on the fibre and vitamins. When vegetables are considered in perspective with foods in general, we find that there really is no such thing as a fresh vegetable that is high in sodium.

Asparagus

Wash the asparagus and cut or snap off the pale part of the bottom. Cut the stalks in small pieces (2" or 5 cm) and cook in a vegetable steamer or a saucepan until tender, about 10 minutes. Or bunch the whole stalks and bind them together using a wide rubber band. Set the asparagus in a tall pot with the cut ends down. Add water to level of 3 inches (8 cm), cover and cook until the asparagus is tender, about 15 minutes. (This is a good method because the tender top end of the stalk is cooked less than the tough woody end.) Serve asparagus with lemon wedges to add a refreshing flavor.

Sodium, 1 cup (250 mL):
Fresh, 3 mgs
Frozen, 2 mgs
Canned, 740 mgs

Green and Wax Beans

Cook plain frozen green or wax beans according to the directions on the package, except leave out the salt in the cooking water.

To cook fresh green beans, wash beans and cut or snap off the ends; cut lengthwise into strips, or snap them into pieces or on the diagonal for a fancy look; or leave the beans whole. Steam beans or cook them in a small amount of boiling water for 15 to 20 minutes. Never add baking soda to the water since baking soda is very high in sodium.

Sodium, 1 cup (250 mL):
Fresh, 8 mgs
Canned wax beans, 690 mgs
Canned green beans, 710 mgs
Frozen cut green beans, 6 mgs
Frozen French green beans with toasted almonds, 670 mgs

Green Beans with Mushrooms and Almonds

More like the fancy frozen green beans.

1 lb.	fresh green beans or frozen green beans	450 g
2 T.	unsalted margarine	30 mL
1	small onion, diced	1

10	small mushrooms, sliced	10
dash	white pepper	dash
3 T.	sliced almonds	45 mL

In a saucepan with a small amount of water, put the fresh or frozen green beans; cook until tender; drain. Meanwhile, melt the margarine and add the onion, mushroom and white pepper. Cook gently 5 minutes or so. Add the almonds and cook for another 2 or 3 minutes. Toss with the hot cooked beans just before serving.

Serves 4
Sodium per serving: 12 mgs
Calories: 148

Lima Beans

Fresh limas are low in sodium. To cook fresh limas, just remove them from their pods and then cook in a small amount of unsalted water for a half hour or so.

Beets

Fresh beets are higher in sodium than most vegetables, with 22 mgs in a medium-size beet. Canned beets are even higher with 545 mgs in a 1-cup (250-mL) serving.

Broccoli

To cook frozen broccoli just follow the package directions, except leave out the salt.

To prepare fresh broccoli, cut a slice off the bottom of each stem. Leave the broccoli whole or slice the stalk into "coins" and divide the top into florets. Steam broccoli or cook it in a small amount of unsalted water for 15 minutes or so.

Sodium, 1 cup (250 mL):
Fresh, 16 mgs
Frozen deluxe florets, 30 mgs
Frozen broccoli spears in butter sauce, 875 mgs

Lemon and "Butter" Sauce for Broccoli

Make your broccoli more like the packaged kind with butter sauce by using the following recipe.

2 T.	unsalted margarine	30 mL
1 T.	lemon juice	15 mL
dash	pepper	dash

Melt the margarine. Stir in the lemon juice and pepper. Toss over cooked, drained broccoli.

Serves 4
Sodium per serving: trace
Calories: 52

Brussels Sprouts

Cook plain frozen brussels sprouts according to package directions but leave out the salt in the water.

To prepare fresh brussels sprouts, trim the bottom, discard any discolored leaves; with a sharp knife score an "X" on the flat bottom. Steam brussels sprouts or cook them in a small amount of unsalted water for about 15 or 20 minutes until tender.

Brussels sprouts are traditionally served with brown butter. The following recipe can be made for fresh or frozen brussels sprouts.

Sodium, 1 cup (250 mL):
Fresh, 16 mgs
Frozen, 15 mgs
Frozen baby brussels sprouts in butter sauce, 865 mgs

Brown "Butter" for Brussels Sprouts

2 T.	unsalted margarine	30 mL
1 T.	lemon juice	15 mL
grind	black pepper	grind

Melt the margarine and cook over low heat until brown. Stir in the lemon juice and pepper. Toss with cooked brussels sprouts.

Serves 4
Sodium per serving: trace
Calories: 52

Cabbage

A medium-sized cabbage has 218 mgs of sodium, but when cabbage is bought as coleslaw or sauerkraut, both versions are *high* in sodium. For example, canned sauerkraut (shredded cabbage in brine) has 1,554 mgs in 1 cup (250 mL). Prepared "deli" coleslaw varies but may have as much as 322 mgs in 1 cup (250 mL). There are two delicious low-sodium coleslaw recipes in the salad chapter (page 122). Unfortunately, there is no way to make sauerkraut without salt since it's essential to the process.

Cabbage with Apples

1	*medium head of red or white cabbage*	1
2	*medium apples, peeled and sliced*	2
1	*medium onion, chopped*	1
2 T.	*unsalted margarine*	30 mL
¼ c.	*vinegar*	60 mL
2 T.	*sugar*	30 mL
1 t.	*crushed caraway seeds*	5 mL
2 T.	*water*	30 mL

Shred the cabbage using a food processor, hand grater or a knife. Mix the apples and onion with the cabbage. Melt the margarine in a large saucepan. Add the vegetables and cook and stir for about 5 minutes. Add the remaining ingredients; cover the pot and cook gently for 35 minutes; add more water, if needed. Remove the cover and cook for 10 minutes more to boil down any excess liquid.

Serves 8
Sodium per serving: 29 mgs
Calories: 91

Carrots

If you are on a sodium-restricted diet, you may be advised to eat fresh carrots in measured amounts. This may seem strange at first, since most of us think of carrots as a food to munch freely when trying to lose weight.

Peel or just scrub carrots before cooking; slice into rings or into sticks. Then steam or cook in a small amount of water until crisp, about 6 minutes, longer if you like them tender.

Sodium, 1 cup (250 mL):
Fresh, grated, 52 mgs
Canned, 510 mgs
Frozen carrots with brown sugar glaze, 1,000 mgs

Queen Cauliflower

If you want to "dress up" plain caulifower, try this recipe.

1	cauliflower	1
1 T.	unsalted margarine	15 mL
1 T.	oil	15 mL
1 T.	wheat germ	15 mL
1 T.	unsalted bread crumbs or crushed low-sodium cornflakes	15 mL

Trim leaves and stem of the cauliflower but leave it whole and put into a cooking pot with a tight-fitting lid. Add 2 cups (500 mL) water and cover tightly. Cook over high heat until the water begins to boil; turn down the heat and allow cauliflower to cook in the steam until fork tender, about 15 to 20 minutes, depending on the size of the cauliflower. In a saucepan melt the margarine. Stir in the oil, wheat germ and bread crumbs. Press the mixture onto the top of the cauliflower, like a crown. (This can be done ahead of time.) Just before serving, set the cauliflower in a pie plate and bake in a 350° F (175° C) oven 5 to 10 minutes until warm.

Serves 8
Sodium per serving: 6 mgs
Calories: 77

Celery

Celery is higher in sodium than most vegetables—25 mgs in a single stalk. For that reason, celery is usually used only in small amounts to flavor a sodium-restricted diet.

Corn

Fresh or frozen ears of corn can be served plain or with unsalted margarine. Add onion or garlic powder (or both) to melted margarine or keep the Unsalt Shaker (page 52) on the table.

You can use fresh or frozen cut corn to make the delicious Corn Relish (page 63).

Sodium, 1 cup (250 mL) except where noted:
Fresh, 1 ear, 1 mg
Frozen, 1 small ear, 4 mgs
Frozen kernels, 2 mgs
Frozen cream-style corn, 480 mgs
Frozen corn in butter sauce, 765 mgs
Canned whole kernel corn, 420 mgs
Canned cream-style corn, 530 mgs

Barbecued Corn on the Cob

This is the oven method. Or cook outdoors on a grill. Follow the same instructions except roast corn over glowing coals, turning occasionally.

2 T.	unsalted margarine	30 mL
1 c.	low-sodium ketchup	250 mL
2 T.	vinegar	30 mL
2 t.	dry mustard	10 mL
¼ t.	ginger	1 mL
¼ t.	onion powder	1 mL
¼ t.	liquid hickory smoke (optional)	1 mL
4	ears of corn, fresh or frozen	4

To make the barbecue sauce, combine all of the ingredients except the corn in a small saucepan; heat gently and stir until the margarine melts. Cut 4 pieces of aluminum foil into approximately 12-inch (30-cm) squares. Lay an ear of corn on each square. Brush the sauce on each ear, spreading the sauce over the surface of the corn. Seal the foil but don't wrap it tightly around the corn, allowing room for steam. Arrange the ears on a cookie sheet, seam side up. Roast in 400° F (205° C) oven for 45 minutes.

Serves 4
Sodium per serving: 14 mgs
Calories: 123

Corn and Zucchini Casserole

Cut corn is a good addition to vegetable casseroles. The following recipe is a hearty autumn favorite.

4	*medium zucchini, about 1 lb. (450 g)*	4
2 t.	*unsalted margarine*	10 mL
1	*medium onion, diced*	1
10 oz.	*frozen corn*	300 g
4 oz.	*no-salt Swiss cheese, grated*	120 g
2	*eggs or equivalent egg substitute*	2

Wash zucchini, slice into pieces, and put in a saucepan with enough water to cover the zucchini. Cover the pan. Bring to a boil and cook for about 15 minutes. While the zucchini cooks, melt the margarine in a saucepan; add the onion and cook gently until tender. In another saucepan, bring ½ cup (125 mL) water to a boil. Add the corn, cover, and boil 2 to 3 minutes. Drain and set aside. Mash the cooked zucchini with a fork, combine with all of the ingredients in a casserole. Bake in 350° F (175° C) oven for 35 to 40 minutes, until top is golden brown.

Serves 6
Sodium per serving: 28 mgs
Calories: 119

Cucumbers

Cucumbers are very low in sodium, only 10 mgs in a medium-sized one; they are also low in calories with 25 calories in a medium cucumber. There is a recipe for Classic Cucumbers in Vinegar (page 119). You can use cucumbers in salads, with tomatoes (page 118), and in sandwiches for a crunchy addition. Cucumbers are crisper when chilled.

Eggplant

Eggplant is low in sodium with only 5 mgs in a whole medium eggplant. Don't use the traditional eggplant procedure of salting eggplant to draw the bitterness out. And avoid Parmesan cheese which also increases the sodium content.

Eggplant can be delicious if you try the recipe for Moussaka (page 200).

Mushrooms

Fresh mushrooms are low in sodium (17 mgs) and calories (32 calories) per ¼ lb. (120 g). Mushrooms can be a flavorful addition to hot and cold dishes.

But canned mushrooms are very high in sodium with 242 mgs in 2 ounces (60 g). Canned with buttery flavoring, mushrooms are even higher and *cannot* be part of a low-sodium diet.

To prepare fresh mushrooms, wash them carefully but don't use too much water or soak them because they will get spongy; just wipe them off gently with a damp paper towel. If the mushrooms are large, cut the stem into "coins" before cutting the crown. If the mushrooms are small or medium, cut the whole mushroom lengthwise through the stem.

Try the Marinated Mushrooms (page 90) and the Mushroom-Barley Soup (page 108).

Okra

Okra, a flavorful vegetable, is low in sodium and adds body to the liquid in which it's cooked. To cook fresh okra, cut off the stems and tips and steam or cover with water and cook gently for 10 minutes or so.

Sodium, 1 cup (250 mL):
Fresh, 3 mgs
Frozen, 4 mgs
Frozen southern okra gumbo, 210 mgs

Okra and Tomatoes

1 T.	*unsalted margarine*	15 mL
1	*medium onion, diced*	1
½ lb.	*fresh or frozen (defrosted)*	225 g
	okra, sliced	
3	*medium tomatoes, cut into chunks*	3
pinch	*sugar*	pinch
grind	*black pepper*	grind

Melt the margarine in a large skillet. Sauté the onion; slice the okra and add. Fry gently for 5 minutes or so. Add the remaining ingredients. Cook gently, partially covered, for 15 to 20 minutes. Serve in small bowls.

Serves 4
Sodium per serving: 15 mgs
Calories: 84

Onions

Onions add flavor to many hot and cold dishes. Don't miss the recipe for delicious French Onion Soup (page 109) and Vegetable Tempura or Onion Rings (page 93).

Boiled Onions

Serve onions boiled the traditional way. Choose the tiny pearl onions or small white onions; remove the skins and root ends but leave the onions whole. Cover with water and boil until the onions are fork tender; drain. Serve boiled onions with a little unsalted margarine and black pepper.

Sodium, 1 cup (250 mL) except where noted:
1 medium fresh onion, 10 mgs
Fresh diced onion, 17 mgs
6 fresh green onions or scallions, 6 mgs
Small onions in a creamy cheese-flavored sauce, 1 cup, 725 mgs

Parsnips

Parsnips look like pale carrots. A medium parsnip has 19 mgs of sodium. Many soup recipes in this book call for "soup greens." These packages (from your market) contain one or two parsnips and for good reason—they add a lot of flavor.

Baked Pears

A delightful garnish on your dinner plate. Bake pears when you have the oven baking a meat loaf or casserole.

4	firm ripe medium pears	4
¼ c.	apple, orange or lemon juice	60 mL

Wash the pears and slice off the tip of the stem end; core the pear. You may like to cut decorative "V"-shaped wedges or scallops around the edges of the pears. Baste the pears with the juice. Place them cut side up in a pie pan lined with foil for an easy cleanup. Bake in 350° F (175° C) oven for about 30 minutes.

Serves 4
Sodium per serving: 3 mgs
Calories: 88

Peas

Fresh peas can be removed from their pod just before cooking. Steam or cook peas in a small amount of unsalted water, from 10 to 20 minutes to until tender.

Frozen peas, like lima beans, are soaked in brine before freezing to keep them plump, making them fairly high in sodium. A person on a strict low-sodium diet is best advised to *avoid* frozen peas, except in measured amounts.

Sodium, 1 cup (250 mL):
Fresh, 3 mgs
Frozen, 187 mgs
Frozen peas and onions, 612 mgs
Canned early peas, 700 mgs

Potatoes

For those who believe a meal is not a meal unless there are potatoes, here are 8 recipes! Potatoes are readily available, easy to prepare and low in sodium.

Sodium, 1 cup (250 mL) except where noted:
1 medium fresh potato, 5 mgs
Frozen french fries (unsalted), 6 mgs
Frozen hashed brown potatoes, 460 mgs
Packaged au gratin potatoes, 710 mgs
Packaged potato pancakes, per 3 pancakes, 490 mgs
Packaged mashed potatoes, 660 mgs

Baked Potatoes

Just put scrubbed potatoes in the oven and bake them at a temperature between 350°F (175°C to 205°C). You can tell when potatoes are done because they will be tender when pricked with a fork.

For topping your potato, use unsalted margarine. If you are watching your calorie intake and also limiting cholesterol, sour cream and other combinations made from cream are taboo. Chopped chives or diced parsley are great on any kind of potato dish.

Baked New Potatoes

12	*small new potatoes*	12
1½ T.	*safflower oil*	22 mL
dash	*paprika*	dash

Wash, peel and pat dry the potatoes. Line a baking dish with aluminum foil to make cleanup easier. Brush the safflower oil on the baking dish. Add the potatoes and turn each one well to coat with oil. Sprinkle with paprika, turning the potatoes again. Bake in 400° F (205° C) oven for about 1 hour, or until the potatoes are brown and soft.

Serves 4
Sodium per serving: 3 mgs
Calories: 250

Boiled Potatoes

These boiled potatoes have seasonings added to the *cooking water* to increase the flavor. You can also add other seasonings that appeal to you—chopped chives, chopped parsley, a clove of garlic (remove before serving), a peeled onion, thyme, rosemary, curry, dry mustard, a dash from the Unsalt Shaker (page 52).

5	*medium potatoes*	5
1	*bay leaf*	1
¼ t.	*onion powder*	1 mL
dash	*white pepper*	dash

Wash and peel potatoes but leave whole, if small; quarter if large. Drop in saucepan, add cold water to cover, with a seasoning or two that appeal to you. Bring to a boil and boil gently for about 20 minutes or until tender to the touch of a fork. Drain and serve.

Serves 4
Sodium per serving: 5 mgs
Calories: 130

Mashed Potatoes

This trick—adding a bay leaf, onion powder and a hearty dash of white pepper—also helps to take away the bland taste from other cooked potato recipes.

5	*medium potatoes*	5
¼ t.	*onion powder*	1 mL

1	bay leaf	1
dash	white pepper	dash
⅓ c.	skim milk	90 mL
3 T.	unsalted margarine	45 mL

Wash, peel and quarter the potatoes; put potatoes in a saucepan with cold water to just cover. Add onion powder, bay leaf, and white pepper. Boil for about 20 minutes or until fork tender. Drain off the water by putting potatoes in colander (you can save the potato cooking water to add to homemade soups). Remove the bay leaf. While the potatoes are in the colander, combine milk and margarine in the saucepan; heat briefly. In a bowl, add the cooked potatoes. Mash with a potato masher or an electric mixer. Serve immediately or keep hot in a double boiler.

Serves 4
Sodium per serving: 16 mgs
Calories: 190

Scandinavian Mashed Potatoes

To add flavor to plain mashed potatoes, borrow a trick from Scandinavians and add a turnip to the potatoes. You can substitute a turnip for one potato and cook in the same pan. Since turnip is tougher than potato, dice the turnip into smaller pieces. Mash as for Mashed Potatoes (above).

Oven Fries

This is a tastier version of the fries you get in restaurants.

4	good quality baking potatoes	4
2 T.	safflower oil	30 mL
1 t.	paprika	5 mL
½ t.	onion powder	2 mL

Wash the potatoes and peel, if you like. Cut the potatoes lengthwise and then cut each half into 3 long strips. Place on foil-lined cookie sheet. Combine the oil, paprika, and onion powder in a small bowl. Brush on potato sticks (clean fingers are fine). Roast in oven 350° to 475° F (175° to 260° C) until fork tender, about 20 to 30 minutes.

Serves 4
Sodium per serving: 5 mgs
Calories: 269

Parsley Potatoes

A nice way to serve potatoes when you're serving meat without gravy or sauce. Small new potatoes, about 3 per person, are excellent choices.

4	medium potatoes	4
4 T.	unsalted margarine	60 mL
1	clove garlic, crushed	1
dash	dry mustard	dash
2 T.	chopped fresh parsley	30 mL
½ t.	lemon juice	2 mL
grind	fresh pepper	grind

Peel the potatoes or leave unpeeled, if you prefer; halve or quarter them. Place them in a saucepan with cold water to cover and cook over high heat until they start to boil. Lower heat and cook gently until fork tender, 15 to 20 minutes. Melt the margarine in a saucepan and remove from heat. Stir in the garlic, mustard, parsley, lemon juice and pepper. Let stand until potatoes are done (this will increase the flavor). Before serving, gently re-heat margarine mixture and pour over the potatoes; or you can strain by pouring through a sieve.

Serves 4
Sodium per serving: 7 mgs
Calories: 196

Potato Pancakes

A delicious addition to any meal, but especially good with plain meats such as pork chops. Applesauce is often served with potato pancakes. Make just before serving.

3	medium potatoes	3
1	small onion (optional)	1
1 T.	flour	15 mL
1	egg or equivalent egg substitute	1
2 T.	skim milk	30 mL
1 T.	unsalted margarine, melted	15 mL

Preheat a griddle or frying pan over medium heat. Peel the potatoes and onion, if using, and cut them into small pieces. Put them into a blender or food processor. Sprinkle with flour, add the egg and milk, and blend just enough to mix (if you blend too much you'll liquefy the potatoes). Add the margarine. Spoon the batter onto the hot frying pan, about ¼ cup (60 mL) for each pancake. When the pancakes are brown around the edges, turn them over and cook on the other side.

Serves 8
Sodium per pancake (with egg): 12 mgs
Calories: 66

Sweet Potatoes and Yams

Sweet potatoes and yams are flavorful, almost as versatile as white potatoes. A medium sweet potato has only 14 mgs of sodium. But canned sweet potatoes are high in sodium, 122 mgs in 1 cup (250 mL).

Don't overlook the easiest way to cook sweet potatoes—bake them as you would white potatoes. Depending on the oven temperature and the size of the potato, it will take 45 to 70 minutes to cook a sweet potato until it's fork tender.

Cook sweet potatoes or yams in their jackets in unsalted water; drain and peel.

Candied Sweet Potatoes

This is the way many people expect sweet potatoes on special occasions.

4	medium sweet potatoes	4
1 T.	unsalted margarine	15 mL
½ c.	brown sugar	125 mL
¼ c.	water	60 mL

In a large saucepan, cover potatoes with water and boil for 30 minutes or so until they are fork tender. Drain and cool slightly; remove their skins and cut them in half. Melt the margarine in a large frying pan. Mix in the brown sugar and water. Add the potatoes and cook very gently over low heat; turn the potatoes every now and then, and cook for about 15 minutes to "candy" the potatoes.

Serves 4
Sodium per serving: 23 mgs
Calories: 276

Spinach and Other Leafy Greens

Spinach is rather high in sodium—94 mgs in 1 cup (250 mL), cooked without salt. Plain frozen spinach is about the same as fresh. A strict low-sodium dieter is advised to eat fresh or frozen spinach in measured amounts. And canned spinach has more than 900 mgs in a cup (250 mL). Frozen spinach in cream or butter sauce is as high in sodium as canned spinach.

Kale, collards, beet greens, curly-leafed endive, escarole and turnip greens can be cooked the same as spinach. Pick over greens carefully, remove any tough or split stems and wash thoroughly. Cut the leaves before cooking, if you like, using sharp scissors. Steam the leaves or cook them in very little water until tender, not mushy, from 5 to 15 minutes.

Baked Acorn Squash

Acorn squash, the easiest of all squashes to prepare, is a good choice when your oven is on for other dishes.

2	*large acorn squashes (more if they're small)*	2
4 T.	*maple syrup*	60 mL
4 t.	*unsalted margarine*	20 mL

Cut the squash in half, remove the seeds and stringy part to make a "well" in the center; put the halves on a cookie sheet, cut side up. Add a fourth of the maple syrup and a fourth of the unsalted margarine in each "well." (Some cooks like to substitute another syrup or brown sugar.) Bake in 400° F (205° C) oven until soft when pierced with a fork.

Serves 4
Sodium per serving: 4 mgs
Calories: 168

Winter Squashes

All winter squashes or marrows are low in sodium—1 cup (250 mL) has only 2 mgs of sodium. Peel and cut up butternut and hubbard squash before cooking. Partially cover with water and boil until fork tender, a half hour or so. You may like to mash the squash before serving.

Frozen butternut and hubbard squash, easier to prepare, are also low in sodium.

Tomatoes

Enjoy the tomato sauce recipes (pages 73–74).

Sodium, 1 cup (250 mL) except where noted:
1 fresh tomato, 4 mgs
Canned whole peeled tomatoes, 1 cup, 440 mgs
Canned stewed tomatoes, 1 cup, 710 mgs
Canned Libby's stewed tomatoes, 1 cup, 585 mgs
Canned low-sodium tomatoes, 1 cup, 30 mgs

Fried Tomatoes

Have you ever fried fresh tomatoes? They are an old-fashioned favorite that can really round out a meal.

4	*medium tomatoes (ripe or green as you prefer or have available)*	4
¼ c.	*cornmeal*	60 mL
¼ t.	*pepper*	1 mL
½ t.	*sugar*	2 mL
1 t.	*paprika*	5 mL
1 T.	*safflower oil*	15 mL

Slice the tomatoes into ¼-inch (6-mm) slices. Combine cornmeal, pepper, sugar and paprika in a shallow bowl. Dip the tomato slices into the cornmeal mixture and turn to coat well on both sides. Heat the oil in a skillet over medium-high heat. Fry the tomato slices until brown on both sides, turning with a pancake turner; drain on paper towels and serve hot.

Serves 4
Sodium per serving: 14 mgs
Calories: 101

Turnips

Cooked white turnips have 78 mgs of sodium in a 1-cup (250-mL) serving; yellow turnips are not so high, with only 10 mgs in the same amount. Turnips are often tucked into "soup greens" because they contribute so much taste to the soup. Scandinavian Mashed Potatoes (page 139) are flavored with turnips.

To cook fresh turnips, wash, peel, dice and cook until tender in boiling, unsalted water. Drain and mash with a potato masher. Season with unsalted margarine, pepper or grated nutmeg.

Zucchini and Summer Squash

Fresh summer squash and zucchini cook in the same time and so easily. Scrub vegetables and cut large ones into slices or wedges and leave very small ones whole. Cook in a small amount of water about 10 to 15 minutes or until tender. You can also steam them; the exact time depends on the size of the slices. Serve hot or cold.

Sodium, 1 cup (250 mL):
Fresh, 2 mgs of sodium
Frozen baby zucchini, 4 mgs
Canned zucchini in tomato sauce, 832 mgs

Five-Minute Zucchini

Faster than a frozen vegetable and delicious, this recipe can be made just before serving. It also works with summer squash. Good with freshly ground pepper and a sprinkling of garlic powder.

2	*medium zucchini or summer squash*	2
1 T.	*unsalted margarine*	15 mL
1 T.	*olive oil*	15 mL

Wash the zucchini and shred using a food processor or hand grater. Heat the margarine and oil over medium heat. Add the shredded squash. Cook for a few minutes, stirring frequently. Serve warm.

Serves 4
Sodium per serving: 2 mgs
Calories: 62

PASTA
AND
PIZZA

Spaghetti and other shapes of pasta are logical parts of a low-sodium diet because they have only a very small amount of sodium, plus no fat or cholesterol!

Pasta has protein, but it's an incomplete protein. For this reason, it's traditionally served with a small amount of a complete protein food, such as cheese or meat. If you are able to find a supplier of low-sodium cheese that tastes good, you can grate a small amount to add to plain pasta. Otherwise, leave it out or measure the small amounts of regular salted cheese that you use *very carefully*.

A serving of pasta is supposed to be two ounces (60 g), which is a small serving.

The traditional ingredients in commercial spaghetti sauces are so high in sodium that they must be avoided: canned plum tomatoes, canned tomato sauce or puree and most prepared spaghetti sauces.

Fresh tomatoes would be a nutritious addition to a sauce when and if they are available where you live.

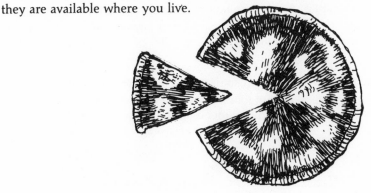

Spaghetti and White Clam Sauce

Canned clams and clam juice may be convenient, but they are outrageously high in sodium. If you and your family love clam sauce, wait to buy fresh clams. Hard-shelled clams (also called quahogs, cherry stones, little necks) are quite high in sodium—465 mgs in 1 cup (250 mL). Soft-shelled clams are much lower—82 mgs in 1 cup (250 mL)—but very perishable. If you live where soft-shelled clams are available, substitute them.

¼ c.	raw clams,* diced	60 mL
⅓ c.	olive oil	90 mL
3	cloves garlic, finely minced	3
2 T.	parsley, finely chopped (optional)	30 mL
2 t.	cornstarch	10 mL
½ c.	water	125 mL
½ c.	vermouth	125 mL
dash	white pepper	dash
½ t.	oregano (optional)	2 mL
	garlic powder (optional)	
8 oz.	linguini or spaghetti cooked without salt	225 g

Prepare the clams: use a knife or steam them open. To steam: Pour 1 cup (250 mL) water in a large saucepan; cover and bring to a boil. Scrub the outsides of the clams with a vegetable brush; add the clams to the boiling water. Cover and steam over high heat, approximately 5 minutes. Check after 2 minutes to see if the shells are open. When they are open, turn off the heat. Remove the clams from the shells and dice. Some cooks prefer to use only the parts with a firm texture and discard the soft "bellies."

To make the clam sauce: Heat the olive oil in a frying pan and sauté the garlic, parsley and clams over *low* heat for 3 to 5 minutes. While this is cooking, in a small bowl stir the cornstarch in the water and vermouth until smooth; add to the olive oil and clams. Sprinkle with pepper and oregano, if desired. Cook over low heat for a minute or so until sauce thickens slightly. Cook linguini according to package directions, except leave out the salt. Drain linguini and turn into a serving dish. Pour the sauce over the linguini and toss.

*Since clams are fairly high in sodium, the amount used must be small. To get the ¼ cup (60 mL) of diced clams, you can buy approximately 12 very small hard-shelled clams (2 inches or 5 cm across at the widest), or 5 medium-size clams (3 inches or 8 cm across at the widest), or 3 large clams.

Serves 4
Sodium per serving: 35 mgs
Calories: 318

Spaghetti with Tuna

Substitute one small can of low-sodium tuna for the clams in Spaghetti and White Clam Sauce (page 146).

Chicken Fajitas

Chicken and yummy vegetables are combined in tortillas to make Mexican-style pizza wrap-ups. In restaurants, the flour tortillas are kept warm in special little dishes. You can keep yours warm by covering the dish with a clean dish towel.

1¼ lb.	*boneless chicken breasts or cutlets*	600 g.
4 T.	*lime juice*	60 mL
2 T.	*olive oil*	30 mL
1 t.	*garlic powder*	5 mL
1 grind	*black pepper*	1 grind
½ t.	*Tabasco sauce (more if you like)*	2.5 mL
2	*large onions, sliced*	2
2	*large green or red peppers, sliced*	2
1 T.	*olive oil*	15 mL
	Flour Tortillas (page 209)	

Wash the chicken and, using scissors, cut into strips ½ inch wide. In a large bowl, combine the lime juice, 2 T. of olive oil, garlic powder, black pepper and Tabasco sauce. Add the chicken, stir and refrigerate for 20–30 minutes. Now is a good time to make the flour tortillas. Before serving, remove the chicken from the marinade and broil on a foil-lined pan 3 to 4 inches from the broiler, until lightly browned. Stir-fry the sliced onion and pepper in the 1 T. of olive oil. At the table, each person takes a heated tortilla and heaps some of the chicken and some of the vegetable onto it. Then the fajita is rolled together, to be eaten while held in the hand.

Serves 4
Sodium per serving: 48 mgs
Calories: 215

Lasagne

1 lb.	*very lean ground beef*	*450 g*
12 oz.	*no-salt-added tomato paste*	*340 g*
2 c.	*water*	*500 mL*
1 t.	*basil*	*5 mL*
⅛ t.	*pepper*	*.5 mL*
1 t.	*onion powder*	*5 mL*
½ t.	*garlic powder*	*2 mL*
2 T.	*sugar*	*30 mL*
2 T.	*cider vinegar*	*30 mL*
3 T.	*unsalted margarine*	*45 mL*
¼ c.	*flour*	*60 mL*
1 c.	*skim milk*	*250 mL*
½ lb.	*low-sodium low-fat cheese grated*	*225 g*
½ lb.	*lasagne noodles*	*225 g*

Make the sauce: In a large skillet, brown the meat; drain off any fat. Add the tomato paste, water, seasonings and vinegar; simmer 25 minutes.

While the sauce is simmering, make the cheese sauce: Melt the margarine over low heat and add the flour; stir with a wire whisk for a couple of minutes; add the milk and stir with the wire whisk; cook over low heat for about 5 to 10 minutes; remove from the heat and stir in the grated cheese. Cook the lasagne noodles as directed on the box, *except* do not add salt to the cooking water; drain.

In a shallow baking dish assemble the lasagne: Spoon a little of the ground beef sauce, spread a layer of a third of the cooked noodles, add a layer of cheese sauce. Repeat until are all ingredients are used up, ending with a cheese layer. Bake in 350°F (175°C) oven for about 30 minutes; let stand for about 10 minutes before cutting. You can also assemble the lasagne ahead of time, refrigerate, and heat later. Allow more time to heat through, if it has been refrigerated.

Serves 6
Sodium per serving: 86 mgs
Calories: 435

Vegetarian Lasagne

You can have this lasagne ready to pop in the oven in the time it takes to boil the noodles, if your sauce is all ready.

4 T.	unsalted margarine	60 mL
2	small zucchini, sliced thin	2
½ lb.	mushrooms, thin sliced	225 g
2 T.	cornstarch	30 mL
2 T.	cold water	30 mL
½ c.	skim milk	125 mL
8 oz.	lasagne noodles	225 g
3 c.	Tomato Sauce (page 74)	750 mL
½ lb.	low-fat low-sodium cheese, grated	225 g

To make the vegetable-cream sauce: Melt the margarine over low heat in a skillet; add the sliced zucchini and mushrooms and cook until they are lightly browned. In a small bowl, dissolve the cornstarch in the water. Add the milk and stir together. Add this mixture to the zucchini and mushrooms. Cook over medium heat for about 10 minutes, or until the sauce is smooth and thick.

Meanwhile, cook the lasagne noodles as directed on the box, except leave out the salt.

To assemble, start with a thin layer of the tomato sauce. Add a layer of cooked drained noodles. Cover with approximately a third of the mushroom-zucchini mixture. Add a third of the grated cheese. Repeat with layers of tomato sauce, noodles, mushroom-zucchini and end with cheese. Bake in 350°F (175°C) oven for about 20 minutes; let stand for a few minutes before slicing.

Serves 6
Sodium per serving: 51 mgs
Calories: 354

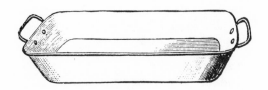

Stuffed Shells

This vegetarian meal can be made ahead and baked just before dinner. It calls for tofu, which is becoming relatively popular. It is made from soy and has virtually no sodium, fat or cholesterol. You will find it in the produce section of the grocery store. If you don't see it, ask! You may want to double the filling recipe so that you will not have cheese and tofu left over. If so, freeze the filling for a future convenient meal.

8 oz.	jumbo shells	225 g
1 T.	olive or safflower oil	15 mL
1	medium onion, finely chopped	1
1	clove garlic, finely minced	1
¼ c.	water	60 mL
2 T.	lemon juice	30 mL
1 c.	tofu	250 mL
2 T.	flour	30 mL
1	egg or equivalent egg substitute	1
1 c.	low-fat cottage cheese	250 mL
3 T.	parsley, finely chopped	45 mL
¼ t.	onion powder	1 mL
¼ t.	garlic powder	1 mL
½ t.	oregano	2 mL
⅛ t.	white pepper	.5 mL
1 c.	grated low-sodium, low-fat cheese	250 mL
2 c.	Tomato Sauce (page 74)	500 mL

Cook the shells in boiling water as directed on the box, except do not add salt to the cooking water; drain. Meanwhile, heat the oil in a large skillet. Pan-fry the onion and garlic. Put the water, lemon juice, tofu and flour into a blender or food processor. Puree until the mixture is *very* smooth. Add this mixture to the onion and garlic. In a bowl, beat the egg or egg substitute lightly. Add the cottage cheese, parsley, seasonings and grated cheese. Stir to combine. Spoon a thin layer of the tomato sauce in a large baking dish. Using a spoon, fill each cooked and drained shell with the cheese mixture. Place the stuffed shells in a single layer in the dish. Cover with tomato sauce. You may wish to reserve part of the tomato sauce to serve heated with the shells. Bake in 350°F (175°C) oven for approximately 30 minutes.

Serves 6
Sodium per serving: 102 mgs
Calories: 369

Pasta Primavera

An easy side dish that combines vegetables with pasta (carbohydrate). Yet, it's fancy enough for any company meal. If you want to make it the main dish, you may want to add small amounts of a protein food, such as small pieces of cooked chicken or other meat, low-sodium canned tuna, or low-sodium cheese.

2 T.	olive oil	30 mL
2 T.	unsalted margarine	30 mL
2	cloves garlic, finely minced	2
2 c.	broccoli,* fresh or frozen, cut into fairly small pieces	500 mL
1 c.	sweet red or green peppers,* cut into thin strips	250 mL
1 c.	carrots,* cut into thin strips, approximately 1 to 1½ inches (2.5 to 4 cm) long	250 mL
8 oz.	linguini or another pasta	225 g
grind	black pepper	grind
	garlic powder (optional)	

Heat the oil and margarine in a frying pan; add the garlic and vegetables and cook for approximately 10 minutes. The vegetables should still have some crispness. Cook the linguini as directed on the box, but leave out the salt. Drain the linguini and toss in a large bowl with the vegetables using two large spoons. Grind the pepper on top and toss again. Garlic lovers will want garlic powder sprinkled on top. It helps to make up for the missing Parmesan cheese.

* You can also add or substitute other fresh vegetables that are available, such as mushroom slices, cherry tomatoes, sliced zucchini or yellow summer squash. As long as the total is approximately 4 cups (1 L) of small vegetable pieces, the choice is up to you. It's most appealing when there are vegetables in more than one color.

Serves 4
Sodium per serving: 32 mgs
Calories: 372

Macaroni and Beef Casserole

1 lb.	lean *ground beef*	450 g
1	small onion, finely chopped	1
1 T.	safflower oil	15 mL
1 t.	oregano	5 mL
6 oz.	no-salt-added tomato paste, diluted with 1 cup (250 mL) water	170 mL
8 oz.	macaroni	225 g
⅛ t.	cumin (optional)	1 mL

Over medium heat, cook ground beef in skillet, breaking up with a fork; cook until no pink color remains. Drain off any fat by spreading meat on a paper towel. Sauté chopped onion in oil until soft. Add oregano, tomato paste and water and stir to combine. Add cooked meat. Cook macaroni in unsalted water for about 9 to 12 minutes; drain macaroni. Toss with the beef sauce.

Serves 4
Sodium per serving: 75 mgs
Calories: 470

Noodles

Noodles are low in sodium—1 mg in a 2-ounce (60-g) serving. Commercially prepared noodle dishes, however, are very high. A person eating one-fourth box of Betty Crocker noodles romanoff takes in 705 mgs of sodium. Although "egg noodles" are made with egg, the amount of egg and cholesterol is quite small. A two-ounce (60-g) serving of cooked noodles has 18 mgs of cholesterol. (To put this in perspective, remember that the yolk of a large egg has 250 mgs of cholesterol.) Cholesterol-free egg noodles are available in many markets.

Ideas for noodles cooked in unsalted water and served with unsalted margarine: Serve noodles with other dishes that have a flavorful sauce such as Beef Goulash (page 182), Chicken Marsala (page 175), Chicken Marengo (page 169), Beef Bourguignon (page 183) or Swiss Steak (page 182); use noodles in recipes that traditionally call for other types of pasta, such as Pasta Primavera (page 151); toss noodles with small amounts of leftover Tomato Sauce (page 74). Make a flavorful noodle dish such as Garlic-Flavored Noodles or Fresh Parsley Pesto and Fettucine (page 153).

Fresh Parsley Pesto and Fettucine

Green sauce for noodles? Yes. Try this when you feel adventurous and are pressed for time. This is especially good when served with a generous tossed salad. Fresh basil in place of fresh parsley is the traditional pesto. In addition to the fresh basil, traditional pesto is made with pine nuts. Use pine nuts, or substitute less expensive walnuts, as we have.

½ t.	basil, dried or double amount of fresh basil	2 mL
½ c.	fresh parsley clusters	125 mL
2	large cloves garlic	2
½ c.	walnuts	125 mL
4 t.	lemon juice	20 mL
4 oz.	no-salt Swiss cheese	120 g
2 t.	olive oil	10 mL
8 oz.	fettucine or egg noodles	225 g

Combine the basil, parsley, garlic, walnuts, cheese and lemon juice in the blender or food processor. Turn on the blender and slowly add the olive oil; blend until smooth. Stop the blender and scrape down the sides. Cook the fettucine without salt. Drain and turn into a warm bowl. Pour sauce over the fettucine. Serve warm.

Serves 4
Sodium per serving: 15 mgs
Calories: 439

Garlic-Flavored Noodles

2 T.	unsalted margarine	45 mL
1 T.	olive oil	15 mL
1	clove garlic, crushed	1
1 T.	fresh parsley, chopped fine	15 mL
1 t.	lemon juice	5 mL
8 oz.	noodles	225 g

Melt the margarine in a skillet; add the oil and garlic. Cook gently for 5 minutes; add the parsley and lemon juice; stir to combine. Cook the noodles in boiling water according to package directions—except leave out the salt in the cooking water; drain. Combine the noodles and sauce in a bowl; toss well before serving.

Serves 4
Sodium per serving: 2 mgs
Calories: 317

Pizza

You can make this family-pleasing pizza quickly, possibly in less time than it would take to have it delivered from a pizza parlor. The dough doesn't need to rise so you can make and eat it right away. To prevent the pizza from sticking to the pan, you can use a non-stick pan, or sprinkle a fine layer of corn meal on the pan, or coat the pan with vegetable or olive oil.

How many pizzas do you want to make? If you like to make extra, *double* this recipe. You can roll the extra dough into pizzas that would be the right size for your family and bake and freeze the baked dough. Or you can wrap the raw dough and freeze it for a short time.

¾ c.	*lukewarm water (neither hot nor cold to the touch)*	185 mL
1 env.	*packaged dry yeast*	1 env.
1 T.	*sugar*	15 mL
2 c.	*flour, preferably bread flour or all-purpose flour (not self-rising flour)*	500 mL
3 grinds	*black pepper*	3 grinds
2 T.	*olive oil*	30 mL
	corn meal to sprinkle on the pans	
½ recipe	*Tomato Sauce (page 74)*	½ recipe
	Pizza Toppings (recipe follows)	
	low-fat low-sodium cheese	

Pour ¼ cup (60 mL) of the lukewarm water into a small bowl; stir in the yeast and sugar; let stand for 5 minutes. In a large mixing bowl, combine the yeast mixture, the remaining ½ cup (125 mL) of lukewarm water, about 1½ cups (375 mL) of flour, the pepper and the olive oil. Stir with a large spoon.

Dust a little of the remaining flour on your work area or breadboard; make a pile of the rest of the flour off to one side of the work area. Put the dough on the floured surface; knead for about 3 to 5 minutes until the dough is shiny and elastic; use the reserved flour while you knead to keep the dough from sticking to the work surface. Divide the dough into parts according to the number and size of pizzas you want to make. (One 12" (30-cm) pizza and one 8" (20-cm) pizza is a popular choice.) Use a rolling pin to roll out the dough into "pizza" shapes and the thickness you like. Sprinkle a light coating of corn meal on your pie pans, cookie sheets or pizza pans. Shape the dough on the pans. Spread the sauce and top with your favorite topping and cheese. Bake in 450°F (230°C)

15 to 20 minutes; using a pancake turner, you can carefully lift an edge of the pizza to see if the bottom is lightly browned. Serve warm. You might like to try a sprinkle of garlic powder on your pizza just before serving.

It would be almost impossible to list how many mgs of sodium or calories you are getting. How thick is the crust? What are the toppings?

Serves 4

Pizza Toppings

Pan-fry thin slices of mushrooms, green or red peppers or onion in a small amount of olive oil with a dash of basil and oregano. Or, leave the vegetables raw if you like a crunchy topping.

To make ground beef taste like sausage (which is too high in sodium): Make fennel tea by pouring ¼ cup (60 mL) boiling water over 1 tablespoon (15 mL) fennel seeds; steep for a few minutes. Strain the fennel tea into a skillet. Add ¼ pound (120 g) of ground beef and pan-fry. Drain the meat on paper before using it as a pizza topping.

FISH AND SEAFOOD

IF YOU OR SOMEONE in your family has been placed on any kind of diet, chances are that fish was recommended because it is low in calories and fat. Commercially frozen fish is usually immersed in brine during the freezing process. Good fresh fish does taste better. Ideally, you should try to find a local market or department with a quick fish turnover. Buy and serve fish the same day for maximum flavor and freshness.

Even though "saltwater" fish swim around in the salty ocean, the sodium content is *not* higher than that of freshwater fish. Although the sodium content varies in different fish, it should not be your first consideration. Select fresh fish according to availability and reasonable prices.

Freezing Fish

If you have fresh fish and would like to freeze it for later use, here is the way an old New England fisherman recommends that you do it: Choose only the freshest fish for freezing. To prepare the fish, first clean and fillet it, then rinse well. Select sturdy freezer containers. If the container is not adequate, the fish will dry out. Place the fillets in the freezer container in the amount of fish you will defrost for one meal. Cover the fish with fresh water. Leave an inch head space for expansion. Seal the container.

Use your frozen fish in recipes that have a tasty sauce: Shrimp or Fish Creole (page 165); Horseradish Gravy (page 58).

If you are absolutely unable to find fresh fish, buy frozen fish and rinse it before cooking. It has been shown that rinsing canned tuna fish through a plastic strainer drastically reduces the sodium content. Rinsing the tuna under running tap water for three minutes removes nearly all of the sodium that had been added during processing. You may want to rinse defrosted fish fillets and use them in place of fresh fillets.

Choosing Fish

Regular fish is a healthier choice than shellfish, although shellfish do not seem as undesirable as we thought a few years ago.

Many people love shrimp, scallops and lobster. It makes sense to eat these fish in moderate amounts. When you are splurging, you want the shellfish to taste as good as possible. This means fresh.

Be sure to buy fresh shrimp, since canned and frozen shrimp have much added sodium. If you can't buy fresh shrimp, don't buy it at all. A 3-ounce (90-g) portion of fresh shrimp has 119 mgs of sodium, fairly high for a protein food; the same amount of chicken has only 56 mgs of sodium. Buy 1 pound (450 g) to serve four, leaving 12 ounces (340 g) of shrimp after the shells are discarded.

You may be fortunate enough to live in an area where people go crabbing to catch fresh crabs. If so, you probably know how to cook fresh crabs. Just remember to leave out all the salty cooking aids; read the label on anything you plan to use. Crabmeat that comes in the small expensive packages may have been "freshened" in brine.

Fish Baked in Foil

The method works well on an outdoor grill—easy and very little mess to clean up.

1 lb.	fresh fish fillets	450 g
dash	paprika	dash
4	onion slices	4
4	green pepper slices	4
4	fresh lemon slices	4
grind	black pepper	grind

Rinse, pat dry, and cut the fish into four pieces. Cut heavy aluminum foil into 4 pieces about 12″ × 12″ (30 cm × 30 cm). Put a piece of fish on each square of foil; sprinkle generously with paprika. Lay a slice of onion and green pepper on each piece; squeeze the lemon slice over the fish and lay it on the top. Fold the foil around the fish to seal. For oven baking, put the foil packages on a cookie sheet. Bake in 425° F (220° C) oven for 15 minutes or so. For an outdoor grill, put the packages on the grill. Fish will flake easily when it's done.

Serves 4
Sodium per serving: 78 mgs
Calories: 98

Broiled Fish Steaks

Good for salmon or swordfish steaks. Using a charcoal grill is another good way to cook fish steaks.

1 lb.	salmon or cod steaks	450 g
2 T.	safflower oil	30 mL
2 T.	lemon juice	30 mL

Preheat the broiler with the broiler pan six inches from the heat. Combine the oil and lemon juice and brush the broiler rack lightly with some of the mixture to prevent the fish from sticking. Brush both sides of the fish lightly with more of the lemon juice and oil. Broil for five minutes. Baste the fish again; turn it over and baste again. Broil for another five minutes or until the fish flakes easily when touched with a fork.

Serves 4
Sodium per serving: 73 mgs
Calories: 196

Broiled Marinated Fish or Shrimp

2 T.	olive oil	30 mL
1 T.	parsley, finely chopped	15 mL
¼ c.	lemon juice	60 mL
2	cloves garlic, chopped	2
1 c.	white wine	250 mL
⅛ t.	black or white pepper	.5 mL
1 lb.	boneless fish fillets or shrimp, cleaned	450 g

Mix oil, parsley, lemon juice, garlic, wine and pepper in a nonmetal bowl. Put the fish fillets into marinade and refrigerate for at least two hours. Preheat the broiler and brush the hot rack with the marinade. Broil close to the heat for approximately 5 minutes until fish flakes when touched with a fork; broil shrimp about 3 minutes.

Serves 4
Sodium per serving (fish): 80 mgs
Calories: 250
Sodium per serving (shrimp): 114 mgs
Calories: 237

Broiled Fish

1 lb.	fresh fish fillets	450 g
2 T.	unsalted margarine	30 mL
2 t.	lemon juice	10 mL
grind	black pepper	grind

Wash and dry the fillets. Place the margarine, lemon juice and pepper in a saucepan over low heat. Brush a broiler pan with some of the melted margarine mixture. Place the fish on the rack. Brush with remaining margarine mixture. Broil a few inches from the heat for about 10 minutes turning once, or until the fish flakes easily with a fork.

Serves 4
Sodium per serving: 76 mgs
Calories: 141

Baked Stuffed Fish

This recipe is especially good for large fish and takes very little effort.

1	*large fish, cleaned with head and tail removed*	1
1	*medium onion*	1
1	*green pepper*	1
3 T.	*lemon juice*	45 mL
2 T.	*chopped fresh parsley*	30 mL
¼ t.	*paprika*	1 mL
grind	*black pepper*	grind

Wash the fish and pat dry. Put the fish on its side in a pan large enough to accommodate the fish. Slice the onion and the green pepper. Lift the top half of the fish and arrange the vegetables in the cavity. Sprinkle lemon juice, parsley, paprika and pepper over the vegetables. Pull the top of the fish over the filling; cover the pan loosely with foil. Bake in 425° F (220° C) oven for about 30 minutes until the fish flakes easily with a fork.

Serves 6
Sodium and calorie content vary according to size of fish

Baked Breaded Fish

This is a great way to serve fish to guests who usually don't eat fish. The fish is moist and tender when it's baked in Roll and Bake Coating Mix.

1 lb.	fresh fish fillets	450 g
1 c.	Roll and Bake Coating Mix	250 mL
	(page 55)	
⅓ c.	lemon juice	90 mL

Wash, dry and cut fish into serving-size pieces. Put the coating mix in one bowl and the juice in another. Line a baking pan with aluminum foil to make cleanup easier. Dip each piece of fish into the juice and into the coating mix, using your hand to press the mix onto the fish. Place in a baking pan; bake in 350° F (175° C) oven for about 10 to 15 minutes, depending on the thickness of the fish; fish is done when it flakes easily with a fork.

Serves 4
Sodium per serving: 77 mgs
Calories: 141

Fish in Wine

If you've never cooked fish before, this is a good first recipe. The fish and wine may vary somewhat in the sodium content depending on the variety you choose.

1 lb.	fresh fish fillets	450 g
1	medium onion, thinly sliced	1
1	green pepper, thinly sliced	1
3 T.	lemon juice	45 mL
¾ c.	dry white wine, not cooking wine	190 mL
¼ c.	Roll and Bake Coating Mix	60 mL
	(page 55)	

Wash the fillets and leave them whole. Line a baking pan with aluminum foil to make cleanup easier and spread fillets on the foil. Dot with the vegetables and the lemon juice. Pour the wine over the top and sprinkle on the coating mix. Bake in 350° F (175° C) oven until tender, about 20 minutes.

Serves 4
Sodium per serving: 84 mgs
Calories: 172

Sautéed Fish

This method of cooking fish on the stove top is easy and tasty.

1 lb.	fresh fish fillets	450 g
⅓ c.	lemon juice	90 mL
⅓ c.	Roll and Bake Coating Mix (page 55)	90 mL
1 T.	safflower oil	15 mL
1	medium onion, chopped	1
1	clove garlic, chopped	1

Wash, dry and cut the fish into serving-size pieces. Pour lemon juice into one bowl and coating mix into another. Dip each piece in lemon juice, then place each in coating mix and use your hand to press the coating on. Heat the oil in a skillet. Sauté the onion and garlic gently for about 5 minutes. Slip in the fish and sauté for about 5 minutes; turn the fish over with a pancake turner and fry gently until browned.

Serves 4
Sodium per serving: 79 mgs
Calories: 148

Batter-Fried Fish or Shrimp

4 T.	flour	60 mL
1 T.	cornstarch	15 mL
½ t.	low-sodium baking powder (shake before using)	2 mL
¼ c.	water	60 mL
1 T.	egg substitute	15 mL
1 lb.	boneless fish fillets or shrimp oil for frying	450 g

Mix 3 tablespoons (45 mL) flour, cornstarch, baking powder, water and egg substitute in a bowl. Beat with a wire whisk until the batter is smooth and foamy. Wash the fish, pat dry and cut into serving-size pieces; dust lightly with the remaining flour. Turn each piece over in the batter to coat well. Pour oil in a frying pan and heat to 375° F (190° C); an electric frying pan is best. Slip each fish slice into the hot oil. Cook fish from 5 to 7 minutes on each side, until golden brown; fry shrimp for 3 minutes. Drain on a double layer of paper towels. Serve plain or with lemon juice or vinegar.

Serves 4
Sodium per serving: 77 mgs
Calories: 200

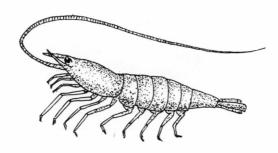

Pan-Fried Fish

This is a recipe traditionally used for fresh trout which is not filleted before cooking.

1 lb.	fresh fish fillets, or whole cleaned fish*	450 g
2 T.	flour	30 mL
¼ t.	paprika	1 mL
dash	white pepper	dash
1 T.	unsalted margarine	15 mL
1 T.	safflower oil	15 mL

Rinse the fish, pat dry and cut into serving pieces. Meanwhile, mix the flour, paprika and white pepper together on a large plate. Coat each piece of fish with the flour mixture. Melt the margarine in a frying pan. Add the oil and heat so it's good and hot. Slide the fish into the hot frying pan and cook for 3 or 4 minutes on each side. The fish should be golden brown and flake easily. Whole fish will need to cook longer.

* You may want to pan-fry your fish Southern style: Dip the fish into the flour mixture, then into egg substitute and coat with cornmeal.

Serves 4
Sodium per serving: 75 mgs
Calories: 161

Serving Fish and Seafood

Just about any fish tastes better with lemon juice, and lemon wedges add a nice touch. Some people prefer to sprinkle vinegar on their fish when served. Specialty fish restaurants often keep malt vinegar on the tables. Tartar Sauce (page 60) is low in sodium, but high in fat and calories.

Shrimp Scampi

Scampi is traditionally served with spaghetti or linguini tossed with olive oil. Two ounces of pasta add 210 calories, but only a trace of sodium.

1 lb.	fresh shrimp in shells	450 g
3 T.	unsalted margarine	45 mL
1 T.	olive or safflower oil	15 mL
1	clove garlic, halved	1
1 T.	parsley, chopped	15 mL
1 t.	lemon juice	5 mL

Remove the shrimp shells and black "vein." Wash the shrimp. Melt the margarine in a frying pan. Add the oil and garlic, sauté for a few minutes. Add the shrimp, parsley and lemon juice. Cook slowly over low heat, turning, until shrimp turns pink, about 5 minutes. Remove the garlic. Serve immediately.

Serves 4
Sodium per serving: 111 mgs
Calories: 179

Shrimp or Fish Creole

Don't think that only convenience foods are convenient. This dish is very fast and easy.

1 T.	olive oil	15 mL
1	medium onion, finely chopped	1
½	green pepper, finely chopped	½
6 oz.	no-salt-added tomato paste	170 mL
grind	black pepper	grind
½ t.	onion powder	2 mL
2 t.	sugar	10 mL
2 t.	lemon juice	10 mL
3 dashes	Tabasco sauce (more if you like it hotter)	3 dashes
1½ c.	water	375 mL
1 lb.	fresh shrimp, shelled, or fish fillets, washed	450 g

Heat the oil in a large frying pan. Add the onion and green pepper and sauté over medium heat for approximately five minutes. Add the tomato paste, seasonings, lemon juice and water and simmer over low heat. Add the shrimp or fish to the sauce and simmer for approximately 5 to 8 minutes, depending on the size of the shrimp or fish.

Serves 8
Sodium per serving (fish): 96 mgs
Calories: 185
Sodium per serving (shrimp): 132 mgs
Calories: 156

POULTRY

CHICKEN IS ECONOMICAL, low in fat and cholesterol and fairly low in sodium. No wonder anyone on a special diet is usually advised to eat the white meat, which comes from the chicken breast—lower in sodium and calories. Therefore, the recipes in *this book* call for chicken breasts. Whole chickens, however, are less expensive and you may prefer to use them cut in serving pieces. If you do substitute the whole chicken, serve the breast portion to the person who needs to be especially careful about his or her diet.

If you are trying to cut down on fat or calories, it makes sense to remove the chicken skin *before* you cook it. A person who is on a strict diet is usually told to limit the serving to 3 ounces (90 g) of cooked chicken or about one breast. A kitchen scale is the most accurate way to know how large a serving is.

With the recipes that follow you can substitute other cuts of chicken. Allow less time for boneless chicken cutlets to cook.

Barbecued Chicken

If you like barbecue chicken the way restaurants serve it, use Barbecue Sauce.

4 (2 lbs.)	chicken breasts, trimmed	4 (1 kg)
	Barbecue Sauce (page 59) or a	
	marinade (pages 70–72)	

Several hours or the day before planning to serve, wash chicken and discard the skin. Mix together the barbecue sauce or marinade in a nonmetal bowl. Put chicken pieces in the sauce or marinade; cover and refrigerate for several hours or overnight.

To barbecue, oven method: Preheat the oven to 400° F (205° C). Arrange the chicken in a baking pan and spoon about a third of the sauce or marinade over the chicken. Cover with aluminum foil. Bake for about 20 minutes. Uncover, turn the chicken over and baste. Cover again and continue baking 20 minutes. Remove aluminum foil, and cook uncovered for 5 to 10 minutes to brown. Serve warm with extra sauce or marinade and with cooked rice.

Indoor or outdoor charcoal broiling method: Arrange the chicken on the broiler pan; brush with sauce or marinade. Broil, checking every 2 to 3 minutes to avoid overcooking. After 5 to 6 minutes, turn the chicken. Brush again with the marinade and broil until the chicken is tender.

Serves 4
Sodium, 1 chicken breast: 67 mgs (more with sauce)
Calories: vary with each recipe

Chicken Fricassee

A classic recipe that is so easy to fix. It almost cooks by itself. Excellent with Quick Biscuits (page 81).

4 (2 lb.)	chicken breasts, trimmed	4 (1 kg)
¼ c.	flour	60 mL
½ t.	white pepper	2 mL
2 T.	safflower oil	30 mL
1	medium onion, diced fine	1
1	clove garlic, minced	1
2 c.	water	500 mL
2 T.	cornstarch	30 mL
⅓ c.	fresh parsley, chopped	90 mL

Wash and skin the chicken. Remove any visible fat. Mix the flour and pepper together on a plate. Coat each piece of chicken by rolling it in the flour mixture. Heat the oil in a large saucepan or Dutch oven. Add the onion and garlic; cook gently for 2 to 3 minutes; add the chicken and cook for a few minutes on each side until golden brown. Add the water; cover the pot tightly and gently simmer for about 45 minutes, or until tender; remove the chicken to a plate.

Measure the cornstarch into a bowl. Gradually stir in a cup of the cooking liquid and pour back into the cooking pot. Heat and stir until sauce thickens. Stir in the parsley. Slip the chicken back in and reheat.

Serves 4
Sodium per serving: 72 mgs
Calories: 252

Quick Lemon Chicken

You can also use *thin* slices of turkey cutlets or veal cutlets and garnish with freshly chopped parsley.

⅓ c.	*flour*	90 mL
dash	*white or black pepper*	dash
1¼ lb.	*boneless chicken breasts or cutlets*	600 g
1 T.	*unsalted margarine*	15 mL
1 T.	*safflower oil*	15 mL
6 T.	*lemon juice*	90 mL
2 T.	*sugar*	30 mL

Mix the flour and pepper together in a bowl. Coat the cutlets with the flour mixture. Heat the margarine with the oil in a large frying pan. Add the chicken and cook over medium high heat until golden brown on both sides. Remove the chicken to a platter and keep warm. Sprinkle lemon juice and sugar into the frying pan and stir over low heat, scraping the bottom of the pan frequently, about 2 to 3 minutes; pour it over the cooked chicken. Serve warm.

Serves 4
Sodium per serving: 56 mgs
Calories: 242

Honey Chicken

Easy enough for everyday and special enough for company!

4 (2 lb.)	*chicken breasts, trimmed*	4 (1 kg)
4 T.	*unsalted margarine*	60 mL
½ c.	*honey*	125 mL
1 t.	*curry powder*	5 mL
½ t.	*dry mustard*	2 mL

Wash, dry, remove skin and fat from chicken. In a saucepan, melt the margarine, stir in the honey, curry powder and dry mustard; remove from heat. Pour about half the sauce mixture into a baking dish. Roll each piece of chicken in the baking dish and arrange with the round side up. Pour any remaining sauce over the chicken. Bake in 375°F (190°C) oven for about 1 hour.

Serves 4
Sodium per serving: 70 mgs
Calories: 368

Baked Chicken in Wine

Wonderful for company.*

4 (2 lb.)	chicken breasts, trimmed	4 (1 kg)
1 c.	white wine (not cooking wine)	250 mL
1 t.	garlic powder	5 mL
1 t.	onion powder	5 mL
1 t.	paprika	5 mL
2 T.	fresh parsley, minced	30 mL

Wash the chicken, remove and discard skin. If you like, line a baking pan with aluminum foil to make cleanup easier. Place chicken pieces on the foil. Mix remaining ingredients in a small bowl. Pour over chicken and cover with aluminum foil. Bake for about 40 minutes or until fork tender.

To roast whole chicken, see note under Roast Turkey (page 178).

Serves 4
Sodium per serving: 72 mgs
Calories: 243

Chicken Marengo

Since this recipe makes a tasty sauce, serve rice or noodles at the same meal.

4 (2 lbs.)	trimmed chicken breasts	4 (1 kg)
2 T.	olive oil	30 mL
1	onion, minced	1
1	clove garlic, mashed	1
2	large tomatoes, peeled	2
½ t.	paprika	2 mL
½ c.	vermouth	125 mL
1 c.	mushrooms, sliced	250 mL

Wash the chicken and discard the skin. Heat the oil in a large casserole. Add the chicken breasts and sauté briefly until golden brown on both sides. Remove the chicken. Add the onions and garlic to the casserole and cook gently for about 5 minutes. Add the tomatoes to the onion and garlic and cook until mushy. Tuck the chicken into the sauce. Add the paprika, vermouth and mushrooms. Simmer for about 40 minutes, or until done.

Serves 4
Sodium per serving: 79 mgs
Calories: 282

Chicken Cacciatore

If you are using a whole fryer, serve the breast to the person who needs to cut down on sodium.

4 (2 lb.)	chicken breasts, trimmed	4 (1 kg)
3 T.	flour	45 mL
2 T.	safflower oil	30 mL
1	medium onion, chopped	1
1	clove garlic, finely chopped	1
1	fresh tomato, cut up	1
½	green pepper, chopped	½
1 c.	fresh mushrooms, chopped	250 mL
6 oz.	no-salt-added tomato paste	170 mL
1⅓ c.	water	340 mL
½ t.	basil	2 mL
1	bay leaf	1
grind	black pepper	grind

In a paper bag, shake the chicken pieces with the flour. Heat the oil in a large frying pan. Brown the chicken pieces lightly on all sides. Add all the vegetables; cook gently over low heat. Dilute the tomato paste with the water. Add the basil, bay leaf and pepper to the sauce and pour over the chicken and vegetables. Cover and continue simmering over low heat until the chicken is tender, about 45 minutes or longer if you like it very tender. Remove the bay leaf. Serve the chicken cacciatore over spaghetti or other pasta, cooked without salt, of course.

Serves 4
Sodium per serving: 91 mgs
Calories: 286

Creamed Chicken

Serve over toast, or for a fancier touch, use as filling for Crepes (page 249) or in Popovers (page 223). If you like, you can add sliced mushrooms, diced green pepper or pimentos as you melt the margarine to make the cream sauce. Creamed chicken can be seasoned at the table with a sprinkling from the Unsalt Shaker (page 52).

3 c.	water	750 mL
1	medium onion, peeled and quartered	1
1½ lb.	chicken breasts	670 g
4 T.	unsalted margarine	60 mL
¼ c.	flour	60 mL
2 T.	sherry (not cooking sherry)	30 mL
dash	white pepper	dash
½ t.	onion powder	2 mL

Combine water and onion in a large saucepan. Remove the skin from the chicken. Cut each breast in half down the back. Add to the saucepan; you may need to cut the chicken into smaller pieces so that it is covered by the water. Bring to a boil, reduce the heat and simmer until tender, approximately 45 minutes. Remove the chicken from the broth and place on a plate to cool. Using a slotted spoon, discard onion, save the broth.

While the chicken is cooling, make a white sauce in a separate saucepan: Melt the margarine over low heat, add the flour and cook over low heat for a few minutes, stirring with a wire whisk. Measure 2 cups (500 mL) of the broth and add to the saucepan; add the sherry and seasonings and stir the mixture over low heat until the sauce is thickened. Cut up the chicken into small chunks, discarding the bones, and add chicken to the sauce and stir. If this is more than you need at the meal, refrigerate or freeze the extra for a convenient meal at another time.

Serves 6 (filling for 12 crepes or popovers)
Sodium per serving: 31 mgs
Calories: 189

Baked "Fried" Chicken

Quick and easy to pop in the oven for a tasty family favorite. Especially good for people who don't want the fat and calories in traditional fried chicken.

4 (2 lb.)	chicken breasts, trimmed	4 (1 kg)
½ c.	lemon juice or orange juice	125 mL
⅓ c.	Roll and Bake Coating Mix (page 55)	90 mL

Remove and discard skin from chicken. Pour juice into a bowl or flat pan, and the coating mix in another. If you like, line a baking pan with aluminum foil to make cleanup easier. Dip each piece of chicken into the juice to moisten, then into the coating mix; use your fingers to press the mix onto the chicken. Arrange in a baking pan and bake in 350° F (175° C) oven until tender, about 45 to 50 minutes.

Serves 4
Sodium per serving: 67 mgs
Calories: 159

Southern Fried Chicken

4 (2 lb.)	chicken breasts, trimmed	4 (1 kg)
½ c.	flour	125 mL
½ t.	white or black pepper	2 mL
½ t.	paprika	2 mL
	safflower or other oil for frying	

Wash the chicken, remove the skin and discard. Mix together the flour, pepper and paprika. Dredge the chicken pieces with the spice mixture. (To dredge, you can put the mixture and chicken into a bag and shake to coat.) Let the chicken stand.

Meanwhile, pour oil ½ inch (1 cm) deep into the skillet. Heat over moderate heat until hot. Add the chicken and cover tightly; brown on one side and turn over. Turn the heat down so that the chicken will brown more slowly; do not replace cover. Continue cooking until done, about 30 additional minutes.

Serves 4
Sodium per serving: 67 mgs
Calories: 261

Stir-Fried Chicken

It's fun to cook this in a wok but a large saucepan or Dutch oven can be used. Traditionally, Chinese foods have smaller amounts of the protein food, and lots of vegetables. Prepare chicken and vegetables in advance and have ready. Cooking takes a few minutes.

2 T.	oil, preferably peanut oil	30 mL
¼ t.	thyme	1 mL
pinch	rosemary	pinch
pinch	oregano	pinch
¼ t.	onion powder	1 mL
1	clove garlic, crushed	1
1	medium onion, chopped	1
1	carrot, sliced	1
½	green pepper, diced	½
¼	head of cabbage, shredded fine	¼
10 oz.	chicken* breast, cut into ½" wide strips	300 g
1 T.	sherry wine (optional)	15 mL

Heat the oil, thyme, rosemary, oregano, onion powder and seasonings in the wok until the oil is very hot and you can smell the seasonings. Add the onion and stir-fry in the hot oil for about 10 seconds. Add the green pepper and carrot and stir-fry for about 10 seconds. Toss in the cabbage and stir-fry until limp and golden. Move vegetables to one side, drop the chicken into the wok and stir-fry until color changes from pink to white and the pieces are cooked through, about 4 minutes. Drizzle in the sherry, if using. Mix chicken with the vegetables. Delicious with rice, cooked without salt, of course.

* If you buy chicken breasts with the bone in, buy about 1¼ pounds (600 g) and bone before cooking. Also, you may want to make some chicken stock by cooking the bones with herbs in water. See Chicken Stock (page 107).

Serves 4
Sodium per serving: 63 mgs
Calories: 170

Maryland Fried Chicken

4 (2 lb.)	*chicken breasts, trimmed*	4 (1 kg)
⅓ c.	*flour*	90 mL
1	*egg* or equivalent egg substitute*	1
1 T.	*water*	15 mL
½ c.	*Roll and Bake Coating Mix (page 55)*	125 mL
	safflower or other oil for frying	

Wash the chicken, remove skin and discard. Sprinkle the flour into a large paper bag, add the chicken and shake. Mix egg with water in a pan; spread Roll and Bake in another pan. Dip each piece in the egg and the coating mix; repeat with each piece of chicken. (If you always use one hand for the egg and the other hand for crumbs, the process is much less messy.) Let the chicken stand.

Meanwhile pour enough oil into the skillet to make a layer ½ inch (1 cm) deep. Brown chicken on one side and turn over. Turn the heat down so that the chicken will brown more slowly. Do not replace cover. Continue cooking until done, about 30 additional minutes.

* Actually, very little of the egg and flour cling to the chicken.

Serves 4
Sodium per serving: 82 mgs
Calories: 310

Chicken or Veal Scaloppine

A delicious special treat. Or use sliced turkey breast, an economical "veal substitute." Good with pasta, garlic bread and a green salad.

1¼ lb.	*boneless chicken breasts, sliced, or lean veal, cut for "scaloppine"*	600 g
3 T.	*flour*	45 mL
dash	*white pepper*	dash
1 T.	*unsalted margarine*	15 mL
1 T.	*safflower oil*	15 mL
⅔ c.	*dry vermouth*	180 mL
½ t.	*basil*	2 mL
1 T.	*lemon juice*	15 mL
1	*onion, finely chopped*	1
1	*clove garlic, finely minced*	1
6 oz.	*no-salt-added tomato paste*	170 mL
1¼ c.	*water*	310 mL

Using a mallet or rolling pin, pound the chicken between 2 slices of waxed paper until very thin, careful not to break the flesh apart. Combine flour and white pepper on a dinner plate. Coat chicken with flour on both sides, shaking off excess flour.

Heat oil and margarine in a large skillet. Add chicken and cook on both sides, about 8 minutes. Remove chicken and add the vermouth to the skillet. Cook over fairly high heat for about 5 minutes, stirring frequently. Turn down heat and add remaining ingredients. Stir and add the cooked chicken and cook over low heat for another 5 minutes.

Serves 4
Sodium per serving (chicken): 78 mgs
Calories (chicken): 292

Chicken, Turkey or Veal Marsala

This recipe is traditionally made with thin slices of veal, but you can save money: substitute 6 boneless chicken cutlets, fresh turkey slices or thinly sliced turkey "cutlets."

¼ c.	*flour*	60 mL
dash	*white pepper*	dash
dash	*oregano*	dash
dash	*basil*	dash
1¼ lb.	*cutlets (chicken, turkey or veal)*	600 g
1 T.	*safflower oil*	15 mL
1 T.	*unsalted margarine*	15 mL
½ lb.	*mushrooms, sliced*	225 g
1 c.	*marsala wine or dry sherry*	250 mL

Mix flour, white pepper, oregano and basil together on a plate. Wash and dry the cutlets and coat each with the flour mixture. Reserve any leftover flour. Heat oil and margarine in a frying pan. Add the cutlets and sauté gently until brown on both sides and tender, about 15 minutes. Remove the cutlets to a dish. Add the mushrooms and ¼ cup (60 mL) of the wine; cook for about 5 minutes over low heat. Scrape the bottom of the pan to loosen any flour. Stir in any reserved flour and the remaining marsala. Simmer until the mixture thickens, stirring constantly. Slip the cooked cutlets into the sauce. Cook gently for about 5 minutes or more.

Serves 4
Sodium per serving (chicken): 67 mgs
Calories (chicken): 301

Sweet-and-Sour Chicken

A family pleaser, very fast and good with rice.

1¼ lb.	boneless chicken breast cutlets	600 g
1 T.	safflower oil	15 mL
1	medium onion, finely chopped	1
2	cloves garlic, finely minced	2
1 c.	water	250 mL
½ c.	juice drained from pineapple can	125 mL
1 T.	molasses	15 mL
3 T.	sugar, more if you like it sweeter	45 mL
¼ t.	ginger	1 mL
½ c.	vinegar	125 mL
3 T.	cornstarch	45 mL
1 c.	pineapple chunks, drained	250 mL
1	green pepper, cut in chunks	1

Trim and remove any fat or skin from the chicken; leave whole or cut into chunks, as you prefer. Heat oil in skillet and cook onion and garlic for about 5 minutes; push onion and garlic to side of pan. Add chicken and brown on both sides. Add ¾ cup (190 mL) of the water. Turn heat down to simmer and cook over low heat, about 10 minutes for small strips of chicken, 15 minutes for larger pieces of chicken.

Remove chicken to a plate. To make Sweet-and-Sour Sauce: Stir pineapple juice, remaining ¼ c. (60 mL) water, molasses, sugar, ginger, vinegar and cornstarch in skillet. Add pineapple and green pepper chunks; bring to boil. Stir, turn down heat and simmer for about 10 minutes. Add chicken and heat through. Serve warm.

Serves 4
Sodium per serving: 66 mgs
Calories: 300

Cornish Game Hens with Rice Stuffing

The cooked meat averages 6 ounces (180 g) per game hen. You can serve half of a game hen to a strict dieter.

1 T.	unsalted margarine	15 mL
1	small onion, minced	1
1	small apple, cored, peeled and minced	1
2 c.	cooked rice (cooked without salt)	500 mL
½ t.	sage	2 mL
½ t.	thyme	2 mL
⅓ c.	vermouth	90 mL
dash	pepper	dash
4	Cornish game hens—each weighs about 1 lb. (450 g) when wrapping and giblets are removed	4

To make the stuffing, melt the margarine in a small pan, add the onion and apple and cook gently for 5 minutes or so, stirring occasionally. Combine with the rice, sage, thyme, vermouth and pepper in a bowl. Wash the hens and spoon the stuffing into the cavities without overfilling. Place the hens on a rack in a shallow pan. Add a layer of water to the bottom of the pan. Cover pan with a tent of aluminum foil. Set pan in 400° F (205° C) oven and immediately turn the heat down to 325° F (165° C). Roast about 50 to 60 minutes until tender. Serve warm.

Serves 4 or 8
Sodium (half a hen): 72 mgs
Calories: 206

Roast Turkey

Buy a turkey that is *not* prebasted with salted butter. A fresh turkey may be best. Clean the turkey and dry it. Brush with a small amount of un-salted margarine, if desired.

To roast, plan 20 minutes per pound for birds up to 6 pounds. For larger birds allow 15 minutes per pound (450 g). If the bird is stuffed, add an extra 5 minutes per pound. Roast in 325° F (165° C) oven.* If you use a tent of aluminum foil, remove it the last half hour of cooking to brown.

*To roast chicken, follow the same directions.

Stuffings

Many people are used to the taste of stuffing, sold dry and packaged in bags. No matter how you "doctor" it up, the product is still very salty (about 4,000 mgs in a small bag). Although sage and other seasonings are used, the major seasoning is still salt. If you stuff a turkey with packaged stuffing, the saltiness is bound to be in the liquid that drips out. If you baste the bird with the pan drippings, you will be, in effect, basting with a salted liquid. A person who really needs to cut down on salt should not eat turkey meat from a bird that was basted with a salted liquid. But fortu-nately, it is very easy to make the salty stuffing in a separate dish, for fam-ily members who do not need to cut down.

We do not think you can make flavorful stuffing from low-sodium bread and unsalted margarine. You may want to try some combinations of seasonings. Or better, try our rice stuffing.

Rice Stuffing for Turkey

Double the stuffing recipe for Cornish Game Hens with Rice Stuffing (page 177) to make enough stuffing for a 12-pound (5.4-kg) turkey.

MEATS

Red meats—beef, veal, lamb, pork, especially—have been criticized for their high fat and cholesterol, expense, and for taking a disproportionally high share of the world's agricultural resources. Animals consume 90 percent of corn, barley, oats and soy. But the fact remains that people love meats and choose them for dinner over other foods.

Organ meats, such as liver, have not been very popular. Although they are rich in iron, they are often not recommended for a person who needs to cut down on cholesterol. You may want to check with your doctor or dietitian to see if he/she recommends organ meats.

Red meats are relatively low in sodium and beef is the lowest; you can figure that a small serving (three ounces or 90 g) of cooked meat has: beef, 55 mgs of sodium; lamb, 58 mgs of sodium; pork, 59 mgs of sodium; veal, 69 mgs of sodium.

If the doctor has told you, or someone you cook for, to limit the number of times per week that red meat is eaten, then you certainly want the meat to taste as good as possible.

Many of the most popular ways of cooking meat don't require any special low-sodium recipes. Just roast, broil, pan-fry or cook over charcoal grill. As *New York Times* food editor and author Craig Claiborne says, charcoal broiling is an excellent way of adding flavor to unsalted meats. Just be sure to leave out all of the high-sodium cooking aids (soy sauce, tenderizer, MSG, etc.)

Veal is often recommended as being a better choice than beef or pork for people who need to cut down on fat. Major drawbacks to veal are the price and higher sodium and calorie contents than chicken. If veal fits into your economic and sodium budget, you can use some of the recipes in the chapter on chicken, such as Chicken, Turkey or Veal Marsala (page 175) or Scaloppine (page 174).

Lean cuts of red meat are the best choice because they have less saturated fat. The lean cuts, such as round, can be tenderized in any of the following ways: braise or cook in a liquid over low heat for several hours; marinate the meat for several hours; pound with a meat mallet; use unsalted meat tenderizer (which became available in late 1982), approximately 1 teaspoon (5 mL) per pound (450 g) of meat—a very generous coating. The tenderizer not only works very well on tough meat cuts but also is made without the potassium chloride, a chemical in many commercial low-sodium products that leaves an unpleasant aftertaste.

Beef

Broiled Steak

1 lb.	boneless beef steak (buy more if there is bone)	450 g
1 t.	unsalted meat tenderizer (optional)	5 mL

Prepare the cooking surface: preheat the broiler or prepare a charcoal fire. If you are using a less than perfectly tender cut of meat, sprinkle it generously with *unsalted* meat tenderizer. (Do not use regular meat tenderizer, which is very high in sodium.) Place the meat on a broiler pan (or on the charcoal grill) and broil a few inches from the heat. Turn over after 2 to 3 minutes; broil on the second side. A rare steak may take *approximately* 3 minutes; a well-done steak may take 6 minutes. Cut into the steak as soon as you think it may be done to see if the steak has cooked long enough. You can always cook it a minute or two longer.

Serves 4
Sodium per serving: 58 mgs
Calories: 162

Steak au Poivre

Steak with pepper has so much flavor you won't miss the salt!

2 T.	freshly ground black pepper	30 mL
1 lb.	boneless, tender beef steak (buy more if there is bone)	450 g

Sprinkle one-half the pepper onto one side of the meat and pound it in with a meat mallet; repeat on the other side. Broil the meat over a charcoal grill or on the broiler rack; or pan-fry the meat in an oiled skillet.

Serves 4
Sodium per serving: 58 mgs
Calories: 162

London Broil

To marinate 2 to 3 pounds (900–1,400 g) of a less tender cut of beef: Select a marinade (page 70–72) and double the amounts.

Marinate for several hours or overnight. Broil until done as described in Broiled Steak (page 180). Slice the meat on the diagonal.

Serves 12
Sodium and calorie content vary with the cut of beef.

Beef Teriyaki

Served with rice and a crisp salad.

1 lb.	*lean boneless beef, such as sirloin or round*	*450 g*
¼ c.	*Soy Sauce Substitute (page 62)*	*60 mL*
¼ t.	*dry mustard*	*1 mL*
3 T.	*sherry, not cooking sherry*	*45 mL*
¼ c.	*water*	*60 mL*

Place the meat in the freezer to partially freeze it so that it will be easier to slice. Meanwhile, make the marinade: combine soy sauce substitute, mustard, sherry and water in a nonmetal bowl. Remove meat from freezer and slice across the grain into *thin* slices. Place the pieces of meat in the marinade; cover. Refrigerate it if you will be marinating it for more than 15 minutes.*

When ready to cook, preheat the broiler. Broil the meat a few inches from the heat for 5 minutes. Turn over and broil for an additional 3 to 8 minutes, depending on how rare or well-done you like it. You can also cube the beef and skewer before broiling, as for shish kebab. If you want to serve the marinade as a sauce, heat it in a saucepan just to the boiling point, reduce heat and simmer.

* If you use a tough cut of meat such as round, let it sit in the marinade for at least several hours or overnight. If you use a tender cut of meat such as sirloin or tenderloin, you can marinate it for just 15 minutes and make the process much quicker.

Serves 4
Sodium per serving: 68 mgs
Calories: 206

Swiss Steak

Slow cooking can really tenderize bottom round cut 1 inch (2.5 cm) or so.

2 T.	flour	30 mL
¼ t.	dry mustard	1 mL
grind	black pepper	grind
¼ t.	paprika	1 mL
1 lb.	round beef steak	450 g
1 T.	safflower oil	15 mL
1	large onion, sliced into thin rings	1
1	clove garlic, minced	1
1	fresh tomato, peeled and chopped	1
6 oz.	no-salt-added tomato paste	170 mL
2 c.	water	500 mL
1 t.	unsalted meat tenderizer. Sprinkle on right before cooking. (optional)	5 mL

Combine the flour, mustard, pepper and paprika and spread half of this mixture onto one side of the meat. Pound it in with a meat mallet (or the side of a heavy saucer). Sprinkle the remaining flour mixture on the other side of the meat and pound it in.

Heat the oil in a skillet over medium heat; brown the meat on both sides. Remove the meat, temporarily, to a plate. To the skillet add the onion, garlic, tomato, the tomato paste and water; stir to combine. Add the meat to the sauce. Cover the pan and simmer over low heat for approximately 1½ hours or until tender.

Serves 4
Sodium per serving: 80 mgs
Calories: 225

Beef Goulash

Serve with noodles or boiled potatoes.

2 T.	safflower oil	30 mL
1	large onion, chopped	1
1–2	cloves garlic, finely minced	1–2
1 lb.	lean beef, cubed	450 g
grind	fresh pepper	grind
1 t.	marjoram	5 mL
2 c.	water	435 mL

¼ c.	low-sodium ketchup or Ketchup (page 55)	60 mL
2 T.	paprika	30 mL
¼ c.	yogurt (optional)	60 mL

Heat the oil in a Dutch oven or casserole. Add the onion and garlic and stir over low heat for a few minutes. Add the cubes of meat and brown on all sides over medium heat. Add the pepper, marjoram and 1½ cups (375 mL) of the water. Bring to a boil, reduce heat, and simmer for about 1 hour. Mix the ketchup, paprika and remaining water and add to the goulash. Simmer for about 10 minutes more. If you like, add the yogurt and stir over low heat without boiling.

Serves 4
Sodium per serving: 63 mgs
Calories: 222

Beef Bourguignon

Good with noodles.

1½ T.	safflower oil	22 mL
1	medium onion, finely chopped	1
1	clove garlic, finely minced	1
1 lb.	lean beef, trimmed of fat and cubed	450 g
12	small onions, peeled	12
grind	fresh pepper	grind
¼ t.	thyme	1 mL
1 T.	lemon juice	15 mL
½ t.	marjoram	2 mL
1	bay leaf	1
1 c.	water	250 mL
1 c.	Burgundy	250 mL
1 c.	fresh mushrooms, sliced	250 mL

Heat the oil in a Dutch oven or casserole. Add onion and garlic and sauté for a few minutes. Add the cubes of meat and brown on all sides. Add the onions, seasonings, water and Burgundy; simmer for about 1½ to 2 hours. Add mushrooms and simmer for another 30 minutes.

Serves 4
Sodium per serving: 78 mgs
Calories: 263

Old-Fashioned Beef Stew

2 T.	flour	30 mL
grind	black pepper	grind
1 lb.	lean beef, cut into cubes	450 g
2 T.	safflower oil	30 mL
1 T.	wine vinegar	15 mL
2	bay leaves	2
½ t.	onion powder	2 mL
½ t.	garlic powder	2 mL
1 t.	no-salt-added tomato paste	5 mL
½ t.	basil	2 mL
3 c.	hot water	750 mL
½ c.	vermouth	125 mL
4	medium potatoes, peeled and cut into chunks	4
2	carrots, peeled and cut into chunks	2
4	medium onions, peeled and quartered	4

In a paper bag, shake the flour and pepper with cubes of meat to coat lightly with flour. Heat the oil in a Dutch oven or casserole. Brown the meat in the oil, turning frequently. Add all the seasonings, water and vermouth; stir to mix. Heat just to the boiling point. Turn down heat, cover and simmer for 1¼ hours, or until almost done. Add the potatoes, carrots and onions and stir; cover and simmer for 40 minutes until potatoes are cooked.

Serves 4
Sodium per serving: 96 mgs
Calories: 386

Beef Roast

Sunday just isn't Sunday for many families without a roast. Roasts are fairly expensive and certainly need attention. Set the roast on a rack in a shallow roasting pan. Use a meat thermometer.

A good rule of thumb: Roast at 325° F (165° C) for 20 minutes a pound for all meat except pork. Pork should be roasted at 350° F (175° C). Remember that meat continues to cook for 15 minutes or so after you've removed it from the oven; take the roast out when the thermometer indicates that it is not quite done for your personal preference.

Pot Roast

When serving a pot roast,* you'll surely have more meat than four moderate servings. Leftover cooked meat can be ground or thinly sliced to make sandwich filling.

1 (4 lb.)	lean trimmed beef suitable for pot roast	1 (1.8 kg)
1	clove garlic, peeled	1
2 T.	flour	30 mL
good grind	black pepper	good grind
2 T.	safflower oil	30 mL
2 c.	water	500 mL
½ c.	vermouth	125 mL
⅛ t.	Tabasco sauce	1 mL
2 t.	leaf thyme	10 mL
3	medium onions, quartered	3
1	potato,* pared and quartered, per person (optional)	1
½	carrot,* pared (optional)	½

Trim off any visible fat. Rub the garlic around the meat. Combine the flour and pepper and coat the meat.

Heat the oil in a Dutch oven or casserole. Brown the meat over medium high heat on all sides. Add the water, vermouth, seasonings, and onions. Reduce the heat to a gentle simmer. Cover and simmer for approximately three hours. Turn the meat over during the cooking process, if convenient, but cook very slowly. Add carrots and potatoes during the last hour of cooking. (You can figure that each potato adds 6 mgs of sodium. Each half of a carrot adds 17 mgs of sodium.)

* If you want to eliminate more fat, make a day early, chill the cooked roast, discard the layer of fat and reheat the meat in the degreased sauce over low heat.

Serves 6–8 (3 oz., 90 g) per serving
Sodium, per potato: 6 mgs
Sodium, per ½ carrot: 17 mgs

Gravy

To make the gravy: After removing fat, there should be about 2 cups (500 mL). Pour half the liquid into a saucepan and the other half in a dish. Add 3 tablespoons (45 mL) of flour to the dish and mix with a fork until there are no lumps and the mixture is smooth. Stir the flour mixture into the saucepan, blending with a wire whisk. Cook over medium heat, stirring constantly until the gravy thickens.

Hash

Still a favorite way to serve leftover beef.

2 T.	*unsalted margarine*	*30 mL*
1	*medium onion, diced*	*1*
12 oz.	*leftover beef, such as pot roast, trimmed of all visible fat and minced or ground*	*360 g*
4	*medium potatoes, boiled and diced*	*4*
grind	*black pepper*	*grind*

Melt margarine in a skillet. Add the onion and cook gently until soft. Add potatoes, stir and cook until the potatoes are browned. Add the meat and heat thoroughly. Sprinkle with pepper. Serve hot.

Serves 4
Sodium per serving: 61 mgs
Calories: 324

Spicy Meat Loaf

1 lb.	*lean ground beef from the round*	*450 g*
2 T.	*chopped parsley*	*30 mL*
½ t.	*basil*	*2 mL*
1 t.	*dry mustard*	*5 mL*
1	*small onion, grated or finely chopped*	*1*
¼ c.	*crumbs from low-sodium bread**	*60 mL*
2 t.	*lemon juice*	*10 mL*
grind	*pepper*	*grind*

Knead all the ingredients together. Spray a meat loaf pan or small individual baking cups or sections of a muffin pan with a vegetable coating spray. Mound the meat loaf in the pan or baking dishes. Bake the loaf in 375° F (190° C) oven for approximately one hour, individual baking dishes for approximately 15 to 25 minutes. When you remove the meat loaf from the oven, drain off the grease by holding the pan at an angle.

* You can substitute ¼ cup (60 mL) dry oatmeal (not instant).

Serves 4
Sodium per serving: 64 mgs
Calories: 228

Family Meat Loaf

1½ lb.	lean *ground beef*	675 g
½ c.	oatmeal, *not instant*	125 mL
¼ c.	wheat germ	60 mL
1	egg or equivalent egg substitute	1
¼ t.	onion powder	1 mL
½ t.	basil	2 mL
grind	fresh pepper	grind
½ t.	oregano	2 mL
¼ c.	no-salt-added tomato paste	60 mL
½ c.	water	125 mL

Mix together all ingredients in a large bowl, kneading with your hands. Bake in a loaf pan in 375° F (190° C) oven for about 1 hour. Individual meat loaves in ovenproof custard cups or muffin pan bake much faster, in about 20 minutes.

Serves 6
Sodium per serving (with egg): 72 mgs
Calories: 258

Swedish Meatballs

These cook without being watched.

1 lb.	very lean ground beef	450 g
1	egg or equivalent egg substitute	1
1	small onion, grated or minced	1
3	pieces of low-sodium bread, made into crumbs, about 1 cup (250 mL) of crumbs	3
¾ t.	allspice	3 mL
1 t.	sugar	5 mL
dash	white pepper	dash
¼ t.	nutmeg	1 mL

Mix all ingredients lightly and form into small meatballs, using one tablespoon (15 mL) per meatball. Put them on a broiler pan (so that the fat will drip down and away from the meat). Bake in 375° F (190° C) oven for approximately 12 to 15 minutes. Good when served with parsley potatoes.

Makes 32 meatballs
Sodium per meatball (with egg): 10 mgs
Calories (with egg): 33

Swedish Meatballs with Gravy

Swedish meatballs are traditionally served with a sauce or gravy made in the same pan. But making a gravy from beef drippings (saturated fat) cannot be recommended. The easiest way out is to make a sauce that uses Beef Stock.

1 lb.	very lean ground beef	450 g
1	egg or equivalent egg substitute	1
1	small onion, grated or minced	1
3	pieces of low-sodium bread, made into crumbs	3
¾ t.	sugar	3 mL
dash	white pepper	dash
¼ t.	nutmeg	1 mL
3 T.	flour	45 mL
½ c.	skim milk	125 mL
½ c.	Beef Stock (page 110) home-made	125 mL

Mix together the meat, onion, bread crumbs and dry seasonings. Form the meat mixture into small meatballs, using one tablespoon (15 mL) per meatball.

Spray your frying pan with a vegetable coating spray and fry the meatballs; turn them to brown evenly. Shake the pan from time to time so that the meatballs do not stick to the pan. After the meatballs are cooked, about 15 minutes, remove them and put them in a bowl. Drain the fat from the pan. Add the flour and stir around in the pan for a few minutes over medium heat. Add the milk and beef stock and stir with a wire whisk. Slip the meatballs back into the pan and simmer 5 to 10 minutes. Good served over noodles or boiled potatoes.

Makes 32 meatballs
Sodium per meatball (with egg): 13 mgs
Calories: 34

Italian Meatballs

By cooking the meatballs in the oven you avoid time and fuss. Using a broiler pan allows the grease to drain off. If you don't have a broiler pan with a rack, you can line a pan that has sides with aluminum foil and support a cookie-cooling rack on the top.

1	egg or equivalent egg substitute	1
1 t.	onion powder	5 mL
1	small onion, finely grated	1
2 T.	no-salt-added tomato paste	30 mL
2 T.	water	30 mL
1 t.	sugar	5 mL
1 t.	basil	5 mL
1 t.	parsley, finely minced	5 mL
3 c.	low-sodium cornflakes, crushed	750 mL
1 lb.	lean ground beef	450 g

Mix together all the ingredients *except* the meat. Let stand for 10 minutes. Mix in the meat. Form meat into balls. Place the meatballs on a broiler pan. Bake in 350° F (175° C) for about 20 to 25 minutes, depending on the size of the meatballs. Serve in Tomato Sauce, Mama's Sauce or Sauce with Peppers and Mushrooms (page 74).

Serves 4
Sodium per serving (with egg): 81 mgs
Calories (with egg): 293

Sweet-and-Sour Meatballs

1 lb.	very lean ground beef such as round	450 g
1	egg or equivalent egg substitute	1
3	pieces low-sodium bread made into crumbs, about 1 cup (250 mL) of crumbs	3
¼ t.	dry mustard	1 mL
¼ t.	ginger	1 mL
	Sweet-and-Sour Sauce (page 61)	

Knead the meat, egg or egg substitute, bread crumbs, mustard and ginger. Shape into 32 meatballs. Place the meatballs on a broiler pan. Bake in 375° F (190° C) oven for about 20 minutes.

Meanwhile make the Sweet-and-Sour Sauce. When the meatballs are done, lift each meatball with a slotted spoon and place in the sauce.

Makes 32 meatballs
Sodium per meatball: 9
Calories: 28

Lamb

Lamb, although fairly low in sodium, is high in fat and price. Roast leg or shoulder of lamb in a 350° F (175° C) oven for approximately 20 to 30 minutes per pound. Before roasting some cooks like to rub the outside surface with a little oil, pepper, rosemary or a cut clove of garlic. Others like to use a knife to make little cuts in the meat into which pieces of garlic are inserted. Set lamb on a rack in your pan.

Lamb is medium rare when the oven thermometer reads 145° F (62° C); well done when the thermometer climbs to 165° F (74° C). Leftover lamb, cut up, can be layered in Moussaka (page 200). Lamb cubes can be transformed into a curry (page 207). Lamb chops, trimmed of excess fat, are broiled a few inches from the heat.

Shish Kebab

A great way to make a small serving of meat look generous. Marinate overnight. You can also substitute lean cubes of beef.

1 lb.	lean lamb	450 g
2	green peppers, cubed	2
12	small onions, peeled	12
12	fresh mushroom caps	12
12	cherry tomatoes	12
	Herb Marinade (page 72)	

Trim off any visible fat and cut the meat into cubes about 1 to 1½ inches (2.5-4 cm). Combine all the marinade ingredients in a bowl. Add the meat, cover and refrigerate for several hours or overnight. When ready to cook, steam the green pepper cubes and onions for 5 minutes. Preheat the broiler, if necessary. (Charcoal broiling is great, if convenient.) Arrange the meat and vegetables on skewers: mushrooms, cherry tomatoes, meat, onion, pepper and repeat. Brush the skewered food with the marinade. Broil until done, about 10 to 15 minutes, turning and brushing with the marinade.

Serves 4
Sodium per serving of lamb: 53 mgs
Calories: 189

Pork

Although pork is fairly low in sodium—59 mgs in a three-ounce (90-g) serving—it is fairly high in fat. If pork is allowed on your diet, be sure to trim off all visible fat.

Pork should *always* be cooked thoroughly, or until the meat is white or grey on the inside—never pink. Another test is to see if the juices run clear when the meat is pricked with a fork.

Pork Chops

To serve four persons three ounces (90 g) of cooked meat, buy approximately 2¼ pounds (1.1 kg) of pork chops to compensate for fat and bone waste, or one chop for each person. If you are feeling more affluent, you can plan to serve two thin chops. If you are buying thicker or medium pork chops, each person eats approximately 3 ounces (90 g) of cooked pork containing 59 mgs of sodium. Broil, pan-fry, or bake your pork chops. Just leave out high-sodium seasonings such as Shake 'n Bake; use Roll and Bake Coating Mix (page 55).

Pork Chops and Apple Rings

A complete stovetop meal with mashed potatoes and a green or yellow steamed vegetable.

2 T.	flour	30 mL
dash	white pepper	dash
4	medium pork chops	4
2 T.	safflower oil	30 mL
3	medium apples, unpeeled	3

Mix flour and white pepper on a dinner plate. Coat both sides of the chops with the flour mixture. Heat the oil in a skillet. Brown the chops on both sides. Turn the heat down slightly and continue cooking until the chops are done, about 35 minutes, depending on the thickness; there should be no pink color left inside the chops. While the chops are cooking, cut the unpeeled apples across the core into slices about ½-inch (1-cm) thick; remove the inside core of each apple slice. When the chops are done, remove them from the skillet and keep warm. Fry the apple slices in the same skillet, on both sides, shaking the skillet from time to time to prevent sticking. Serve the apple slices and chops together.

Serves 4
Sodium per serving: 75 mgs
Calories: 210

Pork Chops and Scalloped Potatoes

1 T.	safflower oil	15 mL
4	medium pork chops, fat trimmed	4
2 T.	unsalted margarine	30 mL
3 T.	flour	45 mL
¼ t.	black pepper	1 mL
2 c.	Chicken Stock (page 107)*	500 mL
4	medium potatoes, peeled and thinly sliced	4
1	medium onion, peeled and thinly sliced	1

Heat oil in a large skillet over medium heat; brown the chops on both sides. Melt the margarine in a saucepan. Add the flour and pepper and stir with whisk for a couple of minutes. Add the chicken stock and cook over medium heat, stirring constantly, until the mixture boils. Layer the potato slices in a 9-inch (23-cm) square or rectangular baking pan which has been sprayed with a vegetable coating spray. Spread onion over the potatoes. Add the chicken stock and pork chops; cover with aluminum foil. Bake in 350° F (175° C) oven for approximately 45 minutes; remove the aluminum foil and bake for an additional 30 minutes.

* You can substitute milk for the broth and get more calcium, but also more sodium.

Serves 4
Sodium per serving: 87 mgs
Calories: 511

Pan-Fried Pork Chops

This is a good way to cook thin chops. Pork needs to be cooked thoroughly, but not overcooked.

1 T.	safflower oil	15 mL
4	thin pork chops, fat trimmed	4
1	medium onion, diced (optional)	1

Heat oil in a skillet over medium high heat. Add the chops and onions. Cook over medium heat for approximately 20 minutes; thicker chops will take longer. Pork should not be pink inside.

Serves 4

Pork Chops with Stuffing

You can use all apple juice instead of mixing with vermouth.

4	medium pork chops, with a "pocket" for stuffing (or just put the stuffing on top)	4
1 T.	unsalted margarine	15 mL
1	medium apple, peeled and chopped	1
1	small onion, peeled and chopped	1
3	slices low-sodium bread, toasted	3
grind	pepper	grind
¼ t.	sage or savory	1 mL
2 T.	apple juice	30 mL
2 T.	vermouth	30 mL

Heat margarine in a saucepan or skillet; add the diced onion and apple and cook over low heat for a few minutes. While that mixture is cooking, crumble the toast into a bowl. Add the seasonings, apple juice and vermouth and the cooked apple and onion.

Place the chops on a broiler pan that has a rack. Spoon the stuffing in the pocket or on top of each chop. Cover with aluminum foil. Bake in 350° F (175° C) for approximately one hour.

Serves 4
Sodium per serving: 69 mgs
Calories: 352

Barbecued Pork Chops

	Barbecue Sauce (page 59)*	
4	medium pork chops, fat trimmed	4

Prepare Barbecue Sauce. Line a baking dish with aluminum foil if you want to make cleanup easier. Arrange chops in pan, cover with sauce and close the aluminum foil. Bake in 350° F (175° C) oven for 30 to 40 minutes, depending on the thickness of the chops.

* There is quite a lot of sauce; approximately one tablespoon of sauce clings to each chop. If you put extra sauce on your noodles, potatoes or rice, you can figure that each additional tablespoon (15 mL) adds 3 mgs of sodium.

Serves 4
Sodium per serving: 67 mgs
Calories: depends on how much sauce is eaten

Sweet-and-Sour Pork Chops

Sweet-and-Sour Chicken (page 176) can also be used for pork without the poultry. Be sure to cook pork longer—at least 30 minutes, longer for thick chops—until the meat pinkness is gone.

Barbecued Spareribs

A person told to limit sodium or red meat intake can really get a lot of chewing satisfaction from eating spareribs! This sauce is so delicious—as good as any restaurant sauce.

2½ lb.	meaty spareribs, country style	1.2 kg
2 T.	unsalted margarine	30 mL
1	medium onion, chopped	1
2 T.	vinegar	30 mL
2 T.	honey	30 mL
¼ c.	lemon juice	60 mL
1 c.	low-sodium ketchup	250 mL
1 t.	dry mustard	5 mL
½ c.	fresh parsley, chopped	125 mL
½ c.	water	125 mL

Trim the fat that you can see from the spareribs. To remove excess fat parboil for 5 minutes: Place the meat in a large pot and cover with cold water; leave the pot uncovered and bring the water to a boil. Turn down the heat and simmer for about 5 minutes; drain ribs in a colander. Refill the pot with cold water; plunge ribs in cold water to firm; drain. Place the ribs on the rack of a broiler pan. Bake in 450° F (230° C) oven for 25 minutes. Meanwhile, make the sauce: Melt the margarine in a saucepan; cook the onion gently until soft; add the remaining ingredients and stir; remove from heat. Baste the ribs with the sauce and reduce the heat to 300° F (150° C). Bake 45 minutes, basting frequently with sauce.

Serves 4
Calories: difficult to calculate accurately; when spareribs are parboiled, much of the fat is lost in the water

Pork Roast

Roasts offer more than four moderate servings and leftover pork is delicious served cold. Or pork can be reheated in Barbecue Sauce (page 59); or make Sweet-and-Sour Pork (page 194).

Place the roast, fat side up, on a rack in a shallow pan. If you like a mild garlic taste, rub the outside surface with a cut garlic clove. Insert a meat thermometer into a meaty part. Roast in 350° F (175° C) oven for approximately 30 minutes per pound (450 g). The internal temperature on a meat thermometer should be 160° F (70° C) when you remove the roast from the oven. Let the meat rest for 10 minutes before carving.

Leftover Pork in Fried Rice

Chinese restaurants often serve fried rice with small pieces of cooked pork. Make Fried Rice (page 204) and add the pork after cooking the onions.

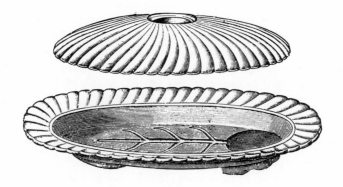

SPECIALTIES
OF THE
HOUSE

MANY POPULAR MEALS for supper or lunch do not fall into the meat and potatoes pattern. Casseroles and hot sandwiches are foods that people often eat, perhaps because they are easy on the food budget or perhaps because they do not require a lot of work, especially at the last minute.

Many ethnic meals that have now become popular because of their good taste, first became commonly used recipes because they could stretch a small amount of the expensive protein food with less expensive foods. Oriental meals with small amounts of pork or seafoods are one example. Italian foods with small amounts of cheese and generous amounts of pasta are another example (Pasta chapter, page 145).

Some ethnic foods are more easily adapted to low-sodium cooking than others. Japanese foods that depend on high-sodium ingredients such as soy sauce (1,319 mgs in 1 tablespoon [15 mL]) are not adaptable to low-sodium cooking. German recipes that call for sausages or "wurst" are not adaptable. Rich French dishes made from heavy cream and butter are probably not what your doctor ordered for you.

Tex-Mex foods, Chinese foods and curry dishes are logical additions to a low-sodium diet. The natural spices, such as chilies and combinations that make a curry, are already low in sodium.

Stuffed Cabbage

You may prefer to substitute crushed low-sodium cornflakes for the rice in this recipe. The low-sodium cornflakes would add slightly more sodium.

12	large cabbage leaves, more if they are small	12
1 lb.	lean ground beef, such as round	450 g
1	medium onion, finely chopped	1
¼ c.	green pepper, finely chopped	60 mL
grind	black pepper	grind
1½ c.	rice, cooked without salt	375 mL
½ t.	paprika	2 mL
¼ t.	dry mustard	1 mL
4 c.	Tomato Sauce (page 74), heated	1 L

Heat some water in the bottom of a vegetable steamer in preparation for steaming the cabbage leaves. Use a knife to cut the stem off a cabbage and separate 12 large leaves. (You may need more than 12 leaves if they are small.) Wash the leaves and place them in the steamer, cover tightly and cook for 5 minutes or so until leaves are limp. Combine the meat, chopped onion and green pepper in a frying pan. Cook gently to brown the meat, breaking it up with a fork as it cooks. Add the black pepper, cooked rice, paprika, dry mustard and ¼ cup (60 mL) of the warm tomato sauce; stir to combine. Select a baking dish that is shallow and just big enough to hold the 12 cabbage rolls close together; a lasagne pan—9 × 13" (23×34 cm) works well, rub with vegetable oil to prevent sticking, or line the pan with aluminum foil for easy cleanup.

Lay out the limp cabbage leaves on a counter or other work surface; divide the meat mixture among the leaves by placing a scoop of meat on each one; roll the leaves around the meat, tucking the ends inside. Place each cabbage roll, seam side down, in the baking pan. Pour tomato sauce over rolls. Cover the pan tightly with aluminum foil. Bake in 350° F (175° C) oven for about 50 minutes. Serve hot.

Serves 4
Sodium per serving: 112 mgs
Calories: 335

Stuffed Zucchini

A good way to use those zucchini that grew too big! Fennel seeds make the beef taste like sweet Italian sausage. Or use a fennel "tea" (see Pizza Toppings, page 155).

4	*medium zucchini, cut in half lengthwise*	4
1	*medium onion, finely diced*	1
1	*clove garlic, minced*	1
1 lb.	*very lean ground beef*	450 g
2 t.	*fennel seeds*	10 mL
1	*slice low-sodium bread, toasted*	1

Half fill a large skillet with water; bring to a boil. Add the zucchini, cut side down, boil for 10 minutes; drain. Scoop out seeds and soft center; reserve. Arrange the zucchini shells in a baking pan; line the pan with foil for easy cleanup. Wrap the fennel seeds in a small piece of cheese cloth and secure the ends of the cloth with a rubber band, wrapped around and around. Put the little package of fennel seeds into skillet with the ground beef. Fry the meat with the fennel in the pan. Stir in the onion and garlic; cook gently until the meat is no longer red. Remove and discard the bag of fennel seeds. Drain the fat off from the cooked meat.

Chop the zucchini flesh and mix with the meat; fill the zucchini shells. Crumble the toast in the blender, to make approximately ⅓ cup (90 mL) of bread crumbs; sprinkle on the stuffed zucchini. Bake in 350° F (175° C) oven for about 20 minutes.

Serves 4
Sodium per serving: 66 mgs
Calories: 256

Stuffed Green Peppers

Make this delicious meal ahead and keep it in the refrigerator until dinner time. If cold, bake for an additional 10 minutes or until hot. Good with Gentle Italian seasoning in the Unsalt Shaker (page 52). Peppers may also be stuffed with Macaroni and Beef Casserole (page 152).

8	*green or sweet red peppers*	8
1 T.	*safflower oil*	15 mL
1	*medium onion, finely chopped*	1
1 lb.	*lean ground beef*	450 g
2 T.	*fresh parsley, finely chopped*	30 mL
1 t.	*basil*	5 mL
¼ c.	*no-salt-added tomato paste diluted*	60 mL
	with ¼ cup (60 mL) water	
2 c.	*cooked rice, cooked without salt*	500 mL
1 c.	*Tomato Sauce (page 74)*	
	(optional)	250 mL

Cut tops off peppers and save; discard seeds and white membranes. Put peppers and tops in a steamer and steam for about 10 minutes. Meanwhile make the filling: Heat oil in a skillet and cook the onion for a few minutes, or until soft; add meat and cook over medium heat until the meat is browned and grainy; drain off any fat; add the seasonings, tomato mixture and the cooked rice. Lightly fill the peppers with the stuffing. Cover with pepper tops. Place in ovenproof baking pan. Add tomato sauce or water to the pan. Bake for about 20 minutes in 350°F (175°C) oven.

Serves 4
Sodium per serving: 88 mgs
Calories: 333

Moussaka

The traditional version of moussaka is layered with lamb and eggplant in a flat pan like a lasagne pan. There are many variations of this casserole using thin slices of potatoes or zucchini, layered with or without the eggplant. When ground lamb is not available, beef is frequently substituted. And leftover meat can be diced and used, if you like.

1	medium eggplant	1
1½ T.	olive oil	25 mL
1 lb.	very lean ground beef, ground lamb or finely diced, cooked lamb*	450 g
1	medium onion, chopped	1
1	clove garlic, minced	1
6 T.	no-salt-added tomato paste	85 mL
½ c.	water	125 mL
¼ t.	cinnamon	1 mL
grind	pepper	grind
2 T.	parsley, finely chopped	30 mL
¼ c. + 1 T.	unsalted margarine	75 mL + 15 mL
½ c.	flour	125 mL
1 c.	skim milk	250 mL
1 c.	Chicken Stock (page 107)**	250 mL
dash	white pepper	dash
¼ c.	Roll and Bake Coating Mix (page 55) or use crumbs from low-sodium bread	60 mL

Slice eggplant ½ inch (2 cm) thick. Brush a *very* thin layer of olive oil over both sides of the eggplant slices. Bake the slices until the top side is lightly browned, about 10 minutes or broil a minute or two on each side. *Make the meat mixture:* Cook the meat, onions, and garlic in a large frying pan over medium heat until no pink color remains; drain off any fat and add the tomato paste, water, cinnamon, pepper and parsley. Turn heat down and simmer until tender, about 25 minutes. While the meat mixture is simmering, *make the white sauce:* Melt ¼ cup (60 mL) of the margarine over low heat; add the flour and stir with a wire whisk until well blended and cook over low heat for a couple of minutes; then add the milk and stock and stir constantly with a whisk until thick.

To assemble the moussaka: Line a flat baking dish with aluminum foil (to make cleanup easier). Layer half the eggplant slices in bottom of baking dish with the meat mixture on top; spread evenly and cover with remaining eggplant slices. Cover with white sauce. Mix the Roll and Bake (or low-sodium bread crumbs) with the remaining tablespoon (15 mL) margarine and sprinkle the mixture on top of the casserole. Bake in 350° F (175° C) oven about 30 to 45 minutes (longer if the casserole has been made ahead of time and refrigerated). Let sit for 10 minutes to make it easier to cut into portions.

* If using cooked, diced meat, add to tomato sauce during last 5 minutes while simmering.

** If you find the taste of prepackaged low-sodium chicken broth acceptable you may use it in place of the homemade stock. You may also want to try plain water as a chicken stock substitute. Using 2 cups (500 mL) of skim milk in place of the stock would increase the calcium (and sodium).

Serves 4
Sodium per serving: 120 mgs
Calories: 525

Zucchini Moussaka

Substitute one pound (450 g) zucchini for the eggplant for a hearty casserole. Slice zucchini into thin slices; no need to broil or bake before layering.

Serves 4
Sodium per serving: 104 mgs
Calories: 475

Beans

Beans may have a plebeian reputation but can make scrumptious meals with imagination. Beans have so many good points that shouldn't be overlooked: They are very low in sodium, fat and cholesterol, very nutritious and can be combined with rice or pasta to make a complete protein meal without the cholesterol and sodium of meat or fish; beans are inexpensive and keep very well. Many favorite ethnic bean recipes suggest beans cooked in delicious ways. Just plan ahead.

To prepare, wash the beans* and cover with water; let them soak *overnight*. If you haven't done this, an alternative method: Place the washed beans in a large cooking pot, cover with water and bring to a boil for one minute. Turn the heat off, cover, and let the beans soak for one hour. To cook: bring to a boil; turn down the heat and simmer until the beans are tender, about 2 hours. Freeze beans in one-meal portions. Beans expand in volume when cooked. For example, one pound or 2½ cups (625 mL) of uncooked kidney beans, will measure 5 cups (1.25 L) after cooking. Each cup (250 mL) of cooked kidney beans contains 6 mgs of sodium.

* Beans do not cook well in hard water. If you substitute bottled water, you should have no problem in the future.

Baked Beans, an American Classic

Dry white beans are called great northern beans or pea beans. They are still a terrific buy and provide excellent nutrition. They also are naturally *low* in sodium. Many people like the convenience of canned pork and beans, but the sodium content is far too high (850 mgs in 1 cup or 250 mL). It's easy to make homemade baked beans as long as you plan ahead. Sweet relish goes well with baked beans.

Beans are a very good source of vegetable protein. But to make the protein more complete, plan to serve the beans with a product that comes from corn or rice. Many traditional recipes use these combinations—beans with corn bread or beans with rice. You may want to add a *small* amount of a complete protein food, such as pork. The traditional ingredient for beans is a piece of salt pork (399 mgs in a small piece). A small trimmed pork chop is a logical substitute, although it can be omitted.

1 lb.	dry white beans	450 g
2	medium onions, cut in half	2
¼ c.	low-sodium ketchup	60 mL
¼ c.	white sugar	60 mL
¼ c.	dark molasses	60 mL
2 t.	dry mustard	10 mL
1	small pork chop trimmed of all fat and bone* (optional)	1

The night before, wash the beans, place in a bowl with water to cover; soak overnight. The next morning, discard the soaking water; mix the beans with all other ingredients in a casserole.** Add water to cover. Cover the casserole. Place in 300° F (150° C) oven and bake for several hours or all day. Check beans from time to time, adding water if necessary. Makes 8 servings.

* Since you can't serve "franks and beans" to people on low-sodium diets, you may want to add additional small, thin pork chops, so that each person gets one chop with his or her beans. Each small chop adds 30 mgs of sodium.

** A bean pot is still the best utensil for cooking beans.

Serves 8
Sodium per serving: 22 mgs
Calories: 261

Rice

Did you know that rice has traditionally been the mainstay of blood-pressure-lowering diets? Rice is a natural for anyone cutting down on sodium, because there are less than 10 mgs in a cup (250 mL) of cooked rice.

The commercial flavored rices, however, are extremely high. For example, a 6-ounce (180-g) package of Uncle Ben's beef-flavored rice has almost 4,000 mgs of sodium.

If plain boiled rice, cooked without salt, tastes bland, make rice more flavorful and avoid the sodium in commercial products. Serve rice with dishes that have a tasty sauce such as Baked Chicken in Wine and Chicken Marengo (page 169), Curry (page 207), Chicken Cacciatore (page 170), Swedish Meatballs with Gravy (page 188), Beef Bourguignon (page 183) and Shrimp or Fish Creole (page 165); cook the rice in chicken or beef broth and add seasonings for more flavor and color; fry the cooked rice in a little oil and add chopped vegetables; toss rice with a little low-sodium tomato sauce.

Fried Rice

Use leftover rice and heat just before eating. To increase the protein value of the dish, add a cup of chopped leftover meat when you add the rice. You can also add ½ cup (125 mL) of sesame seeds after the onions are cooked and before you add the rice to complement the proteins.

2 T.	*safflower oil*	30 mL
2	*medium onions, chopped fine*	2
1	*medium green pepper, chopped fine*	1
¼ t.	*garlic powder*	1 mL
4 c.	*cooked rice (preferably cooked in a flavored broth)*	1 L
½ c.	*water*	125 mL
grind	*black pepper*	grind

Heat the oil in a large skillet. Add the onions and the green pepper, and garlic powder. Cook gently until the onions are soft. Add the cooked rice and water. Stir and cook gently until the rice is heated through. Add the black pepper. Stir again. Serve hot.

Serves 6 (as a side dish)
Sodium per serving: 7 mgs
Calories: 268

Rice Flavored with Chicken Stock

If you use a quick cooking rice, follow the directions on the box but replace the amount of water with homemade stock and add onion powder.

2½ c.	Chicken Stock (page 107)	625 mL
1 c.	raw converted rice	250 mL
1 t.	safflower oil	5 mL
½ t.	onion powder	2 mL

Bring the stock to a boil in a saucepan that has a tight-fitting lid. Stir in the rice, oil and onion powder; cover the pot tightly and cook very gently over low heat for 20 minutes. Remove from heat, uncover, and wrap in towel for 5 minutes.

Serves 6 (as a side dish)
Sodium per serving: 52 mgs
Calories: 196

Hopping John

Black-eyed peas with rice, a traditional ethnic food.

1 c.	black-eyed peas	250 mL
1	small pork chop, trimmed of all visible fat	1
¼ t.	liquid hickory smoke	1 mL
4 c.	water	1 L
1 t.	chili powder (check the sodium content)	5 mL
1	medium onion, chopped	1
2⅔ c.	cooked rice, cooked without salt	680 mL

Wash and drain the beans. Combine in a casserole with pork chop, smoke flavoring and water; cook gently for 45 minutes; add a small amount of water as needed to keep the beans from sticking. Add the chili powder and onion. Continue simmering for 30 minutes or until the beans are tender and most of the liquid is absorbed. Mix the cooked beans and the rice together. Serve warm.

Serves 4
Sodium per serving: 21 mgs
Calories: 181

Louisiana Red Beans and Rice

8 oz.	dry red or kidney beans*	225 g
2	medium onions, chopped	2
4	scallions, chopped	4
1	clove garlic, finely chopped	1
1	green or red pepper, chopped	1
½ c.	fresh parsley, finely chopped	125 mL
½ t.	cayenne pepper	2 mL
dash	ground black pepper	dash
dash	Tabasco sauce	dash
3 oz.	no-salt-added tomato paste	90 g
¼ t.	oregano	1 mL
¼ t.	thyme	1 mL
½ t.	liquid hickory smoke	2 mL
2⅔ c.	cooked rice, cooked without salt	680 mL

Wash red or kidney beans and soak overnight or for several hours in cold water (see page 202 for alternate method). Drain off the *soaking water*; put the beans into a large cooking pot and add enough water to cover. Simmer over medium heat for 15 minutes and add all other ingredients, except the rice. Cook about 2 hours, or until beans are tender. Serve beans over cooked rice.

* You can *double* the recipe and cook all the beans, and freeze for a later low-sodium meal.

Serves 4
Sodium per serving: 30 mgs
Calories: 289

Curry

Anything Curry

With leftovers, you can make this glamorous dish quickly—an exotic way to use leftover meat. Chunks of cooked chicken, lamb, pork or beef, canned low-sodium tuna or cooked fresh shrimp can be used. The curry looks beautiful surrounded by little side dishes.* This recipe does not make a "hot" curry.

If you want to make this dish but don't have any leftover meat, cover 4 chicken breasts in water to simmer for approximately 40 minutes. Then you will have chicken and stock.

3 T.	unsalted margarine	45 mL
1	small onion, finely diced or sliced	1
1 T.	curry powder, less if you like a milder curry flavor	15 mL
¼ c.	flour	60 mL
¾ t.	sugar	3 mL
⅛ t.	ginger	.5 mL
2 c.	Chicken Stock (page 107) or substitute skim milk	500 mL
3 c.	diced cooked chicken, lamb, beef, fish, shrimp, etc.	750 mL
½ t.	lemon juice	2 mL

Melt the margarine in a saucepan or Dutch oven. Add the onion and curry powder. Cook gently over low heat until the onion is soft and yellow. Stir in the flour, sugar and ginger. Add the chicken stock. Blend well and stir until mixture begins to boil. Allow it to boil for about 1 minute.

Just before serving, add chicken and lemon juice. Heat gently. Serve over rice with accompaniments, suggested below.

*Some suggested side dishes: Five-Minute Chutney (page 64); tomato wedges, or chopped tomato; pan-fried onion rings; unsalted, slivered almonds; pineapple chunks; unsalted chopped peanuts; currant jelly; chopped avocado.

Serves 4
Sodium per serving: 88 mgs
Calories: 306

Tex-Mex Cooking

Easy Mexican Sauce

You can buy convenient sauces in jars but unfortunately they all have salt. Fresh unsalted sauces are easy to make. You may prefer a very smooth sauce, or one that has finely chopped fresh vegetables.

6 oz.	no-salt-added tomato paste	170 mL
1 c.	water	250 mL
¼ c.	vinegar	60 mL
1 T.	olive oil	15 mL
2 t.	sugar	10 mL
1 t.	chili powder	5 mL
½ t.	onion powder	2 mL
dash	cayenne pepper	dash
dash	Tabasco sauce	dash

Combine all ingredients in a saucepan and simmer for a few minutes. Add more Tabasco sauce if you like it hotter. This sauce can be frozen.

Makes 1⅔ cups (430 mL)
Sodium, 1 tablespoon (15 mL): 5 mgs
Calories: 12

Fresh Tomato Sauce with Chili

2	medium ripe tomatoes, peeled	2
½	medium green pepper	½
½	small onion, grated	½
¼ t.	oregano	1 mL
¼ t.	garlic powder	1 mL
2	hot peppers or chili peppers* for people who like it hot	2

Finely dice the tomato and green pepper. Dice the hot peppers and combine all the vegetables and spices in a bowl. It's best if the flavors are allowed to blend for several hours.

* If you don't have or don't like fresh chili peppers, you can substitute Salt-free Chili Powder (page 54) or Tabasco sauce to taste.

Makes 1½ cups (375 mL)
Sodium, 1 tablespoon (15 mL): 1 mg
Calories: 3

Tortillas

Tortillas can be made from corn flour or regular white flour. You can make them from scratch from special corn flour called masa harina, a product of Quaker Oats, which is available in some large or Hispanic markets. Regular cornmeal will not work.

Canned tortillas are fairly commonly available, but they contain salt. Each Old El Paso brand tortilla in a can has approximately 118 mgs of sodium. Frozen tortillas may also be available. Check the label to see if salt is an ingredient. Fresh corn tortillas are often refrigerated in markets near the eggs. Check the label; you may be able to find a no-added-salt brand. At home, you can make unsalted tortillas from all-purpose flour.

Flour Tortillas

These are the tortillas used in making burritos.

2½ c.	flour	625 mL
5 T.	unsalted margarine	75 mL
½ c.	warm water	125 mL

Mix 2 cups (500 mL) of the flour in a medium bowl with 4 tablespoons (60 mL) margarine. (Clean fingers work well.) When the margarine is mixed in, gradually stir in the water to make a soft dough. Divide the dough into 12 parts, each one the size of a large walnut; work the dough so as to make each part a smooth ball. Rub some of the reserved margarine on your clean hands and spread on the outside of each ball; place them in the bowl. Cover the bowl with a clean cloth and set it aside for 15 minutes or so.

Heat an ungreased frying pan over medium high heat or heat an electric frying pan to 375° F (190° C). Flatten one ball between the palms of your hands. Flour it on both sides. Use a rolling pin to roll out the tortilla until it is almost paper thin, 7½ to 8″ (20 cm) across. Use small amounts of additional flour as needed. Put the tortilla in the frying pan to cook on one side until the tortilla is bubbled and the underside is lightly flecked with brown. Flip the tortilla over and press it down with a spatula. Cook until the second side is also flecked with brown spots. Some cooks like to roll out all the tortillas first and cook in two or more frying pans at once.

As you cook the tortillas, stack them and cover them with a towel. If the tortillas are to be filled later and have become too brittle to roll without cracking, you can hold them, one at a time, over steaming water, to make them flexible again.

Makes 12 tortillas
Sodium, 1 tortilla: 1 mg
Calories: 146

Burritos

Burritos, a lot of fun to make with a group of friends, are wheat tortillas rolled around a filling. Make the filling and sauces ahead of time, and have people help cook, fill and roll the burritos.

12	Flour Tortillas (page 209)	12
	Meat Filling for Tacos or Burritos	
	(page 211) or Refried Beans	
	(page 213) or both	
	Guacamole (page 212) (optional)	
	Easy Mexican Sauce (page 208)	
	(optional)	
	low-fat, low-sodium cheese, grated	
	(optional)	

On each tortilla center, spoon 2 to 3 tablespoons (30-50 mL) of the meat or refried bean filling, or you can put on a little of each. If you like, add guacamole, sauce and cheese to the filling. Fold each side of the tortilla over about one inch as if you were making an envelope. Start at the bottom and roll the tortilla, keeping the sides tucked in. Serve with optional garnishes as toppings. A burrito can be eaten with a knife and fork or held in the hand like a sandwich.

Makes 12 burritos

Enchiladas

Enchiladas are another popular Mexican food, consisting of a tortilla with a filling inside and sauce on the outside. Enchiladas are often topped with cheese; they also may be baked in the oven until the cheese melts.

Although traditional enchiladas are made from corn tortillas, you can also make the less traditional Flour Tortillas (page 209). "Tortilla" restaurants serve burritos topped with a spicy sauce strewn with cheese. Serve such a Mexican casserole at home!

12	Burritos with your choice of filling	12
	(above)	
2 c.	Easy Mexican Sauce (page 208)	500 mL
4 oz.	low-fat low-sodium cheese, about	
	⅔ cup (180 mL), grated	120 g

Arrange the stuffed burritos in a 9" × 12" (23-cm × 30-cm) flat baking pan. Pour the sauce over them. Sprinkle the cheese on top. Cover with aluminum foil. Bake in 350°F (175°C) oven for approximately 15 minutes.

Makes 12 enchiladas

Tacos

Tacos—Mexican equivalents of sandwiches or snacks—are crispy, corn tortillas that have been folded in the middle and filled with various fillings. Many brands of no-salt-added taco shells are aids to low-sodium cooking. If you can't find a brand without added salt, estimate that each taco adds a little sodium. For example, each Ortega taco shell has 55 mgs.

To heat taco shells turn oven on to 250°F (120°C). Pull oven rack out. Take a taco shell and place it upside down, so that it is hanging suspended over a metal rod of the oven rack. Repeat with number of shells desired. Heat for a few minutes. You can leave the extra ones hanging in the oven while eating the first ones. Reheat if necessary before serving.

To assemble tacos: Scoop about 2 tablespoons (30 mL) of refried beans or other filling of your choice into a warm taco shell. You probably want to put out small bowls of different foods that people can add to their own tacos. Popular garnishes: Refried Beans (page 213), Meat Filling for Tacos or Burritos (below), chopped fresh tomato, chopped onion, chopped cucumber, shredded lettuce, grated low-fat low-sodium cheese, such as no-salt-added Swiss. Sprinkle a small amount of olive oil and vinegar and spices over the chopped vegetables. You can also fill small bowls with sauces and let people spoon on a little sauce if they want to.

Meat Filling for Tacos or Burritos

This seasoned ground beef is a great alternative filling to refried beans. Or use leftover Chili con Carne (page 214) or Sloppy Joe Filling (page 105) as taco filling.

1 lb.	very lean ground beef	450 g
1	medium onion, finely chopped	1
1	clove garlic, minced	1
1 t.	chili powder	5 mL
3 T.	no-salt-added tomato paste	45 mL
1 T.	vinegar	15 mL
dash	Tabasco sauce (optional)	dash

Sauté the hamburger, onion and garlic over medium heat; drain off the fat. Add the chili powder, tomato paste, vinegar and Tabasco sauce. Stir and heat thoroughly.

Makes enough filling for 8 tacos or burritos, with other garnishes
Sodium per serving: 35 mgs
Calories: 87

Tex-Mex Guacamole Topping

It's best served fresh. If you make it a little ahead of time, cover it well with plastic wrap and refrigerate. Guacamole may turn darker, but the flavor is still good.

2	small ripe avocados or 1 large avocado	2
½ t.	garlic powder	2 mL
½ t.	onion powder	2 mL
2 t.	lime or lemon juice	10 mL
dash	Tabasco sauce	dash
1	chopped ripe tomato (optional)	1

Slice the avocados in half; remove the seed. Using a spoon, scoop out the avocado flesh. Put the avocado, lime or lemon juice and seasonings into a food processor or blender. (Ideally, use the mixing blade of a food processor to mash it. If you use a blender, be careful that it does not become totally liquefied.) Or mash with a fork for chunkier consistency. Add the tomato if desired.

Makes about 1½ cups (375 mL)
Sodium, 1 tablespoon (15 mL): 1 mg
Calories: 18

Chicken Filling for Tacos

2 T.	safflower oil	30 mL
1	medium onion, finely chopped	1
1 lb.	boneless chicken breasts	450 g
½ c.	Easy Mexican Sauce (page 208)	125 mL

Heat the oil in a large skillet. Add the onion and garlic and cook gently for a few minutes until the onion is soft. Add the chicken and cook over low heat; use two forks to tear the chicken into shreds as it cooks. Chicken is cooked when it is no longer pink. Add the sauce and stir.

Makes enough for 8 tacos
Sodium per serving: 34 mgs
Calories: 98

Refried Beans for Tacos or Burritos

Delicious as a side dish or for Tacos (page 211) and Burritos (page 210).

8 oz.	red or kidney beans	225 g
2	onions, chopped	2
2	cloves garlic, minced	2
1	bay leaf	1
1 t.	chili powder (check the sodium content)	5 mL
2 T.	safflower oil	30 mL
3 oz.	no-salt-added tomato paste	85 g

Soak beans according to directions under Beans (page 202), and cook beans with one onion, one clove garlic, bay leaf, and chili powder. Cook for about 2 hours, or until the beans are tender, adding water, if necessary, to prevent the beans from going dry; little liquid should be left. Discard the bay leaf. Heat the oil in a large skillet and add the remaining onion and garlic; stir and cook gently for a few minutes; turn off heat. Add about ¼ cup (60 mL) of cooked beans to the skillet with some of the cooking liquid. Mash with a fork or a potato masher. Continue to add beans and mash them in the skillet. Serve warm.

Makes enough for 8 tacos or burritos
Sodium per serving: 13 mgs
Calories: 147

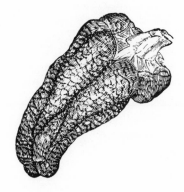

Chili con Carne

With a tossed salad, this is a complete meal. This chili mixture can also be used as a filling for taco shells. If you freeze chili con carne in small amounts (as in an ice cube tray), you can defrost a cube to make a Chili Burger (page 103) out of a plain hamburger.

1 lb.	lean *ground beef*	*450 g*
1 T.	*safflower oil*	*15 mL*
1	*green pepper, chopped*	*1*
1	*medium onion, chopped finely*	*1*
2	*cloves garlic, finely chopped*	*2*
6 oz.	*no-salt-added tomato paste mixed with 2 cans of water*	*170 mL*
3 c.	*kidney beans (cooked without salt)*	*750 mL*
grind	*fresh pepper*	*grind*
1 t.	*oregano*	*5 mL*
½ t.	*paprika*	*2 mL*
1 t.	*cumin*	*5 mL*
1 t.	*chili powder*	*5 mL*

Cook the ground beef in a skillet over medium heat, stirring with a fork and breaking the meat into small chunks until no pink color is left. Drain off any fat. (You can put a double layer of paper towels on a dinner plate and use a slotted spoon to put the cooked meat on the towels.) In the same skillet, heat the oil over medium heat and sauté the onions, chopped pepper and garlic for a few minutes or until tender, stirring frequently. Remove from heat and stir in seasonings. Add the tomato paste and water, drained ground beef and kidney beans. Bring to a boil, lower heat and simmer for about 1 hour.

Serves 6
Sodium per serving: 91 mgs
Calories: 434

Chili non Carne

If you want to make a delicious *vegetarian* version, just leave out the meat. Instead use 3 green peppers, cut into small chunks, and 2 medium onions, chopped. Chili **non** carne is usually served over cooked rice to provide complete proteins.

Popular Chinese Foods

Packaged Chinese convenience foods are high in sodium and Chinese restaurants are off limits for low-sodium eaters. The obvious solution is to cook from scratch at home. But, many of the traditional ingredients in Chinese cooking are high in sodium. Water chestnuts (even fresh ones), soy sauce, canned bean sprouts, dried mushrooms and of course MSG, cannot be used in low-sodium cooking.

Chinese Pepper Steak

Good served over rice or noodles.

1 lb.	boneless steak such as round or sirloin	450 g
1 T.	safflower oil	15 mL
1	clove garlic, peeled	1
4	medium green or red peppers, cut into chunks	4
¼ t.	onion powder	1 mL
3 T.	sherry (not cooking sherry)	45 mL
2 T.	lemon juice	30 mL
1 T.	sugar	15 mL
⅔ c.	boiling water	180 mL
3 T.	cornstarch	45 mL
1 T.	Soy Sauce Substitute (page 62)	15 mL

Place the meat in the freezer to partially freeze it so that it will be easier to slice; slice the meat across the grain into thin strips. If you are using a tough cut of meat, you may want to sprinkle it with an unsalted meat tenderizer.

Heat the oil in a wok or skillet over medium high heat. Add the garlic and cook for a minute or so, or until you can smell the garlic; remove garlic. Add the pieces of pepper to the wok and stir-fry for approximately 3 minutes. If you prefer the peppers less crisp, cook longer. Using a slotted spoon, remove the peppers and reserve. Add the pieces of meat and stir-fry until the pink color is gone, about 4 minutes. Mix onion powder, 2 tablespoons (30 mL) sherry, lemon juice, sugar and boiling water. Add the sauce to the meat with the green peppers. Turn the heat down to medium low; cover and cook for approximately 5 minutes. Meanwhile, combine the cornstarch, soy sauce substitute and remaining sherry, and pour into the wok. Stir for a minute or two, or until the sauce is thickened.

Serves 4
Sodium per serving: 64 mgs
Calories: 279

Egg Rolls

Wonderful for dinner or informal get-togethers. Much better than frozen or store-bought. To make tiny Egg Roll Hors d'Oeuvres, see the instructions in the Snacks and Appetizers chapter (page 83). Buy no-added-salt egg roll wrappers. (We have found them in the vegetable section and in the dairy section of large markets and in oriental specialty stores.)*

¾ c.	onions, diced	190 mL
¾ c.	green peppers, chopped	190 mL
1½ c.	mung bean sprouts or other vegetables, chopped	375 mL
1 c.	cooked chicken or pork	250 mL
1½ T.	sherry (not cooking sherry)	22 mL
1½ T.	lemon juice	22 mL
1½ T.	sugar	22 mL
3 t.	cornstarch	15 mL
1 T.	peanut oil	15 mL
1	clove garlic	1
16	no-salt-added egg roll wrappers	16
	safflower or peanut oil for frying	

Prepare all the vegetables and the chicken or pork: Using a food processor to chop the vegetables or taking the time to dice the vegetables very fine makes the filling look very professional; cut the chicken or pork into narrow strips. Set the vegetables and meat aside. Combine the sherry, lemon juice, sugar and 2 teaspoons (10 mL) cornstarch in a small bowl. Heat one tablespoon (15 mL) of oil in a wok or skillet over medium high heat. Add the garlic and stir-fry for a few seconds; discard the garlic. Add the shredded vegetables to the hot oil and stir-fry for a minute. Add the meat and stir-fry for an additional minute. Add the sherry-lemon sauce and stir to combine all the ingredients. Continue stirring for a minute or two. There should be very little liquid left. Turn off the heat and set aside. To make the sealing liquid, combine the remaining teaspoon (5 mL) cornstarch and ½ cup (125 mL) hot water.

To stuff egg rolls: Place the wrapper on a flat working surface with one of the corners pointing towards you. Spread approximately ¼ cup (60 mL) of filling diagonally on the wrapper. Fold the corner nearest you over the filling. Fold the sides in so that the corners touch. Moisten the last flap with the sealing liquid. Roll the egg roll and seal by smoothing it with your finger. (Egg roll wrappers come with illustrations that make the whole process very easy.) Keep covered to prevent drying.

Pour 2 cups (500 mL) safflower or peanut oil into a wok, skillet, or electric frying pan and heat to 400° F (205° C).

Fry 2 or 3 at a time to maintain the oil temperature. Fry on the first side for 3 minutes or until the underside is crisp and brown. Using tongs or a spatula, turn the egg rolls over and fry for an additional 2 to 3 minutes. Drain on paper towels. Serve hot.

* Egg rolls are often served with dipping sauces. Hot or Mild Mustard are good dips (page 57); Soy Sauce Substitute (page 62) or Sweet and Sour Sauce (page 61) can be used.

Makes 8 egg rolls

Chow Mein

This popular dish can also be made with cooked leftover chicken, turkey or pork and served over rice. The convenient canned fried noodles have approximately 200 milligrams in a small (one-half cup or 125 mL) serving.

1	medium onion	1
½	green pepper	½
6	medium mushrooms	6
1 c.	mung beans, other sprouts, or shredded cabbage	250 mL
10 oz.	boneless chicken breasts	300 g
3 T.	lemon juice	45 mL
1 T.	sugar	15 mL
3 T.	sherry (not cooking sherry)	45 mL
⅔ c.	boiling water	180 mL
1 T.	peanut oil	15 mL
1	clove garlic, peeled	1
2 T.	cornstarch	30 mL

Prepare the vegetables: Cut the onion and green pepper into chunks; slice the mushrooms and sprouts; arrange vegetables on a plate. Cut the chicken into thin strips and have the pieces ready on a plate. Combine 2 tablespoons (30 mL) of the lemon juice, sugar and 2 tablespoons (30 mL) sherry in a small bowl. Stir in the boiling water; set aside.

Heat the oil in a wok or skillet over medium heat. Add the garlic for a minute or so until you can smell the garlic. Add the onions and stir-fry for 30 seconds (push the onion pieces from side to side with a wooden spoon, wok utensil or spatula). Add the green pepper and stir-fry for another 30 seconds. Add the chicken and stir-fry for approximately 2 minutes. (Cooked leftover pieces of meat need only be stirred in for a few seconds to heat.) Add the mushrooms and stir-fry for another minute. Add the sprouts and lemon juice mixture. Stir to combine. Turn the heat down, cover and cook for 3 minutes.

While it is cooking, combine the cornstarch with remaining lemon juice and sherry. Add this to the wok and stir for another minute or two, until the sauce has thickened.

Serves 4
Sodium per serving: 50 mgs
Calories: 206

BREADS

You probably don't know anyone who doesn't like freshly baked bread. But it's too hard and too time-consuming to make, right? Wrong! Just because you have never made bread does *not* mean that you can't. You'll find delicious and quick recipes in this chapter, all low in sodium.

Of course, the companies that make quick bread mixes and ready-to-cook rolls have been telling us for years that only *their* products are convenient. Naturally these companies want us to buy their products. But don't let the ads mislead you into thinking that you need to depend on them.

Those convenient dinner rolls are outrageously high in sodium. For example, two Pillsbury crescent rolls (not packages) contain more than 1,200 mgs of sodium. This is in spite of the fact that the basic ingredients (flour, yeast, shortening) start out with negligible sodium.

For a few minutes of work you can save 1,312 sodium mgs per serving. And you will make the people in your family feel pampered. Extra bread or rolls can be frozen and reheated for later meals.

Homemade bread needs to be sliced thin to make toast. You may want to buy a special "bread knife" or sharpen your old knife. Bread slices more easily after it has cooled. This chapter includes recipes for quick breads, muffins, and yeast breads.

Quick Breads and Muffins

The secret to low-sodium quick breads and muffins: Low-sodium baking powder, unfortunately, is not as easy to use as regular baking powder. We have found that it really helps to do two things: first, always *sift* the flour before measuring it; second, always *shake* and *stir* low-sodium baking powder before measuring it. Do this shaking each time you use it, beginning from the first time you open the jar.

Oat Bran Muffins

The oat bran muffins that you can buy in the supermarket or donut shop may have oat bran, but they also may have more calories, fat and sugar than you would think. As mentioned earlier, an oat bran muffin from a major national donut chain has 122 calories more than the same shop's Bavarian Cream-filled donut covered with chocolate frosting! It also has 35 percent more fat. The recipe below makes delicious oat bran muffins—not dry and tasteless as many homemade oat bran muffins tend to be. They are also a good source of soluble fibre.

1 c.	flour	250 mL
1 c.	oat bran	250 mL
2 t.	baking powder	10 mL
2 t.	cinnamon	10 mL
½ c.	brown sugar	125 mL
½ c.	carrots shredded finely	375 mL
2	large, tart apples (Granny Smith's are a good choice), peeled, cored and shredded finely	2
½ c.	raisins	125 mL
1 c.	chopped nuts (pecans are a good choice)	250 mL
¼ c.	safflower oil	60 mL
½ c.	low-fat milk	125 mL
2	eggs or equivalent egg substitute	2
2 t.	vanilla	10 mL

Prepare muffin pans by spraying with a vegetable coating spray. Combine the flour, oat bran, baking powder, cinnamon and brown sugar in a large bowl. In another bowl, combine the carrots, apples, raisins, nuts, oil, milk, eggs and vanilla. Stir until well-mixed. Pour the wet ingredients over the dry ingredients and stir until well-blended, but don't overmix. Spoon the batter into the muffin tins until they are two-thirds full.

Bake in 375°F (190°C) oven for 15–18 minutes until lightly browned.

Makes 16 muffins
Sodium, 1 muffin (made with egg): 47 mgs
Calories: 158

Blueberry Muffins

3 c.	flour (sift before measuring)	750 mL
½ c.	sugar	125 mL
2 T.	low-sodium baking powder (shake and stir before measuring)	30 mL

½ c.	safflower oil	125 mL
3	eggs or equivalent egg substitute	3
½ c.	skim milk	125 mL
½ c.	water	125 mL
1 c.	fresh or frozen blueberries (don't defrost blueberries before using)	250 mL
	confectioner's sugar (optional)	

Prepare muffin pans by spraying with a vegetable coating spray. Combine the flour, oat bran, baking powder, cinnamon and brown sugar in a large bowl. In another bowl, combine the carrots, apples, raisins, nuts, oil, milk, eggs and vanilla. Stir until well mixed. Pour the wet ingredients over the dry ingredients and stir until well blended, but don't overmix. Spoon the batter into the muffin tins until they are two-thirds full.

Applesauce Muffins

Good to round out a meal any time of day!

1½ c.	flour	375 mL
¼ c.	sugar	60 mL
2 T.	low-sodium baking powder (shake and stir before measuring)	30 mL
½ t.	cinnamon	2 mL
¼ t.	nutmeg	1 mL
1	egg or equivalent egg substitute	1
3 T.	safflower oil	45 mL
½ c.	applesauce	125 mL
¼ c.	skim milk	60 mL
¼ c.	water	60 mL

Prepare 12 muffin cups by coating with a vegetable coating spray or safflower oil. Mix together the flour, sugar, baking powder, cinnamon and nutmeg in a bowl. In another bowl, beat the egg or substitute; add the safflower oil, applesauce, milk and water; mix well. Pour this wet mixture over the dry mixture and stir gently, just enough to moisten. Spoon about ¼ cup (60 mL) of the batter into each muffin cup about ⅔–¾ full.

Bake in 400° F (205° C) oven 15 to 20 minutes.

Makes 12 muffins
Sodium, 1 muffin (made with egg): 8 mgs
Calories: 126

Lemon Bread

¼ c.	unsalted margarine	60 mL
¾ c.	sugar	190 mL
2	eggs or equivalent egg sub- stitute	2
2 t.	grated lemon peel	10 mL
2 T.	low-sodium baking powder	30 mL
2 c.	flour (sift before measuring)	500 mL
¾ c.	skim milk	190 mL
2 t.	fresh lemon juice	10 mL
2 T.	sugar	30 mL

Prepare a bread pan by coating with a vegetable coating or with safflower oil. Combine margarine and sugar in a mixing bowl and beat until the mixture is blended and creamy. Add the eggs or substitute and lemon peel and mix well. Sift together the flour and baking powder. Add about a quarter of the flour mixture to the mixing bowl and blend. Add a splash of milk and blend. Continue alternating flour and milk until all of the flour and milk have been added and the mixture is well blended. Pour the batter into the prepared pan. Bake in 350° F (175° C) oven 50 to 55 minutes until a toothpick inserted in the middle of the bread will come out clean. Mix the 2 teaspoons (10 mL) of lemon juice with the 2 tablespoons (30 mL) of sugar in a small dish. Spoon this mixture over the bread right when hot from the oven. Remove the bread from the pan after it has cooled.

Makes 1 loaf (14 slices)
Sodium, 1 slice: 16 mgs
Calories: 168

Banana Nut Bread

2 c.	flour (sift before measuring)	500 mL
¼ c.	sugar	60 mL
3 T.	low-sodium baking powder (shake and stir before measuring)	45 mL
1	egg or equivalent egg substitute	1
3 T.	unsalted margarine, melted	45 mL
1 c.	mashed banana	250 mL
¼ c.	skim milk	60 mL
¼ c.	water	60 mL
1 t.	vanilla extract	5 mL
¾ c.	chopped walnuts	190 mL

Prepare a bread pan by coating with a vegetable coating spray or unsalted margarine. Melt the unsalted margarine in a small saucepan.

Mix the flour, sugar and baking powder in a bowl. In another bowl, beat the egg or substitute. Mix in the melted margarine, banana, milk, water and vanilla. Pour this wet mixture over the dry ingredients. Add the nuts and stir gently, just enough to moisten. Spoon the batter into the prepared pan. Bake in 350° F (175° C) oven for 50 to 60 minutes. Slice when cool.

Makes 1 loaf (14 slices)
Sodium, 1 slice (made with egg): 8 mgs
Calories: 175

Popovers

Popovers make a special breakfast, brunch or luncheon choice. For a lunch, you may want to serve chicken salad, chicken curry or tuna salad and let people fill their own popovers.

2	*eggs or equivalent egg substitute*	2
1 c.	*skim milk*	250 mL
1 T.	*unsalted margarine*	15 mL
1 c.	*flour*	250 mL

"Butter" or oil 6 custard cups (a vegetable coating spray can also be used). With an electric mixer or a wire whisk, slightly beat the eggs in a bowl. Add the remaining ingredients and beat for about 1 to 2 minutes at medium speed or until smooth; do not overbeat. Ladle the mixture into the custard cups about ⅔ full. Place the cups on a baking pan in a *cold* oven. Turn the oven to 400° F (205° C) and bake for 35 minutes. (It's best not to peek.) Serve immediately (popovers do not stay light and high for very long).

Makes 6 popovers
Sodium, 1 popover (made with egg): 41 mgs
Calories: 142

Yeast Breads

Basic bread ingredients—flour, water, yeast, sugar or honey, oil or un-salted margarine—are all naturally low in sodium. Choose your favorite type of flour, the major ingredient. Most markets carry all-purpose flour, unbleached white flour, rye, whole wheat and bread flour. Be sure *never* to use self-rising flour; it is extremely high in sodium, approximately 1,645 mgs per cup (250 mL). As for bread flour and all-purpose flour, they can be substituted for each other, but you may need slightly more when using all-purpose flour.

Recipes in this book are made with active dry yeast, usually available in packages with three envelopes attached together. In this book, "1 env." refers to one of the envelopes in the package.

Traditional yeast bread recipes always call for some salt to add flavor and control or actually slow down the yeast action. When you leave out the salt, the dough will rise *faster*. This means that you need to be careful *not* to let the dough rise too high to prevent the dough from falling. If the dough drops after it has risen, the baked bread will be flatter and have a coarser texture. It would still be entirely edible, however.

If you are using one of your own bread recipes and you omit the salt, you need to let it rise only about half the time. Recipes in this book have been tested without salt and timings have been adjusted.

Quick Yeast Breads

Quick yeast breads, more like thick batter than traditional kneaded bread, are easy to make because they require no kneading. Even if you have never thought about making your own bread, you can be successful with these bread recipes. And there is nothing like the smell of your own bread baking.

Quick White Bread

Great for people who never thought they could make bread. Also makes very nice toast. A commercial loaf of white bread contains more than 2,300 mgs of sodium.

1 env.	active dry yeast	1 env.
1 c.	warm water	250 mL
2 T.	sugar	30 mL
2¾ c.	bread flour or all-purpose flour	690 mL
2 T.	safflower oil	30 mL
1	egg or equivalent egg substitute	1
1 t.	unsalted margarine (optional)	5 mL

Stir the yeast, warm water and sugar in a large bowl until dissolved. Add about half the flour, oil and the egg or substitute to the yeast mixture. Beat with an electric mixer for 3 to 4 minutes; gradually add remaining flour. Mix until the flour is all blended. The dough will be very sticky. Cover the bowl with a cloth and put it in a warm place to rise until doubled, about 40 minutes.

Oil a loaf pan (non-stick spray is good). Scrape the batter into the loaf pan. Smooth it into the corners. Cover the pan with the cloth and set it in a warm place. Let rise *only* to the top of the pan. While the dough is rising, preheat oven to 375° F (190° C). Bake for about 50 to 55 minutes. If you want the top crust to be soft, rub the margarine over the top as soon as it comes out of the oven.

Makes 1 loaf (20 slices)
Sodium, 1 slice (made with egg): 3 mgs
Calories: 92

Quick Oatmeal Bread

Very quick! It rises once. A commercial loaf of oatmeal bread would have about 3,000 mgs of sodium.

½ c.	boiling water	125 mL
¼ c.	skim milk	60 mL
½ c.	"old-fashioned" oatmeal, not quick or instant oats	125 mL
3 T.	safflower oil	45 mL
¼ c.	molasses	60 mL
¼ c.	warm water	60 mL
pinch	sugar	pinch
1 env.	active dry yeast	1 env.
1	egg or equivalent egg substitute	1
2¾ c.	all-purpose flour	690 mL

Stir together the boiling water, milk, oatmeal, oil and molasses in a mixing bowl. Cool until lukewarm. Meanwhile, put the ¼ cup (60 mL) warm water in a small bowl. Add the pinch of sugar and stir in the yeast. Let sit for 2 to 5 minutes. Add the yeast to the oatmeal mixture. Stir in the egg and about half the flour. Beat for 3 or 4 minutes with an electric mixer, adding the remaining flour gradually. Mix until the flour is blended in and the batter is smooth; it will still be sticky. Oil a loaf pan (you can use a vegetable coating spray). Scrape the dough into the loaf pan; smooth it into the corners. Cover the pan with a cloth and set it in a warm place. Let rise only to the top of the pan. While the dough is rising, preheat oven to 375° F (190° C). Bake for about 50 to 55 minutes.

Makes 1 loaf (20 slices)
Sodium, 1 slice: 6 mgs
Calories: 110

Quick Anadama Bread

Anadama bread combines the flavors of corn and molasses for a delicious taste. It's even better toasted.

½ c.	boiling water	125 mL
¼ c.	milk	60 mL
½ c.	yellow cornmeal	125 mL
3 T.	safflower oil	45 mL
¼ c.	molasses	60 mL
1 env.	active dry yeast	1 env.
¼ c.	warm water	60 mL
pinch	sugar	pinch
1	egg or equivalent egg substitute	1
2¾ c.	all-purpose flour	690 mL

Combine the boiling water, milk, cornmeal, oil and molasses in a mixing bowl; stir. Cool until lukewarm. Meanwhile, pour the warm water into a small bowl, add the sugar, stir in the yeast. Let sit for 2 to 5 minutes, until doubled. Add the swollen yeast to the cornmeal mixture. Stir in the egg and about half the flour. Beat for 3 or 4 minutes with an electric mixer, adding the remaining flour gradually. Mix until the flour is all blended in and smooth but sticky. Oil a loaf pan. Scrape the batter into the loaf pan. Smooth it into the corners. Cover the pan with a cloth and set in a warm place. Let rise *only* to the top of the pan. While the dough is rising, preheat oven to 375° F (190° C). Bake for about 50 to 55 minutes.

Makes 1 loaf (20 slices)
Sodium, 1 slice: 6 mgs
Calories: 100

Quick Whole Wheat Bread

1 c.	warm water	250 mL
1 env.	active dry yeast	1 env.
1 c.	whole wheat flour	250 mL
1¾ c.	white flour	440 mL
⅓ c.	sugar	90 mL
1	egg or equivalent egg substitute	1
¼ c.	safflower oil	60 mL

Pour the warm water in a large mixing bowl, add the yeast and stir. Cover until doubled, about 10 minutes. In another bowl, stir together the whole wheat flour, white flour and sugar. Add about half of the flour mixture to the swollen yeast. Stir and mix in the egg or substitute and oil. Beat for 3 or 4 minutes with an electric mixer and gradually add the rest of the flour. Mix until the flour is blended but moist and sticky. Cover the bowl with a cloth, and set it in a warm place until doubled, around 30 minutes. Spray or oil a loaf pan and scrape the dough into the loaf pan. Smooth it into the corners. Cover the pan with the cloth and set it in a warm place. Let rise *only* to the top of the pan, about 10 minutes. While the dough is rising, preheat oven to 375° F (190° C). Bake for about 50 to 55 minutes.

Makes 1 loaf (20 slices)
Sodium, 1 slice: 3 mgs
Calories: 106

Quick Bran Rolls

Wonderful warmed for breakfast, and they freeze well.

⅓ c.	sugar	90 mL
½ c.	bran	125 mL
½ c.	safflower oil	125 mL
½ c.	boiling water	125 mL
½ c.	warm water	125 mL
pinch	sugar	pinch
1 env.	active dry yeast	1 env.
1	egg or equivalent egg substitute	1
3 c.	all-purpose flour	750 mL

Combine the ⅓ cup (90 mL) sugar, bran, oil and boiling water in a large mixing bowl; stir and cool to lukewarm. In a small bowl pour the warm water, add pinch of sugar and yeast; stir. Let stand for 2 to 5 minutes until doubled. Add the egg to the lukewarm bran mixture and stir well. Mix in the swollen yeast. Gradually stir in the flour. Mix until the flour is blended in and the batter is smooth. Cover the bowl with a cloth and set it in a warm place 2 hours or so, until doubled.

Oil 24 muffin pan cups (non-stick spray is good). Stir the batter and put the batter into the muffin cups, filling each cup about halfway. Cover the pans with the cloth and set it in a warm place. Let rise *only* to the top of the pan. While the dough is rising, preheat oven to 375° F (190° C). Bake for about 50 to 55 minutes.

Makes 24 rolls
Sodium, 1 roll (made with egg): 3 mgs
Calories: 118

Kneaded Yeast Breads

Bread doughs are traditionally made by kneading, although quick "batter" yeast breads, in the previous section, do not require kneading. Kneading is not difficult; a seven-year-old child helped us knead for the recipes in this book.

Usually the wet and dry ingredients are stirred together in a bowl, by hand, electric mixer or food processor, then turned out onto a floured surface, such as a counter top, a kitchen table or a breadboard. Place a small amount, approximately ½ cup (125 mL), of extra flour off to one side of the working area. Use your clean hands to push the dough around fairly vigorously: *push* (with the heel of the hand); *fold* it in on itself and *turn*, a quarter turn; then again, push, fold, and turn. Don't be afraid to keep adding small amounts of additional flour to prevent the dough from sticking. The quantity of flour called for in *any* bread recipe is always approximate. You may have to use more or less.

When dissolving active dry yeast, the temperature of the water is important: It should be 100°–115° F (38°–46° C), slightly warm to the touch. Too high a heat, such as very hot water, will kill the yeast. If you have any doubts about what 100° F (38° C) water feels like, test it with a thermometer until you get used to it.

The fact that temperature affects yeast can be used to your advantage. If you want the dough to rise fairly quickly, you put the dough in a warm place. This is the most common way that it is done. People often put the dough in a turned off oven; a gas oven with a pilot usually provides the ideal temperature. Other warm places around the home include the top of a warm (but not hot) radiator, on top of the refrigerator or any place that is free from drafts.

If you do not find it convenient to bake it right away, slow down the rising action by putting the dough in a covered bowl in the refrigerator. This way the dough will take several hours to rise and you can bake it at your convenience.

After the bread has thoroughly cooled, it can be wrapped. Since homemade low-sodium bread does not have any preservatives, it should be stored in the refrigerator or in the freezer. It may be convenient to slice the bread before freezing it, so that you can take out just one or two slices as needed.

White Bread

2 env.	active dry yeast	2 env.
1¼ c.	warm water	310 mL
2 T.	sugar	30 mL
2 T.	safflower oil	30 mL
¾ c.	warm skim milk	190 mL
5½ c.	bread flour	1.4 L
1 t.	unsalted margarine* (optional)	5 mL

Pour about ¼ cup (60 mL) warm water in a large bowl. Sprinkle the sugar and yeast over the water. Stir and put the bowl in a warm place until the yeast bubbles up, about 5 minutes. If the yeast does not foam up, start with fresh yeast.

Add the remaining cup water, the safflower oil and milk and mix well. Add most of the flour, reserving the rest to work in gradually as needed. Mix well with a large spoon. Sprinkle working surface such as a table or counter top with a thin layer of the reserved flour. Put the rest of the flour in a pile off to the side of the work area. Transfer the dough to the floured surface and knead for about 8 minutes, or until the dough is smooth and elastic; work in small amounts of flour as needed to prevent sticking. To test if you have kneaded enough, press the dough lightly. If it springs back to fill the depression that your fingers made, it has been kneaded enough. Oil bottom of a large bowl. Add the dough and turn it over so it is coated with oil. Cover the bowl with a cloth and put in a warm place until double in bulk, about 45 minutes.

Punch down the dough and turn it onto the working surface. Knead a few minutes. Divide the dough into 2 equal parts and form 2 smooth balls. Spray 2 loaf pans with vegetable spray or brush with oil. Spread the dough into the pans. Cover pans with a clean cloth and rest them in a warm place until doubled, about 30 minutes. Near the end of this rising time, preheat the oven to 375° F (190° C). Bake loaves until golden and they sound hollow when tapped, about 50 minutes.

* If you want the loaves to have a soft crust, brush the top surface of each with a small amount of unsalted margarine right after you take the loaves out of the oven.

Makes 2 loaves (20 slices)
Sodium, 1 slice: 3 mgs
Calories: 80

Soft Rolls

Shape the dough into *round* hamburger rolls or into *long* sandwich rolls. These rolls freeze well. A *commercial* hamburger roll has more than 200 mgs of sodium.

1 env.	dry yeast	1 env.
1 c.	warm water	250 mL
1 T.	sugar	15 mL
1 T.	safflower oil, more to oil the bowl	15 mL
3 c.	bread flour, more if necessary	750 mL
1	egg or equivalent egg substitute (only half is used)	1
3 T.	sesame seeds (optional)	45 mL

Combine ¼ cup (60 mL) of the warm water and the sugar in a large bowl. Sprinkle the yeast over the water and stir. Put the bowl in a warm place until the yeast bubbles up, about 5 minutes. If the yeast does not foam up, start with fresh yeast. Add the remaining ¾ cup water, 1 tablespoon (15 mL) safflower oil and mix well. Add most of the flour, reserving the rest to work in gradually as needed. Mix well with a large spoon or hands. Choose a working surface, such as a table or counter top and sprinkle it with a thin layer of the reserved flour. Put the rest of the flour in a pile off to the side of the work area. Transfer the dough to the floured surface and knead for about 8 to 10 minutes or until the dough is smooth and elastic; work in small amounts of flour if needed to prevent sticking. To test if you have kneaded enough, press the dough lightly. If it springs back to fill the depression that your fingers made, it has been kneaded enough. Oil the bottom of a large bowl. Add the ball of dough and turn it over to coat with oil. Cover the bowl with a cloth and rest in a warm place until doubled, about 45 minutes.

Punch down the dough and knead a few minutes. Divide the dough in 10 equal parts* and roll to form 10 smooth balls. Spray 2 cookie sheets with vegetable spray or brush with oil.

To make *round rolls:* Put the balls of dough onto the cookie sheets, leaving 3 inches (8 cm) between each ball. Fold the edges under to make an even circle. Using the palm of your hands, press each ball to flatten it to 2 to 2½ inches (5 to 6 cm) across.

To make *long rolls,* shape each dough ball between your hands into a sausage shape, about 6 inches (15 cm) long. Place the dough onto the cookie sheets allowing 3 inches (8 cm) between each.

Cover the cookie sheets with a clean cloth and place them in a warm place until doubled in bulk, about 30 minutes. Near the end of this rising time, preheat the oven to 375° F (165° C). If you want sesame seed rolls, use a pastry brush or your fingers to lightly coat the top of each roll with the beaten egg or egg substitute.** Sprinkle the tops with sesame seeds. Bake until the rolls are golden and sound hollow when tapped, about 20 minutes.

* You can make some round and some long rolls. If you want to make larger rolls, divide the dough into fewer pieces before shaping.

** If you want the rolls to have a soft crust, do not put on any glaze before baking. Instead, brush the top surface of each roll with a small amount of safflower oil right after you take the rolls out of the oven.

Makes 10 long or round rolls
Sodium, 1 roll: 6 mgs
Calories: 191

Bread Crumbs

Two easy ways to make low-sodium bread crumbs. You can use commercial low-sodium bread or any homemade bread recipe in this book.

To make bread crumbs in a blender: Toast low-sodium bread; drop small chunks into blender one small piece at a time through the hole in the blender cover.

Rolled bread crumbs: Toast low-sodium bread until dry and crispy. Put the toast in a plastic bag or between two sheets of wax paper, crush with a rolling pin.

It's convenient to make a large batch to store in the freezer. You can take out the amount you need and season as you use it.

Makes ½ cup (125 mL) per slice
Sodium: 7 mgs

Parker House Dinner Rolls

Would you think that rolls with yeast can be ready to eat in just one hour?
Here they are!

2 env.	active dry yeast	2 env.
¼ c.	warm water	60 mL
3 T.	sugar	45 mL
¾ c.	skim milk	190 mL
½ c.	water	125 mL
2 T.	safflower oil	30 mL
4 c.	bread flour or all-purpose flour, more if necessary	1 L
1 T.	unsalted margarine	15 mL

Dissolve the yeast and sugar in the warm water. Set aside for a few minutes until doubled. Meanwhile, pour the milk, ½ cup water and the oil in a
saucepan. Heat until just lukewarm.

Combine the milk mixture, the swollen yeast and all but ½ cup (125 mL)
flour in a large bowl and stir with a large spoon. Knead for 8 minutes, adding extra flour if needed. Cover with a clean cloth and set in a warm place
for 15 minutes.

Turn it out onto a floured countertop. Roll with a rolling pin until it is
approximately ½ inch (1 cm) thick. Cut with a 2-inch (5-cm) biscuit cutter
or plastic top. Fold each circle of dough in half, putting a dot of margarine
in the middle to make Parker House rolls. Place them on a lightly oiled
cookie sheet. Cover with a towel and rest in a warm place until doubled,
approximately 15 minutes. While the rolls are rising, preheat the oven to
350° F (175° C). Bake for 10 minutes.

Makes 24 rolls
Sodium, 1 roll: 10 mgs
Calories: 108

French Bread

Special "French" or "Italian" bread pans, to shape the loaves, are available at hardware and utensil stores. If your family likes long loaves, buy a set; the metal ones are not expensive.

1½ c.	warm water	375 mL
1 env.	active dry yeast	1 env.
2 t.	sugar	10 mL
½ c.	skim milk	125 mL
2 T.	safflower oil, more to oil pan	30 mL
6 c.	bread flour	1.5 L
1 t.	cornmeal for sprinkling	5 mL

Pour ½ cup (125 mL) of the warm water in a bowl and add the yeast and sugar. Stir until it is dissolved; rest for about 5 minutes, or until slightly foamy. Mix the swollen yeast, the remaining cup warm water and 2 T. (30 mL) of oil in a large bowl. Stir in most of the flour with a wooden spoon, reserving a small amount of flour. With the remaining flour, make a small pile on your work surface. Sprinkle a small amount of the flour on the work surface. Turn the dough out and knead about 8 to 10 minutes, working in extra flour to prevent sticking, until smooth and elastic. To test if the dough has been kneaded enough, poke a finger into it. If the dough fills up the hole you poked, it is ready. Brush oil in a large bowl. Put the dough into the bowl and turn it over so that all sides are coated. Cover with a clean cloth and set in a warm place until doubled, about 50 to 60 minutes; do not let the dough rise too long.

Divide the dough into parts: 3 parts for large loaves; 12 parts for hard rolls. To shape the dough, roll into sausage shapes. To prepare the cookie sheets or bread pans, oil and sprinkle with cornmeal. Place the dough on the cookie sheets. Cover with a clean cloth and let rise in a warm spot about 30 minutes. Preheat the oven to 425° F (220° C). While the dough is rising, use a sharp knife to make diagonal slashes 2 inches (5 cm) apart and ¼ inch (.5 cm) deep. Use your hand to brush the surface lightly with water. Bake large loaves about 45 minutes, small rolls about 20 minutes.

Makes 2 loaves (20 slices per loaf)
Sodium, 1 slice: 1 mg
Calories: 84

Garlic Bread

Did you know you could make garlic bread in less than five minutes? Garlic bread is especially delicious when served with chili or spaghetti.

1	French Bread (page 235)	1
2 T.	unsalted margarine	30 mL
2 T.	water	30 mL
1½ T.	garlic powder (not garlic salt)	22 mL

Slice the bread in half lengthwise.

Melt the margarine and mix with the water in a small saucepan. Brush the cut sides of the bread with the melted margarine. Sprinkle with garlic powder. Move the broiler pan 8 inches (20 cm) or so away from the flame. Preheat the broiler.

Broil for 1 to 2 minutes until the top is golden brown. Slice and serve.

Makes 1 loaf

Rye Bread

2 env.	active dry yeast	2 env.
1½ c.	warm water	375 mL
¼ c.	honey	60 mL
3 T.	safflower oil, more to oil pan	45 mL
1¾ c.	rye flour	440 mL
3 c.	bread flour or all-purpose flour	750 mL
2 T.	caraway seeds (optional)	30 mL
	unsalted margarine (optional)	

In a large bowl, combine the yeast, water, safflower oil, honey, caraway seeds, and rye flour. Beat by hand or with an electric mixer until the dough is smooth. Gradually mix in approximately 2½ cups (625 mL) of flour or until the dough can be easily handled; the dough will still be somewhat sticky. Pour the remaining flour to the side of the working area. Knead the dough until it is smooth, about 10 minutes; add extra flour as needed to prevent sticking. To test when the dough has been kneaded enough, touch the top with your finger; it will spring back. Oil a large bowl. Turn the dough around in the oiled surface to coat the dough. Cover with a cloth. Let rise in a warm spot for about 35 minutes.

Punch down the dough and divide it in half. Form each half into a loaf shape.* Place in oiled loaf pans and set pans in a warm spot to rise until doubled, about 45 minutes. Bake in 375° F (190° C) oven for 45 minutes.**

* Rye bread can also be shaped into an oval, placed on a cookie sheet and allowed to double in size. Bake on the cookie sheets the same as above.

** If you want the top crust to be soft, spread with unsalted margarine when they are hot from the oven.

Makes 2 loaves (20 slices per loaf)
Sodium, 1 slice: 1 mg
Calories: 67

Pita Pocket-Bread

You can make your own low-sodium "pocket" bread. Pita only rises once for 30 minutes. That means you can make these delicious sandwich pockets in an hour or so. They are great for lunches and hot sandwiches at home. Make extras for the freezer.

1 env.	active dry yeast	1 env.
1¼ c.	warm water	310 mL
2 t.	sugar	10 mL
3 c.	bread flour, or all-purpose flour	750 mL
1 t.	safflower oil	5 mL

In a large bowl, stir the yeast, water and sugar. Set aside in a warm place until the yeast bubbles up, about 5 minutes. Stir in about 2½ cups (625 mL) of the flour and the oil. Sprinkle a working surface with a thin layer of the reserved flour. Put the rest of the flour off to the side of the work area. Transfer the dough to the floured surface and knead for 8 to 10 minutes until smooth and elastic, working in small amounts of flour to prevent sticking. Divide the dough: If you want mini-pitas, make 12 balls; if you want medium pitas, make 6 balls. Roll each ball into a round about ¼ inch (1 cm) thick. Prepare cookie sheets by coating with a vegetable spray. Place the rounds on the sheets. Cover with a cloth. Let the rounds rise for 30 minutes while you preheat the oven to 500° F (290° C). Bake pita bread for 12 minutes or so until lightly browned.

To serve the mini-pitas slice a lid of about ½ inch (2 cm) off the top of the round. Cut the medium- and large-sized pitas in half and press the inside lightly with your fingers to make the pocket.

Makes 12 small pitas
Sodium, 1 small pita: 1 mg
Calories: 132

Sweet Cinnamon Rolls

These rolls are delicious and great for low-sodium coffee breaks. By comparison, a plain Danish contains 250 mgs of sodium.

¼ c.	warm water	60 mL
1 env.	active dry yeast	1 env.
¼ c.	brown sugar	60 mL
¼ c. + 3 T.	sugar	105 mL
2 t.	ground cinnamon	10 mL
3¾ c.	all-purpose flour	940 mL
1 c.	skim milk	250 mL
1	egg or egg substitute	1
¼ c. + 2 T.	unsalted margarine, melted	90 mL
½ c.	honey	125 mL

Pour the warm water into a small bowl, add the yeast and stir to dissolve; cover until doubled. In another small bowl, mix together the ¼ cup (60 mL) brown sugar, ¼ cup (60 mL) of the sugar and the cinnamon; set aside.

In a large mixing bowl, combine the flour and remaining sugar. Add the milk, the egg, ¼ cup of the melted margarine and the yeast mixture. Stir until combined and put in warm place, covered, for 50 minutes until doubled.

Punch dough down, divide in half and turn onto a lightly floured working surface. Roll half the dough into a 9-inch (23-cm) square. Brush with ½ tablespoon of the melted margarine; sprinkle with half the sugar-cinnamon mixture. Beginning on one end, roll the dough up like a jelly roll. Set roll aside and repeat with remaining half of the dough, ½ tablespoon margarine and sugar-cinnamon mixture. Cut each roll into 9 one-inch (3-cm) slices.

In a small saucepan, combine remaining tablespoon margarine and honey. Pour half the honey mixture into 2, 9-inch (23-cm) round baking pans that have been oiled or sprayed with a vegetable spray. Arrange dough slices, cut side down, in the pans. Cover and let rise until doubled, about 35 minutes. Bake in 350° F (175° C) oven for 25 to 30 minutes. Rest on wire rack for 5 minutes. To remove from pans, invert a plate over the pan, flip the pan over and the glazed part will be on top.

Makes 18 rolls
Sodium, 1 roll (made with egg): 13 mgs
Calories: 209

FRUITS AND OTHER DESSERTS

PEOPLE WHO HAVE been brought up to feel entitled to something sweet after dinner feel deprived without any dessert. Unfortunately, most of the traditional desserts are not good for you; they are high in calories and some are also high in sodium even though they do not taste salty.

If you flip through the dessert chapter in a standard cookbook, you will see recipes that call for ingredients you would never see in cookbooks that promote healthy eating. Saturated fats such as lard, butter and cream, lots of eggs, and sugar are common ingredients in standard cookbooks. Usually the recipes have only a little added salt. But, high-calorie desserts that are made from a lot of eggs, sugar and saturated fats are not good for anyone—even if the desserts are delicious and low in sodium.

Fruit—The Healthy Alternative

Don't overlook fruit for dessert. Fruit is naturally low in sodium and high in vitamins. If a family member expects dessert after dinner, maybe he or she will accept a fruit substitute, at least some of the time.

Fruits are a very logical part of a low-sodium diet because people don't generally feel the urge to salt them. They are also a good source of vitamins and potassium. A high-potassium/low-sodium diet is thought to be even better than a low-sodium diet.

Choose fresh fruit in season. It's pretty easy to know which are in season—look at the prices. The varieties "on special" are your best choice. Some fruits such as bananas are available all year round and the price doesn't seem to fluctuate with the season. Be sure to wash fresh fruits, such as apples, before using.

All frozen fruit is low in sodium. You can buy whole fruit frozen in easy-to-pour bags or packed in syrup. We have called for frozen fruit in several recipes. If you are able to substitute fresh when it is available, this is even better.

Canned fruit is convenient, available all year around and there are a lot of choices of fruit, combinations, syrup and size of the can.

There is no need to buy canned fruit in the low-sodium or diet section of your supermarket. Since canned fruit is already low in sodium, you are just paying extra when you buy no-salt-added fruit.

It's hard to know if there is added sodium in dried fruit without reading the label. *Sodium* bisulfate, for example, may be listed on the label in fine print, even though larger letters say "sun dried."

The USDA booklet, "The Sodium Content of Your Food,"[1] lists these averages: raisins, 17 mgs per cup (250 mL); dried apricots, 12 mgs per cup (250 mL); prunes, 1 mg per prune; dates, 1 mg in 10 dates.

Fruit Desserts

Banana, Pineapple and Rice Dessert

Very low in sodium. Good for people who have used up their daily sodium allowance!

1 c.	cold cooked rice (cooked without salt)	250 mL
1	ripe banana	1
⅓ c.	sugar	90 mL
1½ c.	fresh pineapple, chopped or canned pineapple, drained	375 mL
1 t.	vanilla extract	5 mL

Mash the banana and mix with all ingredients. Blend well. Chill before serving.

Makes 6 servings
Sodium per serving: 2 mgs
Calories: 115

Fruit in Wine

2 T.	sugar	30 mL
2 T.	sweet white wine	30 mL
4	fresh peaches, peeled* and sliced	4
1 c.	fresh or frozen blueberries	250 mL

Heat the sugar and wine in a saucepan over low heat until the sugar dissolves. Add the peaches, cover the saucepan and simmer for approximately 5 minutes over very low heat. Stir in the blueberries. Serve hot or chilled.

* To peel ripe fresh peaches more easily, drop them in boiling water for a minute or so to loosen the skins. If fresh peaches are out of season, substitute canned peaches and omit the cooking step. Instead of peaches, try strawberries with melon, pears with blueberries, cantaloupe with raspberries, nectarines with strawberries or raspberries.

Serves 4
Sodium per serving: 2 mgs
Calories: 104

Apple Crisp

Good warm or cold anytime.

4 c.	apples, sliced	1 L
1 T.	lemon juice	15 mL
¼ c.	flour	60 mL
¾ c.	regular oatmeal (not quick cooking)	190 mL
2 T.	brown sugar	30 mL
3 T.	white sugar	45 mL
1 t.	cinnamon	5 mL
6 T.	unsalted margarine	90 mL
dash	cloves	dash

Arrange the apple slices in a baking pan and sprinkle with lemon juice. In a bowl, combine remaining ingredients to make a crumbly mixture; spoon over the apples. Bake in 375° F (190 ° C) oven for 30 minutes.

Makes 6 servings
Sodium per serving: 3 mgs
Calories: 233

Cherries Jubilee

A spectacular flaming dessert that is traditionally served over vanilla ice cream. If you do not have a chafing dish, you can make it in any ordinary skillet or frying pan.

16 oz.	*dark sweet pitted cherries in light syrup*	*500 mL*
2 T.	*cornstarch*	*30 mL*
2 T.	*sugar*	*30 mL*
¼ c.	*cherry-flavored brandy or Kirsch*	*60 mL*
3 c.	*vanilla frozen yogurt*	*750 mL*

Drain the cherries in a strainer over a bowl; pour the syrup into a measuring cup, add enough water to make 1 cup (250 mL) of liquid.

In a medium saucepan, combine the cornstarch and the syrup mixture, stirring with a wire whisk. Cook over medium heat until the mixture is thickened. Add the cherries; stir. Transfer the mixture to a chafing dish and place over heat. Sprinkle the sugar on top and add the cherry brandy. Using a long-handled wooden match, ignite the dish; allow the brandy to burn itself out. Serve Cherries Jubilee over vanilla frozen yogurt.

Serves 6
Sodium per serving: 2 mgs
Calories: 108
Sodium, ½ cup (125 mL) vanilla: 42 mgs
Calories: 129

Bananas Foster

A spectacular yet easy dessert topping that is traditionally served over vanilla ice cream. This recipe is so delicious, you may prefer it the way we do without the ice cream. It can also be served over lemon sherbet or waffles.

A chafing dish at the dinner table makes a spectacular dessert. But it can be made just as well, and much more conveniently, in a heavy-bottomed frying pan in the kitchen.

4	ripe bananas	4
2 t.	lemon juice	10 mL
4 T.	unsalted margarine	60 mL
2 T.	brown sugar	30 mL
dash	cinnamon	dash
1 T.	white sugar	15 mL
¼ c.	light rum	60 mL

Peel the bananas, cut lengthwise and across into 4 pieces. Sprinkle with lemon juice. In a chafing dish melt the margarine over low heat. Stir in the brown sugar and cinnamon. Add the bananas and cook for approximately 2 minutes, stirring without crushing the bananas. Sprinkle with sugar and add the rum. Use a long wooden match to ignite the rum and serve as soon as it burns itself out.

Serves 4
Sodium per serving: 5 mgs
Calories: 285

Fruit Gelatin

For cooks who would like to make their own gelatin dessert similar to the commercial packages but lower in sodium.

6 oz.	*frozen juice such as orange, defrosted*	*180 g*
2 env. (1 T.)	*unflavored gelatin*	*2 env. (15 mL)*
4 T.	*sugar*	*60 mL*
1 c.	*fruit, such as frozen, sliced strawberries, drained*	*250 mL*

Add enough water to the orange juice concentrate so that you have two cups (500 mL) of liquid. Heat the orange juice in a small saucepan. In a mixing bowl combine the gelatin and sugar. Gradually pour in the heated juice, stirring constantly.

Prepare a gelatin mould or four individual serving dishes by spraying with a vegetable coating spray. Pour the gelatin into the mould or dishes. Refrigerate for 45 minutes. Spoon the drained fruit into the gelatin. Refrigerate again until firm. If you made the gelatin in a mould, unmould before serving.

To unmould: Fill a large bowl with warm water. Put the gelatin mould in the water and hold it there for about 30 seconds. Put a serving plate upside down on top of the mould and flip the whole thing over. The gelatin will come out onto the plate.

Serves 4
Sodium per serving: 3 mgs
Calories: 218

Mandarin Orange Gelatin-Sherbet

11 oz.	canned mandarin oranges	330 g
1 env. (1 T.)	plain gelatin	1 env. (15 mL)
2 T.	sugar	30 mL
1 c.	orange sherbet	250 mL

Drain the liquid from a can of oranges and reserve the oranges. Combine liquid with enough water to make 1 cup (250 mL). Bring to a boil. Dissolve the gelatin and sugar in the liquid. Stir in the sherbet and the oranges and cook over low heat until dissolved.* Spray a mould with vegetable coating spray; pour gelatin into the mould; chill. To unmould, see directions with Fruit Gelatin (page 245).

* If you like, use 2 drops each of red and yellow food color.

Serves 4
Sodium per serving: 8 mgs
Calories: 208

Cool Strawberry Fluff

10 oz. (1¼ c.)	fresh or frozen defrosted straw-berries, sliced	300 g (310 mL)
2 env. (2 T.)	unflavored gelatin	2 env. (30 mL)
1 c.	coarsely crushed ice	250 mL

Drop ½ cup (125 mL) of the strawberries into the blender container and blend the strawberries for about 5 seconds. Turn into a small saucepan and heat over low heat until they begin to boil; pour into the blender. Sprinkle the gelatin over the hot strawberries, cover, and blend for 30 seconds. Add the crushed ice and blend on a low speed for about 20 seconds. Switch to a high speed and blend for about 30 seconds more. Drop remaining strawberries in a bowl and mix in the blended mixture. Pour into individual dishes or a serving bowl. Chill.

Serves 4
Sodium per serving: 1 mg
Calories: 74

Easy Mocha Aspic

½ c.	skim milk	125 mL
1 env. (1 T.)	unflavored gelatin	1 env. (15 mL)
½ c.	cold coffee	125 mL
3 T.	sugar	45 mL
3 T.	non-alkaline cocoa (such as Hershey's)	45 mL
1 t.	vanilla extract	5 mL
1 c.	crushed ice	250 mL

Pour the milk in a small saucepan and heat gently until very hot but not boiling. Combine the milk and gelatin in a blender container; blend on high speed for about 30 seconds. Add the coffee, sugar, cocoa and vanilla; blend for another 30 seconds. Lower speed and begin adding the ice a little at a time (that should take another 30 seconds). Blend on high speed 15 seconds. Chill in individual dishes for at least 30 minutes before serving.

Serves 4
Sodium per serving: 19 mgs
Calories: 79

Ice Cream Sundaes

Ice cream is high in fat and cholesterol. Sherbet is low in both sodium and fat. To make sherbet or frozen yogurt seem a little more special at home, you can add: defrosted frozen strawberries, chilled cut-up fresh fruit, chilled canned fruit, such as canned peach slices, chilled crushed pineapple, a small amount of one of the newer jams made with half the sugar, a liqueur such as green crème de menthe or crème de cacao or Chocolate Sauce (below).

Did you ever consider a fruit sundae? Instead of ice cream or sherbet, use fresh, canned or frozen fruit. Add one of the toppings suggested above. You could make a sundae of crushed pineapple with a little crème de menthe poured on top, for example.

Chocolate Sauce

This not-too-sweet recipe is ideal for your sundae. It makes plain frozen yogurt into a special dessert.

½ c.	*non-alkaline cocoa (such as Hershey's)*	*125 mL*
6 T.	*sugar*	*90 mL*
⅓ c.	*water*	*90 mL*
1 t.	*vanilla extract*	*5 mL*

Combine all ingredients in a saucepan. Stir with a wire whisk over medium heat. Bring to a boil and boil for 2 to 3 minutes, stirring constantly. Remove from heat. Serve immediately or store in the refrigerator. Can be reheated in a double boiler.

Makes ⅔ cup (180 mL)
Sodium, 1 tablespoon (15 mL): 1 mg
Calories: 67

Crepes

This recipe makes 14 five-inch (13-cm) crepes. You can make them in a larger skillet and use Strawberry Filling (below) or a different fruit filling such as blueberries or jam. Try jams with only *half* the sugar added, to cut down on calories.

3 T.	sugar	45 mL
1 c.	skim milk	250 mL
2 T.	safflower oil	30 mL
2	eggs or equivalent egg substitute	2
½ c.	flour	125 mL
2 t.	low-sodium baking powder (shake and stir before measuring)	10 mL
¼ t.	vanilla extract	1 mL
	Strawberry Filling (below)	

Combine all ingredients in a blender container and blend for a minute or so; or mix in electric mixer until batter is smooth. Heat a small oiled skillet or crepe pan until a drop of water "dances" when you splash it on the hot surface. Add ⅓ cup (90 mL) of batter and move the pan around so that the batter covers evenly. Cook over medium heat on one side until edges are browned and there are bubbles throughout the crepe. Turn and cook on the other side to brown. Spoon one-tablespoon (15 mL) strawberries on each crepe and roll crepes up. Spoon remaining strawberries or syrup over the tops.

Makes 14 crepes
Sodium per crepe (made with egg): 18 mgs
Calories: 68

Strawberry Filling

10 oz.	fresh strawberries or frozen strawberries, defrosted	300 g

Slice strawberries. You may use other berries, apples, peaches or other seasonal fruit.

Makes 1¼ cups (310 mL)

Vanilla Pudding

If you're used to pudding mixes, you will be pleasantly surprised at how easy this is and much, much lower in sodium: 76 mgs per half cup (125 mL); commercial, 406 mgs per half cup.

2 c.	skim milk	500 mL
2 T.	unsalted margarine	30 mL
3 T.	cornstarch	45 mL
½ c.	sugar	125 mL
1	egg or equivalent egg substitute	1
1 T.	vanilla extract	15 mL

Heat the milk and the margarine in the top of a double boiler over simmering water. In a bowl, mix together the cornstarch and sugar. Add the eggs or substitute and blend well. Add the vanilla and blend. Pour the cornstarch mixture into the warm milk. Mix with a wire whisk over simmering water until the mixture is thick. A good way to know if it's done is to look for wire whisk patterns; if they stay in the pudding it's done. Cool pudding before serving.

Serves 4
Sodium per serving (made with egg): 79 mgs
Calories: 235

Chocolate Pudding

Enjoyment and calcium from pudding without the added sodium that commercial mixes have. Chocolate pudding from a box mix contains about 400 mgs of sodium in each ½ cup (125 mL) serving, more than 6 *times* the amount in this recipe.

½ c.	sugar	125 mL
2 T.	non-alkaline cocoa (such as Hershey's)	30 mL
3 T.	cornstarch	30 mL
2 c.	skim milk	500 mL
1 t.	vanilla extract	5 mL

Combine the sugar, cocoa and cornstarch in a small saucepan. Add about ½ cup (125 mL) of the milk. Stir with a wire whisk until dissolved and the mixture is smooth. Add remaining milk and vanilla extract. Cook, stirring occasionally until thick, about 5 minutes. Cool before serving.

Serves 4
Sodium per serving: 63 mgs
Calories: 202

Rich Mocha Pudding

To decrease intake of sodium and still have a rich chocolaty pudding, try this recipe.

Substitute 1 cup (250 mL) of brewed or instant coffee (decaffeinated is fine) for an equal amount of milk in the Chocolate Pudding recipe above, or 1 cup (250 mL) each of milk and coffee. Follow the directions for Chocolate Pudding above.

Serves 4
Sodium per serving: 33 mgs
Calories: 165

Scandinavian Pudding

A good dessert to serve to someone who has used up the day's sodium allowance. This is a variation of *Klappgröt*, the traditional Scandinavian dessert.

6 oz.	*frozen pineapple juice concentrate*	*180 g*
2½ c.	*water*	*625 mL*
4 T.	*farina*	*60 mL*
8 oz.	*crushed pineapple, packed in its juice, drained*	*240 g*

Mix the pineapple juice and water in a small saucepan. Bring to a rapid boil. Stir the mixture while gradually adding the farina. Cook gently for 5 minutes or so; remove from heat. Beat by hand or with an electric mixer until the mixture is smooth. Fold in the pineapple. Pour into individual pudding dishes, chill.

Serves 6
Sodium per serving: 2 mgs
Calories: 60

Spicy Fried Apples

This hot dessert is good by itself. But you can fill Crepes (page 249) or top waffles, lemon sherbet, or vanilla ice cream with them, if you are not on a cholesterol-restricted diet.

4	*medium apples*	4
2 T.	*unsalted margarine*	*30 mL*
2 T.	*brown sugar*	*30 mL*
¼ t.	*cinnamon*	*1 mL*
dash	*nutmeg*	*dash*

Peel and core the apples. Slice apples into thin slices. Melt the margarine in a large skillet over low heat. Stir in the brown sugar, cinnamon and nutmeg. Add the apples. Cook gently for 5 minutes or until tender. Stir occasionally so that the apples don't stick but cook on both sides.

Serves 4
Sodium per serving: 2 mgs
Calories: 139

Baked Apples

4	*apples*	4
4 t.	*unsalted margarine*	*20 mL*
8 t.	*sugar*	*40 mL*
4 dashes	*cinnamon*	*4 dashes*
4 dashes	*nutmeg*	*4 dashes*

Use a small paring knife to core the apple; remove the seeds and the hard core. Peel the top quarter of the apple. Line a baking pan with aluminum foil to make cleanup easier. Set the apples in the pan. Into the apple center hole drop 1 teaspoon (5 mL) of margarine, 2 teaspoons (10 mL) of sugar and a dash each of cinnamon and nutmeg. Bake in 350° F (175° C) oven for approximately 40 minutes.

Makes 4 servings
Sodium per apple: 2 mgs
Calories: 126

Elegant Almonds and Fruit

The name says it all!

20 oz.	*pineapple chunks, packed in juice*	*600 g*
16 oz.	*sliced peaches, fresh or canned*	*480 g*
2 T.	*safflower oil*	*30 mL*
4 T.	*slivered almonds (unsalted)*	*60 mL*
1 T.	*lemon juice*	*15 mL*
5 T.	*unsweetened pineapple juice from the can of pineapple chunks*	*75 mL*

Drain the canned fruit, save the juices. Drop the fruit in a serving bowl and refrigerate. Heat oil in a small frying pan, add almonds; cook gently and stir until almonds are lightly browned; remove from heat and cool. Add lemon juice and pineapple juice to almonds and stir; toss over fruit. Refrigerate until serving time. Best served chilled.

Serves 6
Sodium per serving: 3 mgs
Calories: 134

Waffles with Fruit

For a special treat, serve Waffles (page 78) and fruit as a dessert. If you have extra waffles, you can freeze them, defrost, and make them crispy by heating in a toaster or toaster oven. For a delicious and easy topping, slice fresh strawberries or defrost a package of frozen strawberries. Fruit in Wine (page 242) can give you more ideas for toppings.

Fruit and Champagne

This recipe is festive using champagne instead of diet soda. If you decide to substitute champagne for a special occasion, you can estimate that the sodium content will be approximately the same; there will, of course, be more calories in the champagne.

8 oz.	champagne or low-calorie diet soda, such as strawberry or lemon-lime	250 mL
4 c.	fresh fruit, such as strawberries, blueberries or diced peaches	1 L
2 t.	lemon juice	10 mL
1 T.	sugar	15 mL

Chill the champagne or soda. Meanwhile, combine the pieces of fruit in a bowl and sprinkle with lemon juice to prevent darkening. Sprinkle the sugar over the fruit and stir; chill. When ready to serve, place ¼ of the fruit in each of four pretty glass dishes. Pour the champagne or diet soda over the fruit.

Serves 4
Sodium per serving: 6 mgs
Calories (with soda): 68
Calories (with champagne): 218

Cookies and Cakes

Cake mixes and homemade cakes made with regular baking powder are fairly high in sodium. So the way to cut down on the sodium in cakes is to use low-sodium baking powder. We want to warn you, however, that is not nearly as reliable as regular baking powder. Even when you use 1½ times the amount and shake the jar thoroughly, cakes sometimes turn out disappointingly flat. We also tried baking cakes from prepackaged low-sodium cake mixes and were disappointed by the results; the cakes were flat. Convenience products are *high* in sodium: A box of piecrust mix has 2,240 mgs in a box. Try the easy piecrust recipe in this chapter.

Pumpkin Cookies

Soft, moist cookies that pack well and stay fresh longer than other types of cookies.

1 c.	unsalted margarine, more for cookie sheets	250 mL
1 c.	sugar	250 mL
1 c.	canned pumpkin (not pumpkin pie filling)	250 mL
1	egg or equivalent egg substitute	1
1 t.	vanilla extract	5 mL
2 c.	flour	500 mL
2 T.	low-sodium baking powder (shake and stir before measuring)	30 mL
1 t.	cinnamon	5 mL
½ c.	raisins	125 mL
½ c.	unsalted walnuts, chopped	125 mL

Prepare your cookie sheets by spraying with a vegetable spray or by rubbing lightly with unsalted margarine. Beat the margarine until soft; gradually add the sugar and beat until smooth. Add the pumpkin, egg and vanilla. Mix well.

Sift together the flour, baking powder and cinnamon. Add dry mixture to the pumpkin mixture; beat until smooth and rather fluffy. Stir in the raisins and chopped walnuts. Drop the batter by teaspoonfuls on cookie sheets. Bake in 375° F (190° C) oven for 10 to 15 minutes.

Makes 100 cookies
Sodium per cookie: 1 mg
Calories: 80

Holiday Walnut Cookies

These rich cookies are a holiday favorite.

1 c.	unsalted margarine	250 mL
3 T.	sugar	45 mL
1 t.	vanilla extract	5 mL
½ t.	almond extract	2 mL
2 c.	flour	500 mL
1 c.	finely chopped unsalted walnuts	250 mL
	confectioner's sugar for rolling (optional)	

Beat margarine until soft and add the sugar; beat until smooth. Mix in the vanilla, almond extract, flour and walnuts.

Roll dough into balls 1 inch (3 cm) in diameter. Place the balls on cookie sheets. Bake in 350° F (175° C) oven for 20 minutes. If desired, you can roll the cookies in confectioner's sugar while they are still hot.

Makes 50 cookies
Sodium per cookie: 1 mg
Calories: 71

Almond Sugar Cookies

Perfect with a scoop of sherbet.

½ c.	unsalted margarine, softened	125 mL
½ c.	sugar	125 mL
½ c.	sliced almonds, finely chopped	125 mL
1 t.	vanilla extract	5 mL
¼ t.	almond extract	1 mL
1 c.	flour	250 mL

In a mixing bowl, cream the margarine and gradually beat in the sugar. Add the almonds, vanilla, and almond extract. Mix in the flour and blend until the dough is smooth. Shape the dough into a roll about 20 inches long; divide the roll into two sections. Wrap each one in wax paper and refrigerate for at least ½ hour or longer, if you like.

Slice the dough into ¼″ (1-cm) sections. Place the cookies on ungreased cookie sheets. Allow room between them since they spread a little. Bake the cookies in 375° F (190° C) oven for 12 minutes; the edges will be lightly browned. Cool cookies on a rack. Store in an airtight container.

Makes 60 cookies
Sodium per cookie: trace
Calories: 34

Brownies

A cake-like brownie that keeps very well.

10 T.	unsalted margarine	155 mL
6 T.	non-alkaline cocoa	90 mL
2	eggs or equivalent egg substitute	2
½ c.	applesauce	125 mL
½ c.	sugar	125 mL
¼ c.	brown sugar	60 mL
1 t.	vanilla extract	5 mL
1 c.	flour	250 mL
1½ t.	low-sodium baking powder (shake and stir before measuring)	7 mL
½ c.	walnuts, chopped	125 mL

Melt margarine, stir in the cocoa and set aside. In a large bowl beat the eggs with a fork or a wire whisk. Add the applesauce, sugars, and vanilla; mix well. Mix the flour and baking powder and add to batter; stir well to blend. Add the cocoa mixture and the walnuts. Mix until well blended. Prepare a 9-inch (23-cm) square baking pan by spreading lightly with margarine or coating with a vegetable spray. Bake in 350° F (175° C) oven for 30 minutes or so, until a toothpick comes out clean when inserted. Cool and cut into 16 squares.

Makes 16 squares
Sodium per square: 10 mgs
Calories: 178

Pumpkin Oat Bran Squares

Moist and easy to make. You might like to dust the top with confectioner's sugar for a festive look.

1½ c.	flour	375 mL
½ c.	oats, uncooked (not instant or quick-cooking)	125 mL
¼ c.	oat bran	60 mL
2 t.	baking powder	10 mL
1 t.	cinnamon	5 mL
½ t.	ginger	2.5 mL
½ t.	mace	2.5 mL
⅛ t.	cloves	1 mL
2	egg whites	2
1 c.	canned pumpkin	250 mL
½ c.	pecans, chopped	125 mL
½ c.	molasses	125 mL
¾ c.	orange juice	190 mL
¼ c.	safflower oil	60 mL

Prepare a 9-inch (23-cm) square baking pan by spraying with a vegetable coating spray. Mix together the flour, oats, oat bran, baking powder, cinnamon, ginger, mace and cloves in a bowl. In another bowl, beat the egg whites slightly and then add the pumpkin, pecans, molasses, orange juice and oil. Mix well. Pour this wet mixture over the dry mixture and stir gently, just enough to moisten. Spoon into the prepared baking pan. Bake in a 375°F (190°C) oven for 25 minutes or so. Cool before serving.

Makes 16 squares
Sodium per square: 63 mgs
Calories: 138

Peanut Butter Cookies

2 T.	unsalted margarine, more for cookie sheets	30 mL
⅔ c.	unsalted peanut butter	180 mL
¼ c.	sugar	60 mL
¼ c.	brown sugar	60 mL
1	egg or equivalent egg substitute	1
¾ t.	vanilla extract	3 mL
1 t.	low-sodium baking powder	5 mL
1 c.	flour	250 mL

Prepare cookie sheets by spraying with a vegetable spray or by rubbing lightly with unsalted margarine. Combine margarine and peanut butter in a mixer bowl and beat them using an electric mixer. Add the sugars and beat, then add the egg and vanilla; beat well. In a separate bowl, combine the baking powder and the flour; add to the peanut butter mixture and mix thoroughly. Form balls 1 inch (3 cm) in diameter and arrange them on a cookie sheet; leave about 2 inches (6 cm) between the balls. Flatten the balls with a fork. Make a second impression at right angles to the first. Bake in 350° F (175° C) oven for 10 to 12 minutes.

Makes 25 cookies
Sodium per cookie: 4 mgs
Calories: 87

Fudgy Snacks with Peanuts

6 T.	unsalted margarine	90 mL
1½ c.	sugar	375 mL
½ c.	skim milk	125 mL
3 T.	non-alkaline cocoa	45 mL
	(such as Hershey's)	
1 t.	vanilla extract	5 mL
½ c.	unsalted peanut butter	125 mL
3 c.	quick oatmeal (not instant)*	750 mL
¾ c.	unsalted peanuts, chopped	190 mL

Slowly heat margarine in a saucepan, add the sugar and stir until dissolved. Cooking on low heat, add the milk, cocoa, vanilla, and peanut butter; stir. Then add the oatmeal. Cook, stirring constantly, for approximately 3 minutes. Cool slightly. Drop from teaspoon onto wax paper. Using your palms, shape into balls. Roll the balls in the chopped peanuts.

* Or use regular "old fashioned" oats; put them in a blender or food processor to make the pieces smaller.

Makes 52 walnut-sized snacks
Sodium, each snack: 2 mgs
Calories: 94

Oatmeal Cookies

¾ c.	*unsalted margarine*	*190 mL*
¾ c.	*brown sugar*	*190 mL*
½ c.	*sugar*	*125 mL*
1	*egg or equivalent egg substitute*	*1*
¼ c.	*water*	*60 mL*
1 t.	*vanilla extract*	*5 mL*
1 c.	*flour, sifted before measuring*	*250 mL*
2 t.	*low-sodium baking powder* (shake *and stir before measuring)*	*10 mL*
3 c.	*oats, uncooked* (not *instant or quick cooking)*	*750 mL*

Prepare cookie sheets by spraying with a vegetable spray or by rubbing lightly with unsalted margarine. Combine margarine, brown sugar, sugar, egg, water and vanilla in a mixing bowl. Beat until creamy.

Sift together the flour and baking powder and add them to the mixing bowl, mix well; add the oats and mix again. Drop by teaspoonfuls on cookie sheets, leaving room between the cookies to spread. Bake in 350° F (175° C) oven for 12 to 15 minutes. Cool for a minute before lifting them with a spatula.

Makes 80 cookies
Sodium per cookie: 2 mgs
Calories: 47

Strawberry Layer Cake

This unusual cake is made in a way that allows low-sodium baking powder to perform well.

3	eggs or equivalent egg substitute	3
½ c.	sugar	125 mL
1 c.	flour	250 mL
2 t.	low-sodium baking powder (shake and stir before measuring)	10 mL
8 T.	unsalted margarine, melted	125 mL
1 c.	applesauce	250 mL
10 oz.	frozen strawberries, defrosted and drained	300 g

Lightly oil your skillet or griddle and heat it over a low flame on the top of the stove; the skillet should be approximately 6 to 8″ (15 to 20 cm). Beat the eggs and sugar in a mixing bowl on high speed until they are thick. Sift together the flour and baking powder. Add to the egg and sugar; mix gently by hand. Add margarine and mix gently. Pour about ½ cup (125 mL) of batter into the heated skillet; the batter should cover the bottom of the pan and be about the thickness of a pancake. Bake in the oven 5 minutes until the cake is lightly browned. Use a spatula to remove the layer to a serving plate. Pour another ½ cup (125 mL) of batter into the skillet and repeat. Blend the strawberries and applesauce together. Spread a layer of fruit between each of the 3 layers and on the top. Serve within 6 hours for best results.

Serves 8
Sodium per serving: 25 mgs
Calories: 295

Pineapple Upside-Down Cake

⅓ c.	brown sugar	90 mL
1 t.	cinnamon	5 mL
5 slices (7 oz.)	small can pineapple slices	5 slices (210 g)
1 c.	flour	250 mL
1 T.	low-sodium baking powder	15 mL
½ c.	sugar	125 mL
1	egg or equivalent egg substitute	1
¼ c.	skim milk	60 mL
3 T.	unsalted margarine, melted	45 mL

Oil an 8-inch (20-cm) round cake pan or spray with a vegetable spray. Combine brown sugar and cinnamon in a small bowl and sprinkle evenly on the bottom of the pan. Arrange pineapple slices on top of sugar.

To make cake batter: sift together flour and low-sodium baking powder. Add the sugar, egg, milk and melted margarine; beat until well mixed. Pour batter on top of pineapple slices. Bake in 350° F (175° C) oven about 30 minutes or until a cake tester or toothpick inserted in the center comes out clean. Let cool about 10 to 15 minutes. Loosen sides and put a plate upside down over cake. Flip over and remove pan.

Serves 8
Sodium per serving: 16
Calories: 217

Homemade Pies

Homemade pies today are often assembled from piecrust mixes and prepared fillings which, unfortunately, have a lot of added sodium. If you need more information to convince you not to buy them, look at the numbers: 2 crusts from a piecrust mix, 1,968 mgs; Jell-O chocolate instant pudding, 944 (for a small pie).

Fortunately, homemade pies can be made with just a trace of sodium. This does not, however, mean that pie is nutritious. "Mom's homemade apple pie" will always have *many* calories and *few* nutrients. But when you want to bake a pie for a special occasion, at least it can be low in sodium.

Piecrust for Two-Crust Pie

This recipe is for a 9-inch (23-cm) pie with top and bottom crusts.

2 c.	flour	500 mL
11 T.	unsalted margarine	170 mL
⅓ c.	ice water	90 mL

Piecrust for One-Crust Pie

1¼ c.	flour	310 mL
6 T.	unsalted margarine	90 mL
3 T.	ice water	45 mL

Follow the same directions for both.

Put the flour into a bowl. Using two knives or a pastry blender, cut in the margarine until the mixture resembles coarse meal. Add about two tablespoons (30 mL) of water and work it in gently with a fork. Gradually add and mix in the rest of the water using fingers or a pastry blender to work the dough into a ball. Chill dough for 30 minutes; if you are in a hurry, proceed to the next step immediately. If there is enough dough for two crusts, divide the dough in half and let half of the dough wait in the refrigerator while you roll the first crust.

On a lightly floured surface, flatten the dough into a circle with roundish edges. Use a rolling pin to roll the dough into a circle slightly bigger around than the pie pan, rolling from the center outward. Fold the circle of dough over in half and gently lift it onto the pie pan, being careful not to stretch it. Unfold the dough and pat it gently into the pan. Using a kitchen knife, cut off any extra dough that is more than ¾ inch (3 cm) beyond the edge of the pan. Fold the outside dough over to make a double thickness of dough around the rim of the pan. Press the dough edge down with a fork, or use your fingers to make a fluted edge. If the crust will be baked without any filling, prick the crust all over with a fork. Bake in 425° F (220° C) oven for approximately 12 to 15 minutes or until it looks as brown as you would like.

Sodium, ⅛ of a Two-crust pie: 2 mgs
Calories: 265

Pumpkin Pie

1	Piecrust for One-Crust Pie (page 265)	1
½ c.	skim milk	125 mL
½ c.	water	125 mL
1 c.	tofu,* cut into small chunks	250 mL
1 T.	pumpkin pie spice	15 mL
1 T.	unflavored gelatin	15 mL
⅔ c.	sugar	180 mL
1 can (16 oz.)	no-salt-added pumpkin	1 can (450 g)

Prepare piecrust, bake and cool. Put milk, ¼ (60 mL) cup water, tofu and pumpkin pie spice into the blender (in that order). Blend at high speed until the mixture is very smooth. Add the pumpkin to the blender and whip. In a large saucepan dissolve the gelatin in remaining ¼ cup (60 mL) of water. Add the sugar and cook over low heat for about 5 minutes; remove the pan from the heat. Add the contents of the blender to the saucepan. Stir well to combine. Pour into the prepared pie shell. Chill for several hours.

* If your store has more than one kind of tofu (soybean curd), choose the soft one.

Serves 8
Sodium, ⅛ of the pie: 11 mgs
Calories: 128

Cherry Pie

This makes a nine-inch (23-cm) pie.

	Piecrust for Two-Crust Pie (page 265)	
2 lb.	canned, pitted, dark sweet cherries*	900 g
1¼ c.	sugar	310 mL
⅓ c.	cornstarch	90 mL
¼ t.	red food color (optional)	1 mL

Prepare the piecrust dough and chill in the refrigerator while you make the filling. Drain the cherries and reserve the liquid. In a saucepan, mix the sugar and the cornstarch. Stir in one cup (250 mL) of the reserved liquid (discard the rest). Use a wire whisk to stir and cook over medium heat for approximately 7 minutes, or until the mixture is thick; cook for another minute. Remove from the heat and add the cherries and the optional food coloring. Stir to mix. Divide the chilled dough and roll half out to fit a 9-inch (23-cm) pie pan. Crimp the edges. Pour the filling into the prepared bottom crust. Roll out the second half of the dough and place it over the filling. Using a kitchen knife, make a few vent holes in the top crust (this will allow steam to escape). Crimp the edges.

Bake in 400° F (205° C) oven for approximately 50 minutes.

* Comstock new Lite cherry pie filling is made without salt; you may want to try it instead of making homemade. If you are lucky enough to have fresh cherries, you only have to adjust the sugar to taste.

Serves 8
Sodium, ⅛ of the pie: 3 mgs
Calories: 488

Fruit Tart

Really yummy, easy enough for a novice cook and very impressive. Most tart pans are 9½ inches (24 cm) across the bottom. If you do not have a tart pan, you can use a 9-inch (23-cm) pan. Or you could use this recipe and two 8-inch (20-cm) pie pans to make two smaller tarts.

1½ c.	flour	375 mL
8 T.	unsalted margarine	125 mL
3 T.	ice water	45 mL
	Vanilla Pudding (page 250)	
	Fresh or canned fruit, drained*	

Follow the directions for Piecrust (page 250). Prick the crust all over with a fork and bake it at 425° F (220° C) for about 10 minutes. Let the crust cool before adding the filling. Top your tart with slices of fresh or drained canned fruit.

* Sometimes melted jelly is lightly brushed on the top of a fruit tart as a glaze. Apple jelly makes a clear glaze; strawberry jelly makes a pink glaze.

Banana Cream Pie

1	Piecrust for One-Crust Pie (page 265)	1
1	Vanilla Pudding (page 250)	1
2	large or 3 medium bananas, sliced*	2

Prepare piecrust for one-crust pie; bake and cool. Make vanilla pudding and stir bananas into the pudding. Put the pudding into the pie shell. If the pie will not be served right away, cover with plastic wrap and refrigerate.

* If you want the pie to look fancy, add a few slices of banana to the top just before serving.

Serves 8
Sodium, ⅛ of a pie: 40 mgs
Calories: 172

Apple Pie

This recipe makes a nine-inch (23-cm) pie.

	Piecrust for Two-crust Pie (page 265)	
6 c.	apples, peeled and sliced	1.5 L
½ c.	sugar	125 mL
1 T.	cornstarch	15 mL
½ t.	cinnamon	2 mL
¼ t.	nutmeg	1 mL

Roll out one-half of the piecrust and spread in a 9-inch (23-cm) pie pan. In a large bowl, mix the apple slices with sugar, cornstarch, cinnamon and nutmeg. Turn the seasoned apple slices into the pie crust. Roll out the top crust and put it on the pie. Crimp or flute all around the rim of the pie. Cut several holes or vents in the top crust. Bake in 425° F (220° C) oven for approximately 50 minutes.

Serves 8
Sodium, ⅛ of the pie: 4 mgs
Calories: 362

Appendix

The Sodium and Calorie Content
of Fresh and Convenience Foods and Seasonings

(Tables were compiled from United States Dept. of Agriculture (USDA) *Nutritive Value of American Foods in Common Units*—Agriculture Handbook No. 456, USDA *Composition of Foods*—Agriculture Handbook No. 8 and USDA Home and Garden Bulletin No. 233—*The Sodium Content of Your Food* and manufacturers' data. Nutritional information marked with asterisk (*) in Table 2: Cooking Aids and Seasonings (page 270) was supplied by the American Spice Trade Association, which researched and developed the data. Sodium content in prepared and convenience foods is subject to change. Various sources do not always agree on the exact sodium content of specific foods and food products. Trademarks are noted with capitalization of registered names, according to the stylesheet of The United States Trademark Association.)

Table 1: Beverages

Food	Portion	Sodium (milligrams)	Calories
Alcoholic			
Beer	12 fluid ounces	25	151
Gin, rum, whiskey (80			
proof)	2 fluid ounces	1	130
Wine			
Table	¼ cup	4	100
Dessert (sherry, mar-			
sala, etc.)	¼ cup	4	164
Breakfast drink, instant			
Grape	8 fluid ounces	1	125
Citrus fruits	8 fluid ounces	14	124
Carbonated			
Club soda	8 fluid ounces	39	0
Cola			
Pepsi	8 fluid ounces	trace	105
Coke	8 fluid ounces	trace	96
Low-calorie cola ...	8 fluid ounces	21	0
Diet 7-Up	8 fluid ounces	25	3
Fruit-flavored			
Regular	8 fluid ounces	34	128
Low-calorie	8 fluid ounces	46	0

Food	Portion	Sodium (milligrams)	Calories
Ginger ale	8 fluid ounces	13	86
Root beer	8 fluid ounces	24	106
Cocoa mix, water-added, Food Club	6 fluid ounces	150	110
Coffee			
Brewed	8 fluid ounces	2	3
Chase & Sanborn	1 cup	1	2
Instant			
Regular	8 fluid ounces	1	trace
Decaffeinated	8 fluid ounces	1	3
With chicory	8 fluid ounces	7	8
Tea			
Hot			
Brewed	8 fluid ounces	1	0
Tenderleaf bag	1 cup	0	1
Instant	8 fluid ounces	2	4
Iced			
Canned	8 fluid ounces	9	80
Powdered, lemon-flavored			
Sugar-sweetened	8 fluid ounces	1	85
Low-calorie	8 fluid ounces	15	2
Thirst quencher, Gatorade	8 fluid ounces	16	7

Table 2: Cooking Aids and Seasonings

Allspice*	1 teaspoon	1.4	6
Bacon, imitation crumbles, French's	1 teaspoon	40	6
Baking powder	1 tablespoon	1,278	9
Calumet	1 teaspoon	405	
Low-sodium	1 tablespoon	1	23
Featherweight	1 teaspoon	2	8
Baking soda	1 tablespoon	2,463	
Barbecue seasoning, French's	1 teaspoon	70	6
Basil* ,..............	1 teaspoon	0.4	3
Bay leaves*	1 teaspoon	0.3	5
Beef flavor stock base,			

Food	Portion	Sodium (milligrams)	Calories
French's	1 teaspoon	470	8
Caraway seed*	1 teaspoon	0.4	8
Cardamom seed*	1 teaspoon	0.2	
Celery salt, French's	1 teaspoon	1,430	2
Celery seed*	1 teaspoon	4.1	11
Chili powder	1 teaspoon	31	7
French's	1 teaspoon	1	
Chicken flavor stock base,			
French's	1 teaspoon	480	8
Cinnamon*	1 teaspoon	0.2	6
Cinnamon sugar, French's	1 teaspoon	0	16
Cloves*	1 teaspoon	4.2	
Coriander seed*	1 teaspoon	0.3	
Cumin seed*	1 teaspoon	2.6	7
Curry powder, no-salt-			
added	1 teaspoon	1	7
Dill seed*	1 teaspoon	0.2	9
Fennel seed*	1 teaspoon	1.9	8
Garlic			
Fresh	1 clove	1	4
Powder*	1 teaspoon	0.1	5
Salt, French's	1 teaspoon	1,850	4
Salt, French's with			
parsley	1 teaspoon	1,050	6
Ginger*	1 teaspoon	0.5	6
Hickory smoke, Wright's	1 teaspoon	trace	2
Hickory smoke salt,			
French's	1 teaspoon	1,170	2
Horseradish, prepared ...	1 tablespoon	198	
Featherweight, imitation	1 tablespoon	3	100
Horseradish, raw	1 pound	26	
Ketchup			
Regular	1 tablespoon	156	19
Tilli Lewis, imitation ..	1 tablespoon	10	8
Lemon juice	1 teaspoon	0.3	1
Lemon and pepper season-			
ing, French's	1 teaspoon	800	6
Mace*	1 teaspoon	1.3	
Marjoram*	1 teaspoon	1.3	

Meat tenderizer

Food	Portion	Sodium (milligrams)	Calories
Adolph's unseasoned .	1 teaspoon	1,830	2
Adolph's low-sodium .	1 teaspoon	10	2
French's meat tenderizer	1 teaspoon	1,760	2
MSG (monosodium gluta-mate)	1 teaspoon	492	
Mustard			
Powder*	1 teaspoon	0.1	9
Prepared	1 teaspoon	65	8
Maitre Jacques no-salt Dijon	1 teaspoon	1.3	
Nutmeg*	1 teaspoon	0.2	11
Olives			
Green	4 olives	323	
Ripe, mission	3 olives	96	18
Onion			
Powder*	1 teaspoon	0.8	8
Salt	1 teaspoon	1,620	4
French's	1 teaspoon	1,620	6
Oregano*	1 teaspoon	0.3	6
Paprika*	1 teaspoon	0.4	7
Parsley			
Dried	1 teaspoon	6	4
Flakes*	1 teaspoon	5.9	4
Fresh	1 tablespoon	2	2
Pepper			
Black or white*	1 teaspoon	0.2	9
Chili*	1 teaspoon	0.2	
Red*	1 teaspoon	0.2	9
Pickles			
Bread-and-butter	2 slices	101	10
Dill	1 pickle	928	1
Low-sodium dill	1 small pickle	100	
Featherweight			
Sliced cucumber pickles	1 ounce	5	12
Kosher dill	1 ounce	5	4
Sweet	1 pickle	128	18
Poppy seed*	1 teaspoon	0.2	13
Relish, sweet	1 tablespoon	124	21
Rosemary*	1 teaspoon	0.5	5

Food	Portion	Sodium (milligrams)	Calories
Sage*	1 teaspoon	0.1	4
Salt	1 teaspoon	2,325	
Salt, imitation butter-fla-			
vored, French's	1 teaspoon	1,090	8
Sauces			
A-1	1 tablespoon	275	12
Barbecue sauce, Kraft .	1 tablespoon	475	20
Hickory smoke, Kraft	1 tablespoon	475	16
Chili			
Regular	1 tablespoon	227	16
Low-sodium	1 tablespoon	11	16
Featherweight	1 tablespoon	10	8
Soy sauce	1 tablespoon	1,029	11
Tarter sauce, Kraft	1 tablespoon	160	180
Teriyaki	1 tablespoon	690	
Worcestershire	1 tablespoon	206	12
Savory*	1 teaspoon	0.3	
Seafood seasoning,			
French's	1 teaspoon	1,410	2
Seasoning salt, French's .	1 teaspoon	1,230	2
Sesame seed*	1 teaspoon	0.6	9
Sloppy Joe seasoning mix,			
Durkee's	1 ounce	3,512	
Tabasco	¼ teaspoon	6	
Tarragon*	1 teaspoon	1.0	
Tartar	1 tablespoon	182	74
Thyme*	1 teaspoon	1.2	
Turmeric*	1 teaspoon	0.2	
Vanilla extract	1 teaspoon	trace	
Vinegar	1 cup	2	34
Yeast			
Baker's dry	1 envelope	1	20
Fleischmann's active dry	¼ ounce	10	20
Fleischmann's fresh			
active	.6 ounce	5	15

Table 3: Convenience Foods

Food	Portion	Sodium (milligrams)	Calories
Bisquick mix	2 ounces	700	240
Cake, muffin and pie mixes (when mixed)			
Betty Crocker fudge brownie mix	¹⁄₂₄ of 21½-ounce box	95	130
Betty Crocker piecrust mix	¹⁄₁₆ box	140	120
Betty Crocker wild blueberry muffin mix	¹⁄₁₂ pack	155	120
Comstock Lite cherry pie filling	3⅓ ounces	10	80
Duncan Hines carrot cake mix	¹⁄₁₂ box	265	250
Duncan Hines devil's food cake mix	¹⁄₁₂ box	400	200
Featherweight cake and cookie mix	1″ slice	5	170
Pillsbury Plus cake mix, dark chocolate	¹⁄₁₂ cake	440	260
Pillsbury Plus cake mix, chocolate mint	¹⁄₁₂ cake	375	250
Pillsbury Plus cake mix, white	¹⁄₁₂ cake	300	240
Pillsbury Bundt brand cake mix, tunnel of fudge	¹⁄₁₆ cake	315	270
Pillsbury Streusel Swirl, devil's food	¹⁄₁₆ cake	340	260
Pillsbury coffee cake, butter pecan mix	⅛ cake	335	310
Pillsbury gingerbread mix	1-3″ square	340	190
Pillsbury All Ready pie crust	⅛ of 2 pie crusts	325	240
Royal cheesecake mix	⅛ package	450	230
Cakes and cookies (not mixes)			
Featherweight low-sodium cake	½″ slice	6	200
Featherweight chocolate chip cookies	1 cookie	6	40

Food	Portion	Sodium (milligrams)	Calories
Featherweight lemon cookies	1 cookie	3	40
Pillsbury apple turnovers .	1 turnover	305	170
Stella D'Oro peach-apricot pastry	1 pastry	less 10	90
Candy and food bars			
Baby Ruth	1.6 ounces	100	260
Butterfinger	1.6 ounces	70	220
Granola bar, Nature Valley Oats 'n honey, chewy style	1 bar	65	110
Peanut brittle, Kraft	1 ounce	145	140
Reggie! bar	2 ounces	40	290
Pillsbury			
Figurines double chocolate	2 bars	130	275
Figurines chocolate peanut butter	2 bars	115	275
Food sticks chocolate malt	4 sticks	110	180
peanut butter	4 sticks	160	180
Canned products			
Bamboo shoots, La Choy	¼ cup	7	6
Bean sprouts, La Choy ..	⅔ cup	25	8
Chees0s, Franco-American	7½ ounces	852	170
Chicken, chunk, Swanson	2½ ounces	440	120
Chili sauce, Featherweight	1 tablespoon	10	8
Chili sauce with beans, Featherweight	7½ ounces	75	270
Chinese mixed vegetables, La Choy	½ cup	35	12
Chow mein noodles, La Choy	½ cup	205	150
Macaroni and cheese, Franco-American	7⅜ ounces	960	170
Pork and beans in tomato sauce, Libby's	1 cup	850	270
Ravioli, beef, Featherweight	8 ounces	75	260

Food	Portion	Sodium (milligrams)	Calories
Refried beans, Old El Paso	100 grams	360	
Refried beans with sausage, Old El Paso	½ cup	312	194
Refried beans with green chilies, Old El Paso ...	½ cup	279	92
Spaghetti and meatballs, Featherweight	7½ ounces	65	200
Spaghetti in tomato sauce, with cheese, Franco-American	7⅜ ounces	820	170
SpaghettiOs with little meatballs in tomato sauce, Franco-American	7⅜ ounces	1,125	210
Water chestnuts, La Choy	¼ cup	15	16
Cookies and cookie mixes Duncan Hines cookie mix, chocolate chip	2 cookies	95	150
Featherweight chocolate chips	1 cookie	6	40
Featherweight lemon cookies	1 cookie	3	40
Pillsbury slice'n bake Fudge brownies	1 brownie	240	250
Oatmeal raisin cookies .	3 cookies	75	160
Dehydrated potatoes, scalloped, Betty Crocker	½ cup	570	14
Fast foods Burger King Whopper with everything	1 Whopper	990	630
Burger King Whopper double beef with cheese ...	1 Whopper	1,535	950
Burger King french fries ..	1 package	230	210
Burger king vanilla shake .	1 shake	320	340
Frozen products Chicken, fried, breast portions, Swanson	1 dinner (11 ounces)	1,357	590

Food	Portion	Sodium (milligrams)	Calories
Chicken meat pie, Swanson	8 ounces	1,110	450
Hungry-Man boneless chicken dinner, Swanson	19-ounce dinner	2,040	630
Hungry-Man chicken pie, Swanson	16 ounces	2,020	780
Salisbury steak, Swanson	11½ ounces	1,055	500
Three-course dinner, Mexican	18-ounce dinner	2,040	630
Turkey, Swanson	11½ ounces	1,060	360
Gravy, brown Franco-American, canned with onions	2 ounces	340	25
Ice cream toppings Butterscotch, artificial flavor, Kraft	1 tablespoon	65	60
Fudge topping, Kraft ...	1 tablespoon	50	70
Whipped topping, Kraft	¼ cup	10	35
Puddings Chocolate, prepared with whole milk, dark 'n sweet, Royal	½ cup	365	190
Lemon, no-salt-added, pudding and pie filling, Estee reduced calorie .	½ cup	5	100
Pistachio nut, or coconut, prepared with whole milk, Royal	½ cup	320	170
Rice pudding, as prepared	½ cup	155	170
Tapioca, Minute, dry ...	1 tablespoon	2	
Vanilla, butterscotch, coffee, lemon or banana, Royal, as prepared ...	½ cup	245	180
Shake 'n Bake mix	2 ounces	1,925	
Barbecue style	⅕ of envelope	450	

Food	Portion	Sodium (milligrams)	Calories
Snacks			
Chee-tos	1 ounce	360	160
Cheez balls and curls,			
Planters	1 ounce	300	160
Corn chips, Fritos	1 ounce	180	160
Corn chips, Planters	1 ounce	220	170
Cracker Jack	1 ounce	85	120
Nacho cheese tortilla chips			
Doritos	1 ounce	175	140
Planters	1 ounce	170	130
Potato chips			
Lay's	1 ounce	260	150
Lay's sour cream and			
onion	1 ounce	335	160
Planters stackables	1 ounce	210	150
Wise, no-salt-added ..	1 ounce	20	150
Pretzels			
Planters pretzel twists			
and sticks	1 ounce	480	110
Reismann Dutch style,			
unsalted	1 ounce	50	
Rold Gold pretzel twists			
....	1 ounce	410	110
Pringles rippled	1 ounce	250	160
Tortilla chips, Doritos,			
crispy lights	1 ounce	165	150
Soups (canned)			
Bouillon, chicken, Feather-			
weight	1 teaspoon	5	18
Broth, instant low-sodium,			
Herb-Ox	1 packet	5	12
Campbell's			
Chicken noodle, as pre-			
pared	8 ounces	960	70
Low-sodium, chicken			
noodle, ready to serve			
....	8 ounces	100	180
Vegetable soup, as pre-			
pared	8 ounces	820	80

Food	Portion	Sodium (milligrams)	Calories
Chunky chicken with rice	½ can of 9½-ounce can	1,160	140
Chunky beef	½ can of 9½-ounce can	1,025	170
Chunky old-fashioned vegetable-beef	½ can of 9½-ounce can	852	160
Chunky steak and potato	½ can of 9½-ounce can	1,225	170
Featherweight soups with no-added-salt or sugar			
Chicken soup base	5.3 grams	1	25
Chicken noodle	1 cup	40	60
Condensed tomato	1 cup	27	30
Vegetable-beef soup	1 cup	19	85
Health Valley vegetable soup	1 cup	60	
Soups (dehydrated, dry)			
Lipton onion	1 cup	800	
Lipton vegetable-beef and shells	1 cup	1,215	514
Lipton chicken rice	1 cup	1,164	492
Spaghetti sauce (canned)			
Sano's, no-salt meatless	½ cup	40	

Table 4: Dairy Products

Food	Portion	Sodium (milligrams)	Calories
Cheese			
Natural			
Blue	1 ounce	396	104
Brick	1 ounce	159	105
Camembert	1 ounce	239	85
Cheddar			
Regular	1 ounce	198	113
Low-sodium	1 ounce	6	
Kraft Cracker-			
barrel sharp ..	1 ounce	280	90
Featherweight			
no-salt-added .	1 ounce	5	110
Colby	1 ounce	171	
Featherweight no-			
salt-added	1 ounce	5	110
Cottage, regular ...	1 cup	515	239
Cottage, low-fat ...	1 cup	421	125
Cream	3-ounce package	213	318
Kraft whipped			
Philadelphia ..	1 ounce	70	100
Old Pennsylva-			
nia low-			
sodium	1 ounce	30	100
Gouda	1 ounce	232	
No-salt-added ...	100 grams	50	
Gruyère	1 ounce	95	
Limburger	1 ounce	227	98
Monterey	1 ounce	152	
Mozzarella			
Whole milk	1 ounce	106	
Part skim milk ..	1 ounce	132	80
Muenster	1 ounce	178	
New Holland			
natural	1 ounce	100	90
Parmesan			
Grated	1 ounce	247	132
Kraft	1 ounce	455	110
Provolone	1 ounce	248	90

Food	Portion	Sodium (milligrams)	Calories
Ricotta			
Whole milk	½ cup	104	213
Part skim milk ..	½ cup	155	190
Swiss	1 ounce	201	105
Dorman's no-salt-added	1 ounce	8	105
Dorman's no-salt-added, grated	1 cup	32	420
Pasteurized processed cheese			
American	1 ounce	332	105
Kraft singles	1 ounce	405	90
Kraft Light n' Lively singles ...	1 ounce	415	70
Low-sodium	1 ounce	2	
Swiss	1 ounce	388	90
Cheese food			
American	1 ounce	337	92
Kraft Velveeta	1 ounce	430	80
Cheese spread			
American	1 ounce	461	82
Kraft Cheez Whiz .	1 ounce	590	80
Cream products, imitation			
Sour, cultured	1 ounce	29	
Cream, sour, cultured	1 tablespoon	5	28
Cream, sweet			
Light	1 tablespoon	6	32
Heavy whipping	1 cup	76	838
Milk			
Fluid			
Whole 3.5%	1 cup	122	159
Skim	1 cup	127	88
Buttermilk, cul-tured, salted	1 cup	257	88
Canned milk			
Evaporated			
Whole	1 cup	297	345
Skim	1 cup	294	200

Food	Portion	Sodium (milligrams)	Calories
Sweetened con-			
densed	1 cup	343	982
Dry milk			
Nonfat			
Instant	1 cup	425	527
Milk desserts			
Custard, baked	1 cup	209	305
Puddings, made			
from mixes			
Butterscotch			
Regular,			
whole milk	½ cup	245	160
Instant, whole			
milk	½ cup	445	180
Ready to serve			
....	1 can	290	
Chocolate			
Regular,			
whole milk	½ cup	195	180
Instant, whole			
milk	½ cup	470	190
Ready to serve			
....	1 can	262	
Vanilla			
Regular,			
whole milk	½ cup	200	160
Instant, whole			
milk	½ cup	400	180
Ready to serve			
....	1 can	279	
Tapioca, cooked	½ cup	130	160
Milk desserts, frozen			
Ice cream	1 cup	84	257
Ice milk	1 cup	89	199
Sherbet, orange	1 cup	19	259
Yogurt			
Plain			
Regular	8 ounces	106	140
Low-fat	8 ounces	115	113
With fruit	8 ounces	133	

Table 5: Eggs, Fish and Seafood, Meats, Poultry

Food	Portion	Sodium (milligrams)	Calories
Eggs			
Whole	1 egg	59	82
Fleischmann's Egg			
Beaters	¼ cup	90	30
Tilli Lewis Eggstra	½ cup of 7-ounce pack	105	50
Fish and seafood			
Finfish			
Bass, black sea, raw, flesh only	1 pound	308	422
Bluefish, flesh only ..	1 pound	336	531
Catfish, raw, flesh only	1 pound	272	467
Cod, flesh only	1 pound	318	354
Cod, dehydrated	1 pound	36,742	1,701
Flounder, flesh only ..	1 pound	352	358
Haddock, flesh only .	1 pound	277	358
Halibut, flesh only ...	1 pound	245	454
Herring, raw	1 pound	336	445
Herring, smoked	1 pound	28,264	1,361
Perch, ocean, flesh only	1 pound	286	431
Perch, fresh water, flesh only	1 pound	308	413
Pike, flesh only	1 pound	231	422
Rockfish, oven-steamed, flesh only	1 pound	272	440
Salmon steak, not brined	1 pound	290	540
Canned sockeye, salt-added	1 pound	2,368	776
Sardines, canned, drained	1 pound	3,062	755
Snapper, raw, flesh only	1 pound	304	422
Trout, lake, raw	1 pound	357	1,093
Tuna, canned Light meat, chunk			

Food	Portion	Sodium (milligrams)	Calories
Oil pack	6½-ounce can	1,472	530
Water pack	6½-ounce can	1,610	234
Balanced dietetic white .	7-ounce can	100	240
Whitefish, flesh only .	1 pound	236	703
Shellfish			
Clams, raw			
Hard (quahogs, cherrystones, littlenecks)	1 cup	465	182
Soft	1 cup	82	186
Crab			
Canned, drained	1 cup	16,000	162
Fresh	3 ounces	314	108
Lobster, boiled, flesh only	1 pound	953	431
Mussels, raw	3 ounces	243	81
Oysters, raw	1 cup	175	158
Scallops			
Raw	3 ounces	217	95
Shrimp			
Raw, in shell	1 pound	438	285
Canned	1 pound	10,427	337
Chicken			
Chicken breasts, raw with bone	2 pounds	266	546
Chicken, light meat, cooked, flesh only	12 ounces	218	565
Chicken, light meat, roasted, without skin ..	3 ounces	54	141
Cornish Game Hens (one pound raw hen yields approximately 6 ounces of cooked meat)	1 hen	137	232
Cold cuts			
Bologna, beef	1 ounce	220	95
Braunschweiger liverwurst	1 slice	324	78

Food	Portion	Sodium (milligrams)	Calories
Frankfurter	1 frankfurter	639	136
Ham, deviled	1 ounce	253	85
Ham, Dietz & Watson low-salt, cooked	1 ounce	230	
Kielbasa	2 ounces	280	190
Olive loaf	1 ounce	312	65
Pepperoni	1 ounce	122	142
Salami, cooked (beef) ...	1 ounce	255	88
Sausage, cooked (pork) ..	1 ounce	168	135
Turkey breast, Dietz & Watson no-salt-added	1 ounce	23	
Vienna sausage	1 ounce	152	84

Meats
Beef
Raw

Food	Portion	Sodium (milligrams)	Calories
Boneless chuck, flesh only	1 pound	297	1,166
Ground beef, very lean	1 pound	329	812
Round	1 pound	310	863
Sirloin, flesh only	1 pound	268	1,420
T-bone with bone ...	1 pound	207	1,596
Corned, flesh only	1 pound	5,897	1,329
Dried, chipped	1 pound	19,505	921
Hot dogs, Oscar Mayer beef franks ...	1 hot dog	460	140
Lamb, raw, flesh only	1 pound	282	1,007

Liver

Food	Portion	Sodium (milligrams)	Calories
Calf, cooked	1 pound	535	1,184
Chicken, cooked	1 pound	277	748

Pork
Cured
Bacon

Food	Portion	Sodium (milligrams)	Calories
Cooked	2 slices	245	143
Canadian, cooked	1 slice	537	58
Ham	3 ounces	1,114	424
Dietz & Watson low-salt, cooked ...	4 ounces	850	

Food	Portion	Sodium (milligrams)	Calories
Salt pork, raw	1 ounce	399	222
Fresh, raw flesh, cooked, lean only	1 pound	252	1,397
Pork chops, yield from 1 pound, raw with bone	8.2 ounces	141	912
Spareribs, yield from 1 pound, raw with bone and fat	6.3 ounces	65	792
Turkey, cooked, flesh only	1 pound	590	862
Veal, cooked, yield from 1 pound	10.6 ounces	146	703

Table 6: Fats

Food	Portion	Sodium (milligrams)	Calories
Butter			
Regular	1 tablespoon	140	102
Unsalted	1 tablespoon	1	102
Imitation butter flavoring, Durkee's	1 teaspoon	0	
Dips			
Avocado (guacamole), Kraft	2 tablespoons	225	
Clam, Kraft	1 ounce	185	
French onion dip, Kraft .	2 tablespoons	255	
Margarine			
Regular	1 tablespoon	140	102
Blue Bonnet	1 tablespoon	110	100
Fleischmann's soft whipped	1 tablespoon	70	70
Kraft Parkay	1 tablespoon	115	100
Kraft Squeeze Parkay ...	1 tablespoon	110	100
Unsalted	1 tablespoon	1	102
Fleischmann's unsalted ..	1 tablespoon	1	100
Mayonnaise	1 tablespoon	84	101

Food	Portion	Sodium (milligrams)	Calories
Hellmann's real	1 tablespoon	80	100
Kraft real	1 tablespoon	70	100
Oil, vegetable (corn, olive, safflower, sesame, soybean, peanut)	1 tablespoon	0	120
Salad dressing			
Buttermilk, family style, Good Seasons	1 tablespoon	135	
Creamy cucumber, Kraft	1 tablespoon	200	70
French, Kraft	1 tablespoon	125	60
Italian, Good Seasons ...	1 tablespoon	170	
Italian, zesty, Kraft	1 tablespoon	240	80
Italian, oil-free, Kraft ...	1 tablespoon	220	4
Roka blue cheese, Kraft .	1 tablespoon	170	60
French, Kraft (reduced calorie)	1 tablespoon	150	25
Roka, Kraft (reduced calorie)	1 tablespoon	305	14

Table 7: Fruits

Food	Portion	Sodium (milligrams)	Calories
Apples			
Raw or baked	1 small apple	1	61
Slices	1 cup	1	59
Juice	1 cup	2	117
Dried, sulfured ...	8 ounces	11	624
Applesauce, canned			
Sweetened	1 cup	5	232
Unsweetened	1 cup	5	100
Apricots			
Raw	3 apricots	1	55
Dried	1 cup	34	338
Canned, Featherweight blue label	½ cup	10	35

Food	Portion	Sodium (milligrams)	Calories
Avocado, raw	1 large avocado	9	378
Banana, raw	1 medium banana	1	101
Berries			
Blackberries (boy-senberries)			
Raw	1 cup	1	84
Canned	1 cup	2	88
Blueberries			
Raw	1 cup	2	90
Canned, sweet-ened	1 cup	2	242
Frozen	1 cup	2	91
Raspberries			
Raw	1 cup	1	70
Frozen	1 10-ounce package	3	278
Cherries			
Raw, sweet with-out pits	1 cup	3	90
Frozen, sour	1 pound	9	249
Canned, dark sweet, Feather-weight	½ cup	10	60
Canned, sweet-ened	1 cup	3	208
Canned, unsweet-ened	1 cup	2	119
Cranberry, raw whole	1 cup	2	44
Cranberry sauce, sweetened	1 cup	3	404
Currants, raw	1 cup	13	240
Dates, dried	10 dates	1	219
Figs			
Raw	1 medium fig	1	40
Canned	1 cup	5	119
Fruit cocktail,			

Food	Portion	Sodium (milligrams)	Calories
canned, sweet- ened	1 cup	13	194
Grapes, Thompson seedless	10 grapes	2	34
Grapefruit Raw	½ grapefruit	1	40
Canned, sweet- ened	1 cup	3	178
Kumquat	1 kumquat	1	12
Lemon, juice	1 tablespoon	trace	4
Lemon, raw	1 medium lemon	3	22
Mandarin oranges Canned, Three Diamonds	11-ounce can	6	
Canned, Feather- weight blue label	½ cup	10	35
Mangos, raw	1 mango	16	152
Muskmelon Cantaloupe	1 cup	19	48
	1 melon	64	159
Casaba	1 wedge	17	38
Honeydew	1 wedge	18	49
Nectarines, raw	1 nectarine	8	88
Orange juice	1 cup	2	112
Oranges, raw	1 orange	1	71
Peaches Raw	1 peach	1	38
Frozen	1 cup	5	220
Canned, syrup pack	1 cup	5	200
Dried, cooked	1 cup	15	351
Baby food peaches (strained)	1 small jar	trace	100

Food	Portion	Sodium (milligrams)	Calories
Pears			
Raw Bosc	1 pear	3	86
Canned, syrup			
pack	1 cup	3	194
Dried	1 cup	13	482
Pineapple			
Raw	1 cup	2	81
Canned, in syrup	1 cup	3	189
Canned, water			
pack	1 cup	2	96
Plums			
Raw	1 plum	1	32
Canned, in syrup ..	1 cup	3	214
Prunes			
Cooked without			
sugar	1 cup	9	253
Dried, uncooked ..	10 prunes	9	272
Raisins, seedless	1 cup (not packed)	39	419
Sun-Maid	1 ounce	5	96
Rhubarb			
Diced, raw	1 cup	2	20
Cooked with			
sugar	1 cup	5	381
Frozen with sugar			
....	1 cup	8	386
Strawberries			
Raw	1 cup	1	55
Frozen sliced	1 cup	3	278
Watermelon, diced ..	1 cup	2	42

Table 8: Grain Products

Food	Portion	Sodium (milligrams)	Calories
Barley, pearl	1 tablespoon	Trace	44
Breads			
Applesauce spice			
mix, Pillsbury	¹⁄₁₂ loaf	155	150
Boston brown	1 slice	120	
Cracked wheat	1 slice	148	66
French	1 slice	203	102
Melba toast, un-			
salted rye,			
Devonshire	1 slice	1	16
Pita	1	132	
Raisin	1 slice	91	66
Arnold raisin tea	2 slices	225	140
Rye			
Regular	1 slice	139	61
Pumpernickel	1 slice	182	79
Arnold pum-			
pernickel	2 slices	460	150
White			
Regular	1 slice	114	63
Pepperidge			
Farm	1 slice	350	75
Arnold brick			
oven white	2 slices	130	205
Thin	1 slice	79	41
Low-sodium	1 slice	7	63
Whole wheat	1 slice	132	61
Pepperidge Farm			
thin sliced	1 slice	107	70
Bread crumbs			
Pepperidge Farm			
seasoned	1 cup	3,061	
Kellogg's cornflake			
crumbs	1 ounce	305	110
Bread sticks, Stella			
D'Oro, plain	1 stick	less than 10	43
Breakfast cereals			

Food	Portion	Sodium (milligrams)	Calories
Hot, cooked in unsalted water			
Corn (hominy) grits			
Regular, dry	1 cup	2	579
Instant	1 cup	354	80
Quaker instant grits	1 packet	520	80
Quaker quick grits	1 ounce	10	100
Cream of wheat			
Regular, dry	1 cup	2	289
Nabisco instant (half a minute)	1 ounce	10	100
Instant	¾ cup	5	100
Quick	¾ cup	126	100
Mix 'n eat	¾ cup	350	100
Farina	¾ cup	1	80
Pillsbury farina (2 to 3 minutes) ..	2 tablespoons	5	80
Maypo	1 ounce	2	123
Oatmeal or rolled oats, dry			
Regular or quick	¾ cup	1	234
Quaker instant oatmeal ...	1 ounce	400	100
Instant			
Sodium-added	¾ cup	283	
With apples and cinnamon	¾ cup	220	130
With maple and brown sugar	¾ cup	277	160
With raisins and spice	¾ cup	223	160
Wheatena	1 ounce	2	120
Ready to eat			
Bran cereals			
All-Bran	⅓ cup	160	70
Bran Chex	⅔ cup	262	90
40% bran	⅔ cup	251	90
100% bran	½ cup	221	70
Raisin bran	½ cup	209	110

Food	Portion	Sodium (milligrams)	Calories
Cheerios	1¼ cups	304	110
Corn cereals			
Corn bran	⅔ cup	295	110
Corn Chex	1 cup	297	110
Cornflakes			
Low-sodium, Van Brode	1 cup	8	88
Low-sodium, Featherweight	1 ounce	10	110
Regular	1 cup	256	110
Sugarcoated	¾ cup	274	110
Sugar Corn Pops	1 cup	105	110
Fruit 'n Fiber with apples and cinnamon	½ cup	195	90
Granola			
Regular	¼ cup	61	130
Nature Valley	⅓ cup	45	130
Sovex fruit 'n nut granola	1 ounce	4	110
No-sodium-added	¼ cup	16	
Grape-Nuts	¼ cup	195	100
Kix	1½ cups	261	110
Life	⅔ cup	146	120
Product 19	¾ cup	175	110
Rice cereals			
Frosted Krispies	¾ cup	200	110
Low-sodium	1 cup	10	
Puffed rice	2 cups	2	50
Rice Chex	1⅛ cups	238	110
Rice Krispies	1 cup	340	110
Special K	1¼ cups	265	110
Total	1 cup	375	110
Trix	1 cup	160	110

Food	Portion	Sodium (milligrams)	Calories
Wheat cereals			
Frosted Mini-Wheats, Kellogg's	1 ounce	10	110
Puffed wheat	2 cups	2	50
Sugarcoated ...	1 cup	46	
Shredded wheat	1 biscuit	3	75
Wheat Chex	⅔ cup	190	100
Wheaties	1 cup	355	110
Wheat germ, toasted	¼ cup	1	92
Wheat cereal, Nutrigrain	⅔ cup	195	110
Egg roll wrappers, Nasoya	1 wrapper	75	
Nasoya wonton wrappers	1 wrapper	18.75	
Flour			
Bran, Quaker, unprocessed	2 tablespoons	0	20
Bran, Sovex, unprocessed wheat	⅔ cup	5	80
Cornmeal	1 cup	1	502
Cornmeal, yellow, Quaker	1 ounce	10	100
Cornmeal, self-rising	1 cup	1,946	491
Cornstarch	1 tablespoon	trace	29
Gold Medal Wondra	1 cup	5	400
Pillsbury all-purpose	1 cup	less than 5	400
Pillsbury Best bread	1 cup	5	410
Pillsbury enriched self-rising	1 cup	1,645	380
Rye			
Light	1 cup	1	364
Medium	1 cup	1	308

Food	Portion	Sodium (milligrams)	Calories
Pillsbury	1 cup	5	420
Dark	1 cup	1	419
Sauce 'n gravy			
flour, Pillsbury	2 tablespoons	5	50
White and bread			
flour	1 cup	3	499
White self-rising	1 cup	1,349	440
Whole wheat	1 cup	4	400
Pancake mixes			
Aunt Jemima			
complete	3 4" pancakes	870	220
Featherweight mix	3 pancakes	70	130
Hungry Jack extra			
light	3 4" pancakes	495	200
Pillsbury Hungry			
Jack	3 4" pancakes	925	330
Pasta			
Dry (spaghetti,			
macaroni, shells, lasagne			
noodles, etc.)	1 pound	9	1,674
Noodles, cooked	1 cup	3	200
Noodles and beef-			
flavored sauce, Lipton ...	½ cup	555	190
Pasta, cooked	1 cup	2	155
Rice			
Brown, raw	1 cup	17	666
Fried rice mix,			
Minute	1 cup	1,270	320
White, raw	1 cup	10	708
Converted, cooked			
without salt or			
butter	1 cup	3	186
Quick, cooked			
without salt			
or butter	1 cup	9	180
Rolls			
Brown and serve	1 roll	138	
English muffin,			
Arnold	1 muffin	310	150

Food	Portion	Sodium (milligrams)	Calories
English muffin, Pepperidge Farm	1 muffin	633	140
Hamburger, Arnold	1 roll	285	110
Hamburger, Pep- peridge Farm	1 roll	201	100
Hot dog, Arnold	1 roll	290	110
Refrigerated dough	1 roll	342	
Pillsbury butter- flake	1 roll	445	110
Pillsbury crescent	2 rolls	665	200
Pillsbury Hungry Jack, butter- milk	2 biscuits	605	200
Sesame seed bun, Pepperidge Farm	1 roll	205	
Stuffing Pepperidge Farm cube	1 ounce	484	110
Pepperidge Farm herb	1 ounce	491	110
Taco shells Old El Paso	1 shell	50	51
Ortego	1 shell	55	
Tortillas, corn, canned	3.6 ounces	681	267

Table 9: Legumes and Nuts

Food	Portion	Sodium (milligrams)	Calories
Almonds			
Salted, roasted	1 cup	311	984
Planters	1 ounce	220	170
Unsalted, slivered	1 cup	5	688
Beans			
Baked, canned			
Boston style	1 cup	606	287
With or without pork .	1 cup	928	311
Cooked without salt			
Great Northern, raw ..	1 pound	86	1,542
Kidney, cooked	1 cup	6	218
Raw	1 pound	45	1,556
Canned	1 cup	844	230
Navy, cooked	1 cup	13	212
Pinto, calico, red			
Mexican	1 pound	45	1,583
Brazil nuts, shelled	1 cup	1	916
Cashews			
Roasted in oil, unsalted ..	1 cup	1	916
Dry roasted, salted	1 cup	1,200	800
Chestnuts, fresh, shelled ...	1 cup	10	310
Chickpeas or garbanzo beans, dry, raw	1 cup	52	720
Filberts (hazelnuts), chopped	1 cup	2	729
Lentils, raw	1 cup	57	646
Mixed nuts, Planters			
Dry roasted	1 ounce	220	160
Unsalted	1 ounce	10	170
Peanuts			
Dry roasted, salted	1 cup	986	838
Planters	1 ounce	220	160
Roasted, salted	1 cup	602	842
Unsalted	1 cup	8	842

Food	Portion	Sodium (milligrams)	Calories
Planters unsalted	1 ounce	10	170
Peanut butter			
Smooth or crunchy	1 tablespoon	97	94
Food Club	1 tablespoon	170	200
Planters	1 tablespoon	95	95
Low-sodium	1 tablespoon	1	94
Peas			
Blackeye, raw	1 pound	159	1,542
Split, raw	1 pound	181	1,579
Pecans	1 cup	trace	742
Dry roasted, Planters	1 ounce	220	190
Pistachio nuts, dry roasted,			
Planters	1 ounce	220	170
Soybeans			
Cooked	1 cup	4	234
Bean curd (tofu)	1 pound	32	327
Fermented soybeans			
(miso)	¼ pound	379	194
Sunflower seed kernels,			
salted, Planters	1 ounce	220	160
Sunflower seed kernels,			
unsalted, Planters	1 ounce	10	170
Walnuts, English	1 cup	2	781

Table 10: Sugars, Syrup, Chocolate and Gelatin

Food	Portion	Sodium (milligrams)	Calories
Chocolate chips for baking .	6 ounces	6	858
Cocoa, Hershey's cocoa			
powder	⅓ cup	5	120
Coconut, shredded	1 cup	18	277
Gelatin			
Royal	½ cup	90	80
Knox, unflavored	1 envelope	0	23
Featherweight	½ cup	2	10
Honey	1 cup	17	1,031
Jams and jellies			
Jam			
Regular	1 tablespoon	2	54

Food	Portion	Sodium (milligrams)	Calories
Low-calorie	1 tablespoon	19	16
Jelly			
Regular	1 tablespoon	3	49
Low-calorie	1 tablespoon	21	
Sugar			
Brown	1 cup	66	821
Granulated	1 cup	2	770
Granulated	1 tablespoon	trace	46
Powdered	1 tablespoon	trace	31
Syrup			
Chocolate flavored			
Thin	2 tablespoons	20	92
Fudge	2 tablespoons	33	124
Corn	1 tablespoon	14	59
Karo Light	1 tablespoon	25	60
Karo, pancake or			
waffle	1 tablespoon	30	60
Maple			
Regular	1 tablespoon	2	50
Imitation	1 tablespoon	20	1
Molasses			
Light	1 tablespoon	3	50
Medium	1 tablespoon	7	46
Blackstrap	1 tablespoon	19	43

Table 11: Vegetables

Food	Portion	Sodium (milligrams)	Calories
Artichokes, fresh	1 medium	36	12 to 67
Asparagus			
Raw	1 cup	3	35
Frozen	1 pound	9	104
Canned			
Regular	1 cup	564	43
Low-sodium	1 cup	7	38
Beans			
Lima			
Cooked	1 cup	4	262
Frozen	1 cup	232	212
Canned	1 cup	401	163
Snap (green)			

Food	Portion	Sodium (milligrams)	Calories
Fresh	1 cup	8	35
Frozen			
Regular	1 cup	1	33
With almonds	3 ounces	335	50
Birds Eye	3 ounces	335	50
With mushrooms	3 ounces	145	30
Canned			
Regular	1 cup	319	32
Low-sodium	1 cup	5	38
Food Club no-salt	1 cup	10	40
Bean sprouts, mung, raw	1 cup	5	37
Beet greens, cooked	1 cup	110	26
Beets			
Cooked	1 cup	73	54
Canned			
Sliced	1 cup	401	63
Libby's	1 cup	545	70
Low-sodium	1 cup	113	79
Harvard beets, Libby's ...	1 cup	345	160
Pickled beets, Libby's ...	1 cup	425	150
Black-eyed peas, dried	1 pound	159	1,542
Black-eyed peas, canned	1 cup	560	170
Broccoli			
Raw	1 stalk	18	47
Cooked without salt	1 cup	16	40
Frozen			
Cooked without salt	1 cup	28	48
Birds Eye	3.3 ounces	20	25
With cheese sauce, Green			
Giant	½ cup	420	70
Birds Eye	5 ounces	665	170
With hollandaise sauce	3.3 ounces	115	
Birds Eye frozen broccoli			
and cauliflower	3.3 ounces	20	25
Brussels sprouts			
Fresh, cooked	1 cup	16	56
Frozen			

Food	Portion	Sodium (milligrams)	Calories
Cooked without salt	1 cup	22	51
In butter sauce,			
Green Giant	½ cup	275	60
Cabbage			
Green, raw	1 cup	18	22
Green, raw	1 pound	91	109
Red, raw	1 cup	23	28
Carrots			
Raw	1 carrot	34	30
Fresh, cooked			
without salt	1 cup	51	48
Frozen			
Cut or whole			
....	3.3. ounces	43	
In butter sauce	3.3 ounces	350	
With brown sugar			
glaze, Birds Eye	3.3 ounces	500	80
Canned			
Regular	1 cup	581	69
Low-sodium	1 cup	96	54
Cauliflower			
Raw	1 head	112	232
Raw	1 cup	11	28
Cooked without salt	1 cup	13	28
Frozen			
Cooked	1 cup	18	32
With cheese sauce,			
Birds Eye	5 ounces	630	160
Celery, raw	1 small 5″ stalk	21	3
Chard, Swiss, cooked	1 cup	125	26
Collards			
Fresh, cooked	1 cup	36	42
Corn			
Cooked	1 ear	trace	70
Frozen, cooked	1 cup	2	130

Food	Portion	Sodium (milligrams)	Calories
Green Giant	1 ear	4	120
Canned			
Cream style			
Regular	1 cup	604	210
Del Monte low-so-			
dium	1 cup	20	160
Libby's	1 cup	530	170
Low-sodium	1 cup	5	210
Libby's low-sodium .	1 cup	20	160
Vacuum pack	1 cup	577	174
Whole kernel			
Regular vacuum pack			
....	1 cup	496	174
Green Giant	1 cup	440	180
Low-sodium	1 cup	3	152
Featherweight	1 cup	23	160
Cucumber	1 small	9	22
Dandelion greens, cooked .	1 cup	46	35
Eggplant, cooked	1 cup	2	38
Endive, raw	1 cup	7	10
Kale, fresh, cooked	1 cup	47	43
Kohlrabi, cooked	1 cup	10	40
Leek	1 pound	12	123
Lettuce	1 cup	5	8
Mixed vegetables			
Canned	1 cup	380	116
Featherweight	½ cup	25	40
Frozen	3.3 ounces	45	59
Birds Eye corn, green			
beans and pasta	3.3 ounces	285	110
Mushrooms			
Raw	1 cup	11	20
	1 pound	68	127
Canned	½ cup	488	22
Canned, broiled in butter	6-ounce can	710	22

Food	Portion	Sodium (milligrams)	Calories
Mustard greens			
Raw	1 pound	145	141
Cooked	1 cup	25	32
Okra, cooked	10 pods	2	31
Onions			
Mature	1 medium	8	32
Green	1 tablespoon, chopped	trace	2
Parsley, raw	1 tablespoon	2	2
Parsnips, cooked	1 cup	12	102
Peas, green			
Cooked	1 cup	2	114
Frozen			
Regular	1 cup	187	106
In butter sauce, Green			
Giant	1 cup	830	140
In cream sauce	2.6 ounces	420	
With mushrooms	3.3 ounces	215	70
With pearl onions,			
Birds Eye	3.3 ounces	310	70
Canned			
Regular	1 cup	493	150
Del Monte early gar-			
den	17 ounces	375	60
Low-sodium	1 cup	7	137
Food Club low-sodium	1 cup	15	130
Peas and carrots,			
Libby's	1 cup	610	100
Peppers			
Sweet, raw or chopped ..	1 pod	10	16
Sweet, chopped	1 cup	20	
Pimientos, canned	4 ounces	8	31
Potatoes			
Baked or boiled	1 medium	6	104
Frozen			
French fried	10 strips	3	137

Food	Portion	Sodium (milligrams)	Calories
Canned	1 cup	753	190
Instant, reconstituted	1 cup	485	195
Hungry Jack mashed	½ cup	330	140
Mashed with milk and			
salt	1 cup	632	137
Au gratin	1 cup	1,095	355
Pumpkin, canned	1 cup	5	81
Pumpkin pie filling, Libby's	16-ounce can	9	210
Radish	10 medium	8	8
Rutabaga, raw	1 cup	7	64
Sauerkraut, canned	1 cup	1,755	42
Libby's	1 cup	1,480	40
Shallot	1 tablespoon	1	7
Spinach			
Raw	1 cup	39	14
Cooked	1 cup	90	41
Frozen			
Regular	1 cup	107	47
Canned			
Regular	1 cup	484	49
Low-sodium	1 cup	79	49
Squash			
Raw, summer	1 cup	1	25
Winter, cooked without			
salt	1 cup	2	129
Baked, mashed	1 cup	2	113
Frozen	1 cup	2	91
Acorn, cooked	1 large	4	172
Sweet potatoes			
Baked or boiled in skin	1 potato	13	148
Canned, vacuum packed	1 cup	96	216
Tomatoes			
Raw	1 tomato	5	40
Cooked without salt	1 cup	10	63
Canned			
Whole, ...	1 cup	313	51

Food	Portion	Sodium (milligrams)	Calories
Stewed	1 cup	584	60
Diet Delight low-			
sodium	½ cup	15	25
Low-sodium	1 cup	16	
Hunt's low-sodium	4 ounces	15	
Tomato juice, canned			
Regular	1 cup	878	46
Ocean Spray tomato			
vegetable cocktail	6 ounces	600	45
Libby's	6 ounces	455	35
Low-sodium	1 cup	9	46
Diet Delight	1 cup	27	47
Featherweight	6 ounces	20	35
V-8 vegetable juice	6 ounces	720	35
V-8 low-sodium vege-			
table juice	6 ounces	60	35
Tomato paste, canned	1 cup	77	215
Contadina no-salt-added	6 ounces	69	139
Contadina no-salt-added	¼ cup	26	52
Contadina no-salt added .	1 tablespoon	6	13
Balanced dietetic	6 ounces	under 10	150
Balanced dietetic	1 tablespoon	1	14
Featherweight no-salt-			
added	6 ounces	70	150
Tomato sauce, canned	1 cup	1,498	40
Turnips			
Cooked yellow	1 cup	5	36
Cooked white	1 cup	78	36
Turnip greens, cooked	1 cup	17	29

Tips to help you

- **Make a list before you go to the store** so that you can stock your kitchen with many acceptable choices: lots of fruit (apples, pears, strawberries, etc.). You think that strawberries are too expensive? Then buy oranges if they are in season. But how do strawberries really compare in price per pound with bakery delicacies? Buy low-calorie vegetables, low-calorie drinks, low-calorie salad dressing, and high-fibre foods such as whole grain breads and oat bran cereals.

- **Don't buy any foods that you can't resist:** chocolate, ice cream, butter, fatty steaks.

- **Buy the right amount, especially of the protein foods.** If you buy small servings of meat for each person, there won't be leftovers to tempt you.

- **Get into the habit of filling your plate with foods that are not high in calories.** Two servings of vegetables, perhaps one yellow and one green, can help. So can a generous salad or a serving of fruit. It's depressing to look at a dinner plate that looks mostly empty. Some people like to use pretty dishes, glasses and place mats, too.

- **Don't be a martyr—learn to like the way you'll be eating from now on.** If you don't like the taste of diet sodas, try squeezing a little fresh lemon juice in them. Learn to drink your coffee black or use low-fat milk and/or an artificial sweetener. Even restaurants will give you a little milk if you ask. Those "non-dairy" creamers are often made with very unhealthy ingredients such as coconut oil. (This is especially bad for someone with a cholesterol problem.)

- **Stick to your eating plan—don't skip meals.** Unless you are different from every other "dieter" on earth, skipping meals will mean that you will get hungry. Then you will eat something convenient—perhaps cookies or potato chips.

- **Care enough about yourself to have something planned for those times when your willpower is low.** This may be in the evening or the middle of the night. Have fresh fruit or popcorn on hand, for example.

- **If you give in and eat a lot of unhealthy foods, don't get discouraged and say that you just can't do it.** Go back to sensible eating the next day. If you made a mistake in your checkbook, you wouldn't give up writing checks, would you?

You should be aware that other people in your life may react differently to your diet. Many people who eat butter and bacon are not going to be thrilled. If someone in your family misses foods such as butter, ask that person to come in with you to see the doctor or dietitian next time. Perhaps you can bring up the subject of butter.

You deserve a lot of credit for going to the trouble of making delicious healthy foods. You deserve a round of applause.

About the Authors

Edith Tibbets, an instructor for Health Education Associates Inc., Sandwich, Massachusetts, graduated from the University of Illinois (M. Ed.) and Tufts University (A.B.). A former elementary school teacher, she coauthored (with Joanna Goldfarb, M.D.) *The Breastfeeding Handbook* and is a contributor to the *Journal of Continuing Education in Nursing* and the *Journal of Nutrition Education*. With coauthor Karin Cadwell, Edith Tibbetts teaches workshops for Health Education Associates Inc. on health-related subjects to nurses, dietitians and doctors. Married to Donald Tibbetts and mother of three children, Edith Tibbetts lives in Pocasset, Massachusetts, where she has herb and vegetable gardens.

Karin Cadwell, a graduate of the University of Pennsylvania (M.S.N.) and Upsala College (A.B. in English), teaches professional continuing education programs for Health Education Associates Inc., Sandwich, Massachusetts. She is a contributor to the *Journal of Nutrition Education*, *JOGN Nursing* and the *Journal of Continuing Education in Nursing*. Karin Cadwell is a member of Sigma Theta Tau (national nursing honor society). Married to Charles Cadwell, she is the mother of two children and makes her home in Dennisport, Massachusetts.

Index

(Complete sodium and calorie contents of fresh and convenience foods and seasonings may be found in the Appendix, pages 269–305.)

Greens, Leafy, 142
Grilled Cheese Sandwich, 100
Grinder, 96
Ground Beef
  lean, 37
  and Vegetable Soup, 111
Guacamole
  Dip, 87
  Topping, Tex-Mex, 212

H
Hamburger(s), 102
  Fast-Food-Style, 102
  Sauce, 60
Hash, 186
HDL (high-density lipoproteins),
  17–18
Heart failure, congestive, 10
Herb
  Blend Seasoning, 53
  Marinade, 72
Hero Sandwich, 96
High-density lipoproteins (HDL),
  17–18
Hoagie, 96
Holiday Walnut Cookies, 257
Home fries, 82
Honey
  Chicken, 168
  Dressing, 69
Hopping John, 205
Horseradish, 58
  Gravy, 58
Hot
  cocktail sauce, 60
  mustard, 57
  Open-Faced Sandwiches, 98
  peppers, 54
  Pita Sandwiches, 99
  sauce, 54
Hydrogenated oils, 17
Hypertension, 10

I
Ice Cream, 37
  Sundaes, 248
Italian Meatballs, 188–189

K
Ketchup, 27–28, 55

Kidney problems, 10
Kneaded Yeast Breads, 230–239

L
Labels, reading of, 9 , 25, 27,
  28–29, 32–33
Lamb
  Moussaka, 200–201
  Shish Kebab, 190
Lasagne, 148
  Vegetarian, 149
LDL (low-density lipoproteins),
  17–18
Leafy Greens, 142
Lemon
  Bread, 222
  and "Butter" Sauce for Broccoli,
    130
  Chicken, Quick, 168
  juice, 36
Lima Beans, 129
Liquid Hickory Smoke flavoring, 37
London Broil, 181
Louisiana Red Beans and Rice, 206
Low-calorie Italian dressing, 67
Low-density lipoproteins (LDL),
  17–18
Low-sodium diet, 38–39
Lunch
  cold, adding hot items to, 95
  restaurant selections for, 47

M
Macaroni
  and Beef Casserole, 152
  Italian Style Salad, 119
  Salad, 118
Mama's Sauce, 74
Mandarin Orange Gelatin-Sherbet,
  246
Marinade(s)
  Burgundy, 72
  Herb, 72
  Lemony, 70
  Orange Juice, 71
  Sweet-and-Sour, 70
  Tomato-Wine, 71
  White Wine, 71
Marinated
  Bean Salad, 121
  Mushrooms, 90